ATHEISM

WHAT EVERYONE NEEDS TO KNOW®

ATHEISM

WHAT EVERYONE NEEDS TO KNOW®

MICHAEL RUSE

OXFORD
UNIVERSITY PRESS

OXFORD
UNIVERSITY PRESS

Oxford University Press is a department of the University
of Oxford. It furthers the University's objective of excellence in research,
scholarship, and education by publishing worldwide.

Oxford   New York
Auckland   Cape Town   Dar es Salaam   Hong Kong   Karachi
Kuala Lumpur   Madrid   Melbourne   Mexico City   Nairobi
New Delhi   Shanghai   Taipei   Toronto

With offices in
Argentina   Austria   Brazil   Chile   Czech Republic   France   Greece
Guatemala   Hungary   Italy   Japan   Poland   Portugal   Singapore
South Korea   Switzerland   Thailand   Turkey   Ukraine   Vietnam

Oxford is a registered trademark of Oxford University Press
in the UK and certain other countries.

"What Everyone Needs to Know" is a registered trademark of Oxford
University Press.

Published in the United States of America by
Oxford University Press
198 Madison Avenue, New York, NY 10016

© Oxford University Press 2015

Library of Congress Cataloging-in-Publication Data
Ruse, Michael.
Atheism : what everyone needs to know/Michael Ruse.
pages cm. — (What everyone needs to know)
Includes bibliographical references and index.
ISBN 978–0–19–933458–2 (pbk. : alk. paper) — ISBN 978–0–19–933459–9
(hardcover :alk. paper)
1. Atheism.   I. Title.
BL2747.3.R835 2014
211'.8—dc23
2014014796

1 3 5 7 9 8 6 4 2
Printed in the United States of America
on acid-free paper

To the memory of my parents and the other loving Quakers
of my childhood

CONTENTS

ACKNOWLEDGMENTS

First and foremost, I am very grateful to my editor, Peter Ohlin, at Oxford University Press for asking me to write this book. You will soon see that it has become something of a personal journey, and I feel humbled that Peter could see that I was the person to write it. I have just finished co-editing *The Oxford Handbook of Atheism*. It will be no surprise to find that I have made heavy and unapologetic use of the contributions; I wouldn't be much of an editor if I didn't think they were at the cutting edge of the topic. Stephen Bullivant, with whom I worked on this collection, was the Platonic form of collaborator—knowledgeable, hardworking, and never irritable. I simply could not have written this book without this earlier project or without Stephen's ever-helpful advice. I am hugely in the debt of my friend Brian Davies OP. He is one of the world's experts on the thought of St. Thomas Aquinas, and he took time out from his heavy schedule of teaching and research to go over my manuscript with a very careful and critical eye. He is the best of teachers. I count myself privileged to be numbered among his students. I still don't think the God of the great philosophers—Augustine, Anselm, Aquinas—holds water, but Brian has given me a much better understanding of why I don't think it works, and how very much I am giving up by rejecting it.

I never met William and Lucyle Werkmeister, who left monies to fund my professorship and to support my research. Colleagues who did know them tell me with some glee that Lucyle, after whom my professorship is named, was very religious and would not at all agree with the contents of this book. They tell me also that the Werkmeisters would be delighted that their gift is being so used, and I would like to think that this book, and the others that I have written since I have been at Florida State University, are a way of showing my gratitude. Included in the funds is support to run workshops and conferences. I was therefore able to bring together a group of friends (as I would now like to count them) to discuss my manuscript. They included John Kelsay, David McNaughton, Jeffery O'Connell, John Schneider, Kimberly Blessing, Michael Peterson, and Stephen Bullivant. I am very appreciative of their reading and help and also am in debt to Sarah Buck Kachaluba for organizing the workshop. As always, I am incredibly grateful to my wife, Lizzie. As you will see, she is a pretty good sport to put up with me. She is just praying (in an entirely secular way) that I don't follow this book on religion with another on opera.

PROLOGUE

Why Should I Write—Why Should You Read—a Book on Atheism?

On September 11, 2001 (9/11), Muslim fanatics hijacked four planes. Two were flown into the World Trade Center in New York, one into the Pentagon in Washington, D.C., and the fourth failed to find its destination, probably the White House, only because of the incredible bravery of the passengers on board. The next morning, a young graduate student in California took up his pen and began a fiery polemic against what he saw as the root cause of the vile attacks: religion. Sam Harris, now a neurobiologist, was the to-be author of *The End of Faith: Religion, Terror, and the Future of Reason* (published in 2004). In fairly short order, the biologist and popular science writer Richard Dawkins produced *The God Delusion* (2006), the philosopher Daniel Dennett wrote *Breaking the Spell: Religion as a Natural Phenomenon* (2006), and the journalist Christopher Hitchens authored *God Is Not Great: How Religion Poisons Everything* (2007). Christened the "New Atheists," their books were bestsellers, and their ideas were avidly consumed by countless people looking for a solution to something that seemed so mystifying: meaningless attacks on innocent people simply going about their business. Expectedly, this assault soon occasioned a counterresponse, and before long a flood of works argued that the New Atheists were entirely mistaken both about religion and its connection to social unrest and upheaval. *The Dawkins Delusion: Atheist Fundamentalism and the Denial of the Divine* (2007) by Anglican theologian Alister McGrath and his wife, Joanna Collicutt McGrath, and *God and the New Atheism: A Critical Response to Dawkins, Harris, and Hitchens* (2007) by Catholic theologian John Haught are typical. Matters moved from the serious to the farcical when first the religious paid for advertisements on the sides of buses—"Jesus said I am the way and the life"—and then the atheists responded with advertisements of their own: "There probably is no god, so stop worrying and get on with your life."

Without this controversy, I very much doubt that Oxford University Press would have asked me to write this book. Without this controversy, I very much doubt—unless you have the misfortune to be stuck in an undergraduate course in philosophy or religion—you would be reading this book. But there is a controversy. I have written it. You are reading it. Truly, no apologies or misgivings are needed. Although perhaps some explanations and directives are needed. One could write a book just on the New Atheism, and indeed as we have just seen, several have done just this. But one senses that broader issues are at play here. Dreadful as were the events of 9/11, it is clear that the books sparked in response were successful because in some vague sense society was waiting for such works. In other words, there were broader, already existing worries and dissatisfactions with religion, and the New Atheism cashed in on these. After all, it is worth remembering that although *The God Delusion* was a runaway bestseller, selling more than 2 million copies in its first two years, its sales were dwarfed by the thriller of the decade—*The Da Vinci Code* (2003), which sold 40 million copies in its first three years—and that this latter book had as its central plot the conceit that Jesus was not the son of God, that the Catholic Church knows this and conceals the information, and that its sinister organization Opus Dei will stop at no tactics, including murder, to keep the status quo. Hardly a testament to the glories of the faith!

More broadly, survey after survey has shown—we shall look at some in detail—that people, particularly the young, are losing interest in and commitment to religion, particularly organized religion (Bullivant 2010). This is obviously far from a universal trend, but it is true and widespread. Reasons for the withdrawal are easy to find. On the one hand, there is universal disgust at the hypocrisy of so many in positions of religious authority. One thinks not just of the predation on the young by Catholic priests, but the extent to which the hierarchy covered up and to this day fights tooth and nail to avoid acknowledging responsibility. Balancing this have been the sexual and fiscal shenanigans of Protestant so-called televangelists. On the other hand—as Christians (especially evangelicals) are themselves now starting to realize (Kinnaman 2011)—so much claimed and demanded in the name of religion seems out of date and irrelevant, distracting from really significant problems: Pope Paul VI reaffirming the ban on artificial methods of contraception; the refusal to accept gay people as fully functioning and worthwhile members of society; and while insisting on various social doctrines about liberty (including rights about guns), adamant refusal to accept that a woman's body is her body and not the property of the state or the church—and most certainly not of a group of old men who supposedly have never had sex in their lives, nor equally Protestant pastors with a tendentious reading of the supposedly pertinent biblical passages. At the same time, Africans die in hordes from HIV, children the world over go to bed hungry because there is no food, and our fields face drought and our cities face flooding.

This is not to say that everyone is now rushing to nonbelief, to a denial of the existence of God or of gods, to (as I shall understand it in this book) atheism in some sense. In fact, much suggests that this is not so. Catholic novelist J. R. R. Tolkien's *The Lord of the Rings* has sold 150 million copies worldwide, and obviously a major factor in its continuing success (not to mention the film adaptations) is the religious underpinning to the work (Bud 2013). But atheism in some sense is becoming more of a possible option. Hence, this book—one that tries to lay out dispassionately the issues surrounding atheism, the arguments against it and the arguments for it, its critics and its supporters. We need to move beyond the polemics and look at the underlying issues. We need to know the facts, the history, the merits and demerits, the prospects, and hopes and fears. We need, in other words, a balanced look at the question of atheism. Which in itself raises worries, for too often *balanced* means "bland and boring," something that in itself would be very regrettable, for, whatever else one might say about New Atheism and the reactions to it, *boring* is very much not a predicate that jumps at once to mind. I will try to keep this point constantly in view, because I can assure you that if you find this book boring, then that is my problem and not that of the topic. The subject is interesting, and the implications are important. If on finishing this book you do not agree with this, I have failed in what I set out to do.

Who Am I to Presume to Write Such a Book?

Because of the intended scope of such a book as this, truly only God himself is qualified as a potential author. It must be part historical, part sociological, part theological, part philosophical, part anthropological, and more. As the late social psychologist Donald Campbell used to say, any human author must be willing to be inadequate in many fields at once. I have the credentials. My daytime job is as a philosopher, particularly a philosopher of science. I specialize in evolutionary biology, and this has led me back to work on Charles Darwin, to such an extent that I think of myself now as much historian as philosopher of science. In recent years, partly because of the ways in which Darwinian thinking impinges on religion, partly because of the outside threat to biology by the so-called

Creationist movement—more recently, the Intelligent Design theorists—I have been much engaged in work on the relationship between science and religion. A while back, I (along with such luminaries as the late Stephen Jay Gould) was an expert witness for the American Civil Liberties Union in a court case defending evolution against biblical literalism. I am not a religious studies expert, nor am I a theologian, but my work has taken me into those fields, and I have tried to learn from the professionals about the various issues and topics. I was raised as a Quaker, and although it is long since I was a practicing member of the Religious Society of Friends, it would not surprise me if at times you discerned this background in what I write. One tries to be impartial and objective, but childhood training particularly does have a way of showing through. In a real sense, I hope that it does, because the genuine love shown by my parents and their coreligionists to me and other children in our group has infused my whole life with joy and gratitude. Part of that love was the insistence that no one but me can make decisions about who I am and what I believe. This was not intended to be nor has it proven easy. In the just-mentioned court case, I was asked about my present religious beliefs, and I had to confess that although I may be an expert witness on many things, that is one area where my expertise does not extend. This is still true. I know I don't believe in most religious claims, so I suppose in this sense I am an atheist. Whether there is something more, I simply don't know, and in a way I am glad I don't know. I am nevertheless intensely religious, in the sense that these questions about God and the ultimate meaning of life are very important to me. I wouldn't be writing books like this if I weren't. The first reader of everything I write is myself. In this respect, therefore, I am very different from my beloved wife, Lizzie, who is very much part of the newer generation I was talking about. She simply doesn't care about religion. She doesn't know about it and doesn't want to know about it. She is not prejudiced against religion. Her best friend is director of Christian education at a local church. But it is simply not for her. It is for me and it is primarily for those like me, whatever the content of their beliefs, that this book is written.

Is There a Theme?

One final point and we can begin. This book is an overview, an introduction, packed with information. For all that, is there a connecting theme? Binding all together into a whole, do we see the emergence of some particular viewpoint or finding? Most certainly we do. It is that atheism for both supporters and critics is an intensely moral issue. It is not just a matter of the facts, does God exist or not? It is rather whether morally we should believe in God or the gods. The nineteenth-century English mathematician and philosopher William Kingdom Clifford (1845–1879) wrote on the "ethics of belief" (1879), claiming that it is immoral to believe something without sufficient evidence. It is this insight that morality is the key to proper belief that underlies the debate about atheism.

1

FROM THE GREEKS
TO THE ENLIGHTENMENT

How Do We Go about Our Task?

In a perfect world, no doubt, we would consider belief and
nonbelief equally for every society, for every inhabitant of
Planet Earth. Christianity would count no more than, say,
the cargo cult of the Melanesians. The denial of Christianity
would be on a par with the denial of the cargo cult. We do not
live in a perfect world, thank goodness, and so we are going to
have to make decisions about what to consider and what not
to consider. At the risk of seeming narrow and blinkered—
Eurocentric or some such thing—I am going to focus on the
atheism debate as it has occurred and continues to occur in
the West and those areas of the globe influenced by or set-
tled by the West: Europe, America, other parts of the First
World, and places where Western culture predominates. In
other words, while recognizing fully and explicitly the debt
to Jewish thought, my discussion of atheism is going to be
framed within the Christian context. I can show that this is
not just prejudice or laziness, but that in major respects atheism is a Western issue and certainly inasmuch as it is a *problem*, it is a Western issue. Many indeed would argue that in
trying to avoid the Scylla of Eurocentrism one runs the risk
of getting caught in the Charybdis of "mental colonialism,"
where one illicitly assumes that concepts and problems of the

West are mirrored in the rest of the world (Quack 2013). There is truth in this. But it would be wrong to ignore other religions entirely, and so apart from the occasional in-context remark about Judaism and Islam considered as religions in their own right, a separate chapter is devoted to non-Christian religions and the question of atheism. It is just that normally they will not be the focus of discussion.

The battle is about God and whether such an entity exists, and if so, what is this deity's nature and how does it all affect us humans. In the Western context, someone who subscribes to the God of Abraham—that is, someone who is a Jew, a Christian, or a Muslim—is known as a *theist*. This term comes from the Greek word for god, *theos*, and so strictly it ought to apply to anyone who believes in a god or gods. But the tradition is to preserve it for believers from these three religions, and that is how we shall use it. The word *atheist* (*a theos*), therefore, strictly speaking, is already defined in the Western context because it is someone who does not believe in such a God. Somewhat illogically, however, perhaps because it is a derivative word and because its use does go back to Greek times, the term is applied not just to those who deny the Abrahamic God, but to those who deny any and all gods, and this is the usage of this book. Of course, though, if you really want to understand the nature and functioning today of a notion like atheism, you need to dig into its history. Let us therefore turn at once to the past. (Introductions to the topic include Buckley 1987, Bremmer 2007, and Hyman 2010.)

Were There Atheists in Ancient Greece?

In the West, there are two major influences from the past—the Greeks and the Jews. Athens and Jerusalem, head and heart, reason and faith. Let's kick off with the Greeks, and the first thing we can say with some confidence is that if there was any atheism (understanding this, obviously, in the sense of denial of any gods), it was not a major factor in Greek culture (Sedley

2013). The five hundred years or so from the time of Homer (eighth century BC) was the age of the Greek gods that fill the pictures of art galleries—Zeus and his fellow inhabitants of Mount Olympus, the various sea gods (Nereids) and river gods (Nymphs) and spring gods (Naiads) and tree gods (Dryads) and more. This was a world as real as the one we inhabit.

The great philosophers—Socrates (469–399), Plato (427–347), Aristotle (384–322)—started the break from all of this, but they were no less committed to an unseen world, a world of deities or at least of deity, for it is thanks to them we start to see the significant move (by the Greeks) from polytheism, many gods, to monotheism, one god. In the *Republic*, Plato famously posited that there are unseen archetypes, the Forms (or the Ideas), and that it is on these that our world is modeled (Cooper 1997). A horse is a horse and not a cow because it "participates" in the Form of Horse. The Forms come hierarchically, and the ultimate is the Form of the Good. As all life here on Earth owes its being to the sun, so all Forms in some sense owe their being to the Form of the Good. In the *Timaeus*, Plato introduced the notion of the Demiurge, something that molded existing material into the universe (Ruse 2013). Whatever the relationship between the Demiurge and the Form of the Good, they are intimately related (if not identical), with the former working according to the latter. Plato's student Aristotle worried that the Forms omitted the link that makes them meaningful for us, and his Supreme Being explicitly stressed this connection. Invoking the notion of a final cause—something we shall see much of in this book—he argued that things must be understood in terms of ends as well as of proximate causes (Ruse 2003). The eye not only had physiological causes making it but it exists for the end, the purpose, of seeing. Ends can influence people and their actions, even though they themselves do nothing. I strive to finish my doctoral dissertation. It is me, not the completed, accepted dissertation that is doing the work, but in some sense it is that goal that is affecting me right now. The Supreme Being, the Unmoved Mover, affects me as I strive to its perfection. It does nothing for me in return and indeed is probably ignorant of my existence, as it does the only thing a perfect thing could do, namely, contemplate its own perfection!

Against this, what price atheism? We can say a number of things. First, in this time and on down to the Romans and the coming of Christianity, atheism was not going to be a dominant position. The idea was certainly known. The term *atheism* was used against Plato's teacher Socrates when he was put on trial for corrupting the youth of Athens with radical and dangerous ideas. Regardless of whether it was corruption, Socrates was certainly filling young ears with radical ideas. Atheism was not among them, although it is true that he had little time for the traditional gods. Second, many of the figures that you might think atheistic were probably more accurately described as at best weak atheists and more likely *agnostic*, meaning unsure or skeptical about all of the positions, or even believers in a god or gods of some perhaps weird kind. Sophists were teachers who specialized in philosophy and rhetoric. One of the best known, Protagoras (490–420), was notoriously a nonbeliever. But he was certainly more agnostic than atheist. "As regards gods, I am unable to know either that they exist or that they do not, or what form they have. For there are many obstacles to knowing: the obscurity of the matter, and the shortness of human life" (Protagoras fragment 4, in Diels and Kranz 1952, 265). The same is probably true of the members of the school of thinkers known as atomists. On the surface, they seem prime candidates for atheism, believing as they did that everything is simply a matter of random motions of particles in space, sometimes coming together and forming complex entities. But they believed in gods that were, like us, the result of chance happenings among the atoms! One of the later atomists, Epicurus (341–270), stressed that these gods have no interest in us, neither rewarding nor punishing; that there is no soul and death is the end of things; and that as a result, one should aim for tranquility and happiness in this life, because there is and will be nothing more.

Third, all of this notwithstanding, there were almost certainly some full-blooded atheists, although prudently they generally kept silent because the authorities disapproved so strongly of the position. In the *Laws*, Plato criticizes them severely. Already starting the confirmation of the point I made at the end of the *Prologue*, the philosopher's main worry was that without belief in a deity or deities, societal norms crumble. God belief is needed for proper behavior. Thus, as was the case in the charge against Socrates, there was a moral component. Atheism is not just wrong but dangerous. Not that this stopped people from toying with the idea or related notions; by the time Greek culture was coming to an end, many, if not most, of the subsequent arguments about atheism had had an airing. Carneades (214–129), the head of Plato's Academy two centuries after the founder, lit into the subject with a zest that would be much admired in certain quarters today. Does one really believe that every last stream or spring has its own deity? And if one doubts these, why believe in the bigger gods? Do the gods have personalities, and do they act in various ways? If so, how can they be eternal and unchanging? (We shall see this one again.) Do the gods have the virtue of courage, and if so, does this mean that they experience fear? Having one important feature seems to imply having another very inappropriate feature. Carneades was probably not an atheist himself, perhaps an agnostic, but the arguments had been let out of the box.

Do We Find Atheism in the Bible?

In the earliest writings, twelfth and eleventh centuries BC, the god of the Old Testament—Yahweh or, in the Latinized form, Jehovah—is but one god among many. He is the god of the Israelites, and so it is not such a very great surprise that he acted as a bit of an ethnic cleanser toward others. Let their gods defend the peoples of other races and tribes if they can. Monotheism only starts to come to the fore as the Israelites developed a more sophisticated theology (sixth century BC, around the time of the author of the second half of the book of Isaiah, toward the end of the Babylonian exile). But agreed that it was possible to believe in other gods rather than Yahweh—even to the extent of putting other gods before Yahweh—was believing in no god at all an option? One does not have to be a biblical scholar to see that even if it was an option, it was simply not an option that people were going to take. For the Jews (and others at that time), one rather believed in God by default. Notice, however, that by and large, unlike the Greeks, argumentation does not play a large role. There is of course Psalm 19: 1: "The heavens are telling the glory of God; and the firmament proclaims his handiwork." But this is atypical. For the Jews, up to and including Jesus and his followers, it was faith that mattered, not reason, meaning a strong conviction without necessarily having any physical or other direct proof. "Now faith is the assurance of things hoped for, the conviction of things not seen" (Hebrews 11: 1). Moreover, it is made pretty clear throughout that having faith is not a neutral matter. Again thinking of Jesus, remember the story of Thomas, who gets berated for wanting evidence that the man before him was indeed the Risen Christ. "Jesus said to him, 'Have you believed because you have seen me? Blessed are those who have not seen and yet have come to believe'" (John 20: 29).

But let's persist with the question. Was it even conceivable to be an atheist? There is the famous passage from the Psalms: "Fools say in their hearts, 'There is no God'" (14: 1). General opinion among scholars, however, is that this is not so much a denial of the existence of God but a resolve to live without God. The rest of the psalm is about the awful behavior of people who turn from God—more a matter of ethics (morality) than of epistemology (knowledge). Perhaps it is all a question of reason as opposed to faith. With reason, you can get some counterarguments, and they can have real bite. With faith, it is more nebulous and really goes from full conviction to nothing much. One suspects that in biblical times there must have been people who were much like my wife, not really bothered one way or the other. But religion would have been a much more insistent presence back then, and going all the way to positive nonbelief would have been a bit strange. When you don't believe something—that is, you believe in its nonexistence—it is usually because you have a good reason to believe as you do.

Did the Coming of Christianity Make Atheism Less or More Probable?

Christianity set the scene for the next two thousand years. It inherited the God of the Old Testament. By now, one is firmly in the world where one has moved from the one-among-many tribal god Yahweh to a single all-powerful creative deity: "Sovereign Lord, who made the heaven and the earth, the sea, and everything in them" (Acts 4: 24). This, monotheism, is the background against which the discussions are going to be framed, especially when the theologians started to draw on the Greek philosophers to articulate their notion of God. As we shall see, the influence of Plato (more precisely, Neo-Platonism) on Augustine (354–430), the most important of them all, was immeasurable (Brown 1967). Yet, the tradition of Jewish thought persisted. First, there was the total commitment to God as Creator God: "In the beginning when God created the heavens and the earth" (Genesis 1: 1). There is no nonsense about the universe being eternal or a designer god coming along and making a world out of preexisting material. First there was nothing. Then there was something. God was responsible. The second break with Greek thought was in the emphasis on the way that God is, on occasion, prepared to intervene in his creation. He is not a Platonic Form, simply existing as a kind of model for this world of ours, or an Aristotelian Unmoved Mover, unaware of our existence and unable to partake in the doings of daily life. Above all, in the incarnation (the coming of God in a human form) and the subsequent atonement (our forgiveness through God's suffering on the cross), we have a God of miracles. We have what is known as an immanent God. We have a providential God who is intimately concerned in our destiny. "Am I a God near by, says the LORD, and not a God far off? Who can hide in secret places so that I cannot see them? says the LORD. Do I not fill heaven and earth? says the LORD" (Jeremiah 23: 23–24).

In the early part of the new millennium, especially in Roman society, charges of atheism were rife, both by Christians and by critics of Christianity (Edwards 2013). The former thought that beliefs in the traditional gods were wrong and dangerous, and the latter thought that Christianity was both mistaken and a threat to the good order of the state. Note, therefore, that as before, atheism was never just a frame of mind, but something with strong social and moral connotations. But were there any real atheists? If there were, they were few and far between. However, there were some movements that were to have repercussions and influence in centuries far distant in the future. Above all, there were the Skeptics—folks who took agnosticism into all areas of inquiry, refusing to admit certain truths and thus suspending judgment. Particularly important was the school known as Pyrrhonism, the best-known exponent of which was the Roman philosopher Sextus Empiricus (160–210). In respects echoing Carneades, he served up a series of devastating arguments focusing on the tensions between a God of the Jews who is actively involved in the affairs of the world and a God of the Greeks who was eternal and unchanging—a God, that is, that the great Christian philosophers and theologians were trying to forge out of the two traditions. Does God have a body or is he incorporeal? If the former, then he seems subject to decay and change. If the latter, then it is hard to see how he can act and have any effect: "the incorporeal is inanimate and insensitive and incapable of any action" (Sextus Empiricus 1953, 151). Along the same lines, suppose God is a person, that is, a creature or, not to put too fine a point on it, an animal. If so, then he is going to have animal-like features, including emotions. Hence, there are going to be things that vex him, like certain sights and sounds, and so in a sense he is liable to being worsened by them. He will be put in something less than a divine mood. And that seems incompatible with an unchanging God. Even more problematic are certain virtues. Take continence. This is the ability to show restraint. But not any kind of restraint. "For a man, they say, is continent not when he abstains from an old woman with one foot in the grave, but when he has the power of enjoying Lais or Phyrne [two notorious Greek courtesans famed for their beauty] or some such charmer and then abstains" (153). So even if God is continent, it means that he has to struggle and is open to change for the worse. "And if there are some things which are hard for God to abstain from and hard to endure, then there are some things which are able to change him for the worse and to cause him vexation" (157). Courage, too, implies that God has to be scared of something and that he overcomes his emotions.

Sextus was not an atheist. But he was certainly planting seeds that would germinate and fruit, if long after his time.

Is Medieval Europe Important to Our Story?

Well, it is and it isn't (Weltecke 2013)! In some respects, it is perhaps the most relevant of all, for it was then that great philosophers—notably St. Anselm (1033–1109) and St. Thomas Aquinas (1225–1274)—were developing and elaborating their arguments for the existence of God. These are obviously going to be the subjects of much discussion, for and against, before we have finished. In other respects, it isn't really that relevant, at least when it comes to the case for atheism. Right through the time, there were surely people who were basically indifferent to religion, willing indeed to break with its moral dictates. That is true of any age. There were also people, sometimes groups, who were willing and perhaps determined to counter fundamental aspects of belief—Christian, Jewish, and, of course, of growing importance, Muslim. You find people who asserted that the Greek philosophers were right and that matter is eternal. Others denied the immortality of the soul. Generally speaking, these were dangerous things to do and laid one open to charges of heresy and subsequent punishment. But outright denying the existence of God was another matter. A case can be made for saying really no one went there. It wasn't so much considered wrong and dangerous as simply absurd. The sort of thing philosophers could and did posit, because everyone knew that they did not mean to be taken seriously. Thinking in contemporary terms, suppose a philosopher today posited that President John Kennedy was really an alien from Andromeda and that he was assassinated to cover up this fact. No one would take this seriously. Indeed, everyone would think such a hypothesis showed that its inventor was one of those barmy, rather creepy conspiracy fanatics who simply cannot accept that two plus two always equals four. It is just plain crazy, and if its promoter is sane, then he or she is probably a philosopher, only putting forward this hypothesis to make a point—for instance, that even really nutty scenarios are logically possible. The same was true of the denial of God's existence in the Middle Ages.

What Was the Scientific Revolution?

So, let us fast-forward to the middle of the last millennium and to the three big Rs (Robichaud 2013). First, there is the Renaissance with the discovery of the glories of the past and the growth of intellectual humanism as represented by people like Erasmus of Rotterdam (1466–1536), who learned the languages of antiquity and used this knowledge to reignite the intellectual achievements of the great thinkers of Greece particularly, but also of other societies. Then there is the Reformation, the break by many Christians from the rule of Rome and the development (or sometimes refurbishing) of alternative claims and doctrines. One of the biggest moves was the repudiation of the Catholic emphasis on tradition, that the church is authoritative in the handing on of the truth and that salvation can be gained as much as anything through good works. Now the emphasis is on the individual and his or her direct relationship to God. The Bible takes the authoritative role of the church. And salvation is to be purchased through faith, not works. "For by grace you have been saved through faith, and this is not your own doing; it is the gift of God" (Ephesians 2: 8). That was why Protestants condemned the purchase of indulgences—prayers for the dead and that sort of thing and a major spark of all of the trouble. You cannot buy your way into the Kingdom of Heaven.

Third, there is what is known as the Scientific Revolution. This is the growth and development of science, from the Polish astronomer Nicolaus Copernicus (1473–1543) at the beginning of the sixteenth century to the English physicist Isaac Newton (1642–1727) at the end of the seventeenth century. It is the period that sees Copernicus put the sun at the center of the universe and the Earth as one of the planets circling it; that sees Tycho Brahe (1546–1601) map the heavens with incredible accuracy, and then his assistant Johannes Kepler (1571–1630) propose his laws that captured the motions of the planets; that sees Galileo Galilei (1564–1642) do the same for terrestrial motion and giving its laws; and that sees Isaac Newton bringing everything together in one unifying theory, with his force of gravitational attraction at the explanatory heart. There is much else, of course, including William Harvey (1578–1657) working on the mechanism of the heart, William Gilbert's (1544–1603) seminal inquiries into magnetism, and the growth of chemistry from alchemy, as represented by the labors of the Irish aristocrat Robert Boyle (1627–1691).

The Scientific Revolution is many things to many people, then and now. Above all, it was a change of metaphors (Hall 1954; Dijksterhuis 1961). Until that time, very much under the influence of Aristotle, the world was seen in terms of organisms. Unlike Plato, Aristotle did not believe in one unifying world soul, but he did think that everything should be understood organically (Sedley 2008). That is why, for inanimate objects as well as living things, talk of final causes is appropriate. Everything is to be understood in terms of ends (purposes, goals) as well as proximate factors—what made it, how it came to be. After the Scientific Revolution, everything was to be understood in terms of machines, mechanisms. How does it work? What are the laws governing its functioning? But is this such a big deal? You might say, truly, that just as the organic model has some kind of intentionality at play—for Plato the Demiurge, for Aristotle special vital forces—so the machine model has some kind of intentionality at play. Who made the machine and for what purpose? The answer for the Christian is that God is the machine maker. But fairly soon scientists found that talk of God in science really added nothing to the discussion, so it was dropped (Ruse 2010). God became a "retired engineer" (Dijksterhuis 1961, 491).

The scientist-mathematician-philosopher René Descartes (1596–1650) is the key figure here. He divided all things into two different substances—*res extensa*, extended or material things, and *res cogitans*, thinking or conscious things. Humans uniquely link the two, but otherwise it is all one or the other. Science deals with the material, and so it is all a question of finding the unbroken laws governing dead matter, or rather— Descartes was an enthusiastic corpuscular theorist—particles of it. Robert Boyle, as important as a philosopher of the revolution as a contributor to it, made explicit the machine metaphor. Making specific reference to a device built in the late sixteenth century, he argued that the world is "like a rare clock, such as may be that at Strasbourg, where all things are so skillfully contrived that the engine being once set a-moving, all things proceed according to the artificer's first design, and the motions of the little statues that at such hours perform these or those motions do not require (like those of puppets) the peculiar interposing of the artificer or any intelligent agent employed by him, but perform their functions on particular occasions by virtue of the general and primitive contrivance of the whole engine" (Boyle 1996, 12–13).

Did the Scientific Revolution Spell the Death of God?

Most assuredly, it did not. Copernicus was a cleric. (He was not ordained but technically was a kind of clerk working for the Catholic hierarchy. This supported what was a very professional pursuit of astronomy.) Subsequent major figures in the revolution were all committed to Christianity in one way or another. Descartes upset many authorities with his philosophizing—he was quickly put on the Index—but he died as he lived, a sincere Christian. In the *Discourse on Method*, he wrote that we should think of our body "as a machine created by the hand of God, and in consequence incomparably better designed and with more admirable movements than any machine that can be invented by man" (Descartes 1964, 41). Newton privately doubted the divinity of Christ but famously (or notoriously) spent as much time studying the Bible as studying nature. Boyle was explicit that the machine metaphor said nothing against God: "And those things which the school philosophers [followers of Aristotle] ascribe to the agency of nature interposing according to emergencies, I ascribe to the wisdom of God in the first fabric of the universe" (Boyle 1996, 12).

Of course, there is the Galileo episode, without which no account of the Scientific Revolution—no account of the relationship of science to religion in the Scientific Revolution—would be complete (McMullin 2005). That Galileo ran into problems with the church because he endorsed Copernicus's heliocentric (sun-centered) worldview does show that there were significant tensions. But the clash was never quite what later antireligious zealots made it out to be. It occurred a hundred years after Copernicus, during the Counter-Reformation, when the Catholics were firmly shutting the stable door after the fleeing of the Protestants. It should never have happened, but students of the episode all stress that much of the problem was brought on Galileo by himself. To say he was tactless is a bit like saying Hitler had a thing about the Jews. He set out to rub the authorities the wrong way, and having been parodied as a near-moron in Galileo's writings—writings in the vernacular so everyone could read them—it is hardly surprising that the pope reacted badly and strongly.

Are We Now on the Road to Atheism?

Obviously, the Scientific Revolution—as well as the Renaissance and the Reformation—had major aftereffects (Kors 2013). You don't have that kind of earthquake without some follow-up tsunami. The Reformation had a significant, if somewhat indirect, effect on the issue. Luther and Calvin and the others were not themselves in any way moving toward nonbelief. Rather, they were setting out what they thought were the proper conditions for Christian thinking and behavior, especially over the matter of belief versus action, with Protestants favoring the former and Catholics the latter. However, once you allow through the door the idea that there are alternative positions from which to choose, it proves to be the thin end of a very large wedge. If there are two forms of (Western) Christianity, why not three or four? Once you take away the idea that there is one and only one form of true belief, you start people thinking up their own forms of such belief that may not be as Christian-centered or friendly as either Protestantism or Catholicism. Add to this that by the time of the seventeenth century, the way to the East has been opened right up and travelers there are finding very sophisticated forms of what seem to be religious belief—Buddhism, Hinduism, Confucianism—that make no mention of Christian themes whatsoever, and there seems to be a veritable smorgasbord of options.

And then there was science. As the triumphs continued, more and more it seemed that the world could be explained without any direct reference to the deity. It was not a question of rejecting God, but of reconceiving his relationship to his creation. If God was a retired engineer, then acknowledge this fully. Make him do all of the work at the beginning, and then once he had got his machine (the world) up and running, let him sit back and admire his handiwork. This is not atheism, but it is certainly not theism. We have a hands-off god rather than a hands-on god. Introducing another term, it is usual to speak of this kind of god as the God of *deism*, a term derived this time from the Latin word for God (*deus*). In a broad sense, people like Plato and Aristotle could be described as deists, but it is usual to reserve the term for modern times. Lord Herbert of Cherbury (1583–1648) is often known as the father of English deism. As you might expect, the articulation and growth of deism was not necessarily a simple and smooth phenomenon. Lord Herbert actually believed that God would send signs and intervene after prayer! Isaac Newton, for all that he privately denied the divinity of Christ—which in itself takes out a lot of miracles—nevertheless thought that God had to intervene to keep the solar system functioning efficiently. So this one can say: For the deists, the thought that they were simply on the way to atheism would have been totally shocking. Of course, their opponents and critics took the time-honored move of labeling them atheists, and of course, given the opprobrium and sometimes real danger of being labeled an atheist, there were good prudential grounds for not admitting to total non-belief. But generally one can say that if one thought of oneself as a deist in the seventeenth and eighteenth centuries, with reason one could think of oneself as deeply religious—just not a conventional Christian.

But whatever the believers of the moment might think, ideas have their own momentum. With hindsight, surely one can see that deism is just a stopping place on the road to atheism. Methodologically, God is now retired. It is but one more step to make him metaphysically retired also. Yet, interestingly, this did not happen, at least in any straightforward way. For a start, there was somewhat of a backlash. If not consciously, there were those who saw that the rot had set in and traditional Christianity was under threat. They drew a line in the sand and refused to cross it. They saw that the head, the power of reason, was leading to new modes of thinking, and so they declared themselves for the heart, the emotions, and ultimately faith. Pietism in Germany, from which Immanuel Kant (1724–1804) emerged, was one such group reacting against the forces of change. In Britain and then in America, the Methodists were the great counterrevolutionaries. Of course, in a way one can say that these movements were as modern and revolutionary as the groups and ideas they opposed, and certainly no one would say that education and understanding was lacking or despised. John Wesley (1703–1791), the founder of Methodism, was an Oxford graduate. But when he had his conversion experience, it was not reason that led him. He wrote of going to church and of reading Luther on Paul's Epistle to the Romans. Suddenly, "I felt my heart strangely warmed. I felt I did trust in Christ, Christ alone, for salvation; and an assurance was given me that He had taken away my sins, even mine, and saved me from the law of sin and death" (John Wesley's journal entry, May 24, 1738).

But what of those who did go the way of reason? The eighteenth century, the age of the Enlightenment, saw some great skeptics and revolutionaries, but in the end, they remained deists and did not make the move to atheism. This is true of the French writer and wit Voltaire (1694–1778). His novel *Candide* is a withering attack on attempts to defend God in the face of evil, but still he remained a believer. This is almost certainly true of David Hume (1711–1776), the great philosopher. His posthumously published *Dialogues Concerning Natural Religion* (1779) contains some of the most powerful critiques of religious claims—critiques we shall be considering in some detail later—but in the end he hedged about total rejection of the deity, and a case can certainly be made for deism. This is undoubtedly true of Erasmus Darwin (1731–1802), grandfather of Charles Darwin and in his own right an evolutionist.

Darwin's God—the God of the deist—has preprogrammed the world so that he did not have to intervene further. Evolution, therefore, can be seen as the greatest triumph of God. It is the strongest proof of his existence. It is certainly not something that disproves the need for or existence of a creator or designer. In Darwin's own words, "What a magnificent idea of the infinite power of *The Great Architect! The Cause of Causes! Parent of Parents! Ens Entium!*" (Darwin 1794, 509). Across the Atlantic, it is true also of the American revolutionaries. Shortly before he died, Benjamin Franklin (1706–1790) responded to the president of Yale that he certainly believed in a God who was worthy of worship. However, when it comes to Jesus, although the morality preached is the best we have or shall ever have, "I have, with most of the present Dissenters in England, some Doubts as to his Divinity" (Van Doren 1938, 778).

Why Not Go All of the Way?

Why did deism persist? There are probably as many answers as there were deists. For someone like Franklin, religion was entwined with humans functioning in groups, and he saw religion in some form or another as essential for a healthy society. If Christianity is not the answer, then some other answer must be sought. But without generalizing wildly, it is clear that one major factor kept people from total nonbelief: the problem of organisms. Boyle was explicit on this. The world may be machinelike, but organisms demand final-cause thinking! You cannot get away from intention when looking at them, and this implies designing intelligence. "For there are some things in nature so curiously contrived, and so exquisitely fitted for certain operations and uses, . . . that, though they may have been designed for other (and perhaps higher) uses, yet they were designed for this use" (Boyle 1966, 397).

Not everyone bought into this. In the spirit of the atomists and other ancients, there were always those who argued that given enough time, even random motions would create the illusion of design. This convinced no one. Somewhat more enterprising were those who argued that people like Boyle had it backward. It was not so much that the eye was designed for seeing, but that things having come together as they are, nature takes advantage of them and uses them. As it happens, we have eyes, and so use them to see. But if we didn't have eyes, then presumably we would have something else, and we could use that. The neo-Epicurean Guillaume Lamy (1644–1683) argued that to think otherwise, claiming that organisms show design, which can then be used for intended purposes, commits God to having created the clitoris so that women could masturbate (Lamy 1679, 81–82). Apparently no one back then picked up the challenge and explored in full the rather interesting theological implications of this line of thought.

It is debatable as to whether Immanuel Kant was a deist and ultimately not that profitable to speculate on his tortured theological thinking. But he was adamant that organisms are special and that in explanation they seem to require some kind of designing intelligence, even if one may not bring this into science (Kant 1951). For this reason if for no other, many would not have seen deism as a stopping place on the way to atheism. Was this about to change? Let us see.

2

FROM THE ENLIGHTENMENT
TO THE PRESENT

Were There Then No Atheists in the Enlightenment?

In 1762, David Hume left his native Edinburgh, the capital of Calvinist Scotland, and moved to the more open climes of Paris, the capital of freethinking France. Invited to dinner by the notorious Paul-Henri Thiry, Baron d'Holbach (1723–1789), Hume remarked that he had never met an atheist and doubted that such existed. His host laughed and invited the Scot to look around the room at the other dinner guests. "I can show you fifteen atheists right off. The other three haven't yet made up their minds" (Mossner 1954, 483). The baron may have been exaggerating, but he was certainly speaking truly of himself and some others, notably the philosopher and early evolutionist Denis Diderot (1713–1784). D'Holbach, very much a post-Renaissance man, was much influenced by the writings of the Ancients, most particularly the poem *On the Nature of Things* by the Roman poet Lucretius (99–55 BC), himself in turn a follower of the philosophy of Epicurus, the Greek atomist who advocated control of the passions and a simple life free of superstition and fear—wherein lies true happiness. Lucretius did not deny the existence of gods but thought they are irrelevant to us and that all, including humans and their thinking, can be explained naturalistically by the motions of the atoms. D'Holbach—who also knew and appreciated the work of Lamy—took these ideas further and in his *System of Nature* (that may have been partly penned by his friend Diderot) dropped the idea of God entirely and argued for a purely naturalistic account of the whole of existence.

One asks why D'Holbach and the others like Diderot embraced atheism. The answer is simple, namely, that they saw themselves engaged in a moral quest. Religion produces ignorance, superstition, hatred, violence, and much more. In the Epicurean tradition, the Enlightenment atheists wanted people to break with all of this, to accept and rejoice in the natural world that exists and functions without purpose or end or reason, simply as a result of atoms going blindly about their paths. "Many persons acknowledge, that the extravagances to which superstition lends activity, are real evils; many complain of the abuse of superstition, but there are very few who feel that this abuse, together with the evils, are the necessary consequences of the fundamental principles of all superstition; which are founded upon the most grievous notions, which rest themselves on the most tormenting opinions" (D'Holbach 2007, 2: 205). As always, atheism is not just a matter of facts but also of morals and social policy.

Was Christianity Becoming Irrelevant?

By now you will be realizing that it is not just a matter of atheism in isolation, but of atheism in relation to its doppelgänger, theism. When I was a kid, many homes had on their walls a model of a house with two front doors. In one stood a model of a little woman in summer clothing, and in the other stood a little man shivering under an umbrella. I suppose it worked by catgut or something like that, for when it was sunny, the little woman came out of the door, and when it was raining, she was pulled back in and the little man came out. Atheism and theism are a bit like that. As one gains the upper hand, the other sinks and despairs, and conversely. In Europe, the nineteenth century was a pretty rainy time for theism, and conversely, atheism found lots of sunshine (Nash 2013).

In a way, the most important thing is outside our story. In the second half of the eighteenth century and the first half of the nineteenth century, Britain became industrialized, with other major countries following in later years. This meant that folk left the structured society of rural Britain, where the church had a long and important role, moving to cities and working in anonymous factories, where the church found it difficult to follow and keep contact. Increasingly, there were large numbers of people for whom religion meant less and less. From a broader perspective, this is all something that goes back to the Scientific Revolution and the other major upheavals of that time. We see four hundred years or more of a changing world making possible a life without God (Taylor 2007). But things did intensify as we move from the eighteenth to the nineteenth century. Incidental changes are revealing. Rather than religion, secular things like professional sports started to catch people's attention and occupy their time. Of course, this was not true of everyone, and the nonconformist churches—Methodism particularly—started to make major inroads, as did Catholicism, especially where there were large Irish settlements. This does not mean that people declared themselves atheist or even nonreligious, and the state schools did sterling work in keeping alive the flame of Christianity, but the fact is that in Britain and increasingly in large parts of Europe, religion simply ceased to have the magic and the hold that it once had.

Why Was America Different?

This was not the case across the Atlantic. It is difficult to generalize. Excluding the French-speaking, Catholic province of Quebec, which will get special mention later in this chapter, British North America—namely, Canada—has always reflected the mother country in important ways. This was

not so in the United States, particularly in the southern part
of the country and the west as the young country expanded
outward. There, if anything, religion, specifically a strong
form of evangelical Christianity, deeply Bible-based, grew at
great speed and with much effect (Noll 2002; Porterfield 2012).
It was in the first half of the nineteenth century that we see
the beginnings and growth of what today is known as biblical
literalism, Fundamentalism, or, more recently, Creationism or
Creation Science (Numbers 2006). It was also the time when
we start to see the beginnings of distinctively American forms
of religion, like the Seventh-day Adventists and (most notably)
the Church of Jesus Christ of Latter-day Saints, better known
as the Mormons.

There were many reasons for this growth, truly remarkable
when you think that almost to a person the founders of the
country in the late eighteenth century—men like Benjamin
Franklin—were deists. The simple and true answer is that
deism is no religion to build a new country—work that is dangerous, back-breaking, and yet with hope for the future. People
needed rules for the present—how to treat servants, how to
bring up children, what to say to strangers—and the preach-
ers gave them those. Read your Bible! The answers are there.
And don't be worried by your lack of education. Did not St.
Paul say that the words of the wise are foolish (1 Corinthians
3: 18)? This was a religion for the times and even more so as the
country rushed toward the tragedy of the Civil War. Although
the abolitionists were much given to quoting Scripture—it is
hard to justify owning another human being in the face of
the Beatitudes—the slave owners and those who accepted the
practice were no less given to quoting the Holy Word. Hagar,
Sarah's handmaiden, is given to Abraham, who impregnates
her with as little moral concern for the young woman's desires
or integrity as the worst kind of plantation owner. No wonder
that, when it came to the slave question, Christianity was cherished at least as much by the South as by the North. After the
war, Christianity came even more into service in the South.

Sermon after sermon was preached likening the Southerners to the Israelites in captivity. God chastises most those whom he loves the most.

What Is Higher Criticism?

Back in Europe, in the first half of the nineteenth century, there were more than just social factors leading to—shall we say—a recasting of traditional Christianity. If, like Protestants, you make the Bible all important, then you are asking for people to start looking carefully at the text, and as scholars develop skills and techniques for reading and assessing ancient writings— from Greece or Egypt or increasingly from the Far East—they are going to turn these powers on the Holy Writ (Rogerson 2000). As they did—*lower criticism* is the study of the texts as texts, and *higher criticism* is the interpretation of such texts— very quickly they started to find that the Bible reads less like something handed down by the deity from on high and more like a collection of manuscripts telling of ancient peoples and their fables and beliefs and practices, all rather cobbled together into one book. The creation stories of Genesis were soon seen to be mythological accounts of origins, not literal but intended to express great truths about our relationship to the deity. The much-loved stories of the patriarchs and the kings and the prophets were analyzed for their symbolic meanings and less as true happenings in an ancient land, far away and long ago. And even more dramatically, the stories of the Gospels and the rest of the New Testament were now seen to be constructions bolstering the claim of Jesus as Messiah rather than eyewitness testimonies of events that really occurred. Particularly scandalous was *The Life of Jesus* by the young German scholar David Strauss (1808–1874), who saw the accounts of the miracles as storytelling designed to cement the special status of the Savior.

One cannot say that the results of this scholarship were always welcomed. When Marian Evans, later transformed into the novelist George Eliot (1819–1880), translated Strauss into English, the evangelical reformer the Seventh Earl of Shaftesbury (1801–1885) referred to it as "the most pestilential book ever vomited out of the jaws of hell." But higher criticism had a lasting effect, not the least in forcing people to rethink their views on traditional Christian beliefs about such things as eternal damnation for nonbelievers. If the Resurrection was a product of human imagination, would one not want to say much the same about many of the prescriptions that one finds associated with Christianity? John Stuart Mill (1806–1873) wrote of his father James Mill (1773–1836) that he rejected the God of Christianity because he wanted no truck with "a being who would make a Hell—who would create the human race with the infallible foreknowledge, and therefore the intention, that the great majority of them were to be consigned to horrible and everlasting torment" (Hyman 2010, 127). Many felt this way. In the autobiographies of Victorian worthies, again and again one finds that things like this started to tip people toward nonbelief (Budd 1977). The role of science was very much secondary (Ruse 2005).

But Wasn't Science the Death Knell?

Perhaps secondary in a temporal sense, but surely overall it was science that demolished traditional theism. Geology was hacking away at the age of the Earth. Physiology and chemistry were showing that life is no more than material processes. Physics was making implausible a host of beliefs from transubstantiation to the afterlife. Thanks to thermodynamics, we know we are headed for heat death rather than Paradise. And above all, there was Darwin. In his great work, *On the Origin of Species* (1859), he argued that all organisms are the end result of a long, slow, natural process of development, evolution. Moreover, giving a full exposition of an idea hinted by Diderot, he offered a mechanism that provided a naturalistic—law-bound—explanation of final causes in biology. Starting with the propensity of all organisms to explode upward in population numbers, Darwin followed others—particularly the clergyman Robert Malthus (1766–1834)—in thinking that life is an ongoing struggle for existence. Pointing out that the winners in the struggle will tend on average to be different from the losers, Darwin argued that this leads not just to change but to change in the direction of "adaptive advantage"—organisms with eyelike features and handlike features do better than organisms without such features, and so, without the need of divine intervention, the organic world becomes ever-more designlike. Final causes without an immediately intervening creative intelligence. Then, in a later work, the *Descent of Man* (1871), Darwin extended all of this thinking to our own species. Not only are final causes explained but so are those thus shaped, up to and including us. Biology had been brought into the fold with physics. "There is grandeur in this view of life, with its several powers, having been originally breathed into a few forms or into one; and that, whilst this planet has gone cycling on according to the fixed law of gravity, from so simple a beginning endless forms most beautiful and most wonderful have been, and are being, evolved" (Darwin 1859, 489–490).

After Darwin, wasn't Christianity on life support? Perhaps so. These are some of the issues we are going to be raising and discussing later in this book. What we can say is that as the nineteenth century moved along, it became possible to be a respectable nonbeliever. This was the final position of Darwin, although it is interesting to note that he did not jump straight to this after discovering natural selection. Right up through the writing of the *Origin*, he continued to believe that God designed organisms; it was just that he did this at a distance, through unbroken law. "I see no necessity in the belief that the eye was expressly designed. On the other hand I cannot anyhow be contented to view this wonderful universe & especially the nature of man, & to conclude that everything is the result of brute force. I am inclined to look at everything as resulting from designed laws, with the details, whether good or bad, left to the working out of what we may call chance" (Darwin 1985–, 8: 224, letter to Asa Gray, May 22, 1860). When Darwin did move to nonbelief, confirming the pattern just noted, it was because he hated the theological idea of eternal damnation for nonbelievers (who included both his father and his brother) rather than the science.

Starting in antiquity, we have already met the idea of what came to be known as *agnosticism*, but it was Thomas Henry Huxley (1825–1895), Darwin's great supporter and the grandfather of the novelist Aldous Huxley (1894–1963), who invented the term to cover the position of people like him, not believers but at the same time not outright atheists—folk who simply didn't know and were not ashamed to admit this. Huxley tells how he ran through the gamut of possible beliefs—theism, atheism, pantheism (the belief that God and the physical world are one and the same, often ascribed to the Dutch philosopher Baruch Spinoza [1632–1677], who spoke of *deus sive natura*, God or nature)—and decided that none of these categories really applied to his own thinking. He just didn't know. This wasn't indifference—anything but. He felt he didn't have the tools or the facts to give an answer. "So I took thought, and invented what I conceived to be the appropriate title of "agnostic." It came into my head as suggestively antithetic to the "gnostic" of Church history, who professed to know so much about the very things of which I was ignorant; and I took the earliest opportunity of parading it at our Society [a debating club to which he belonged], to show that I, too, had a tail, like the other foxes" (Huxley 1894, 239).

Was Agnosticism a Cop-out?

I used the word *respectable*, and this was intentional. For someone like Huxley, as always, being an agnostic was not simply a matter of epistemology. It was a moral issue. He did not become an agnostic through ignorance or indifference or a desire to stir things up. He became an agnostic because he was driven to such a position. "The one thing in which most of these good people were agreed was the one thing in which I differed from them. They were quite sure that they had attained a certain 'gnosis'—had more or less successfully solved the problem of existence; while I was quite sure I had not, and had a pretty strong conviction that the problem was insoluble. And, with Hume and Kant on my side, I could not think myself presumptuous in holding fast by that opinion" (238). But giving up on God did not mean giving up on morality or one's massive sense of social duty. People like Huxley were deeply involved in the reformation of Victorian Britain, trying to bring modern science (including social science) and technology to the running of a huge, urbanized society. They may not have been Christians, but they took the parable of the talents tremendously seriously. And to succeed at what they were doing, they had to be above reproach. They had to be purer than pure. They could not afford the notoriety of someone like Baron d'Holbach. So even had they been in sympathy with his extreme radicalism, they would have recognized its political liabilities, and they stayed far away. Victorian agnosticism was earnest and sincere. It was also very respectable.

What about the Atheists?

But what about those for whom respectability was very much a secondary issue? Those for whom nonbelief was a burning passion, and that in itself was what counted, not the ways in which it could be fitted into a larger overall agenda? Going into the nineteenth century, it was the French Revolution that set the agenda, both of those who reacted against it and of those who welcomed its meaning and significance, if not the violence into which it degenerated. This second group was the one that might be expected to move in the direction of nonbelief, especially given that so much of the revolution's causal motivation was rejection of the old patterns of belief and behavior—not the least, that represented by established Christianity. In Britain and America, the key work was Thomas Paine's *Age of Reason*, the first part of which was published in 1794. Paradoxically, it was written while Paine (1737–1809) was imprisoned in France, and it was an attempt to prevent the French from sinking into a slough of despair and atheism! Paine himself was openly and flatly a deist. "I believe in one God, and no more; and I hope for happiness beyond this life" (Paine 1907, 21). What made his work controversial, however, was the extent to which he paralleled the more sophisticated higher criticism in taking apart the tales of the Bible and showing them to be myths, fabrications, stories to make a point regardless of the facts. Moreover, so much of the material is about as morally degenerate as it is possible for stories to be. "Whenever we read the obscene stories, the voluptuous debaucheries, the cruel and torturous executions, the unrelenting vindictiveness, with which more than half the Bible [OT] is filled, it would be more consistent that we called it the word of a demon, than the Word of God. It is a history of wickedness, that has served to corrupt and brutalize mankind; and, for my own part, I sincerely detest it, as I detest everything that is cruel" (34). Yet as always we see that Paine was not arguing as he did just for fun or to make philosophical points. His was a moral crusade, to turn people from mistaken and degenerate ways to the paths to true understanding and happiness. "I believe in the equality of man; and I believe that religious duties consist in doing justice, loving mercy, and endeavouring to make our fellow-creatures happy" (21–22).

Paine had little effect in France, but his influence in Britain and in the early years of the American republic was immense, not the least because his Quaker roots had instilled in him the virtues of plain speaking, and this was evident in his writings through and through, thereby making them that much more dangerous because they appealed to so general an audience. From now on, nonbelief in traditional Christianity was part of the public discourse, even though in Britain there were savage prosecutions for the publication of Paine's work, and in America the religious growth at the beginning of the nineteenth century turned popular opinion from enthusiastic endorsement of Paine to rejection and revilement. As the century went on, despite the criticisms, increasingly there were attempts to put society on a nonreligious basis—noteworthy were the efforts of the early socialist, the Scottish mill owner Robert Owen (1771–1858), who tried to found his own utopian societies, although without lasting success. One of his disciples, George Jacob Holyoake (1817–1906), who was also influenced by the French philosopher August Comte's (1798–1859) idea of society passing through three phases—the religious, the metaphysical, and the positivist—managed to be the last person in Britain sent to prison (in 1842) for blasphemy. He was much involved in the nascent cooperative societies in Britain—the "Co-op"—places where the working classes could purchase goods without being burdened by the profits of the capitalists. Holyoake preferred the name *secularist* to the more provocative *atheist*, although in later life he was happy to refer to himself as an agnostic. He was a great founder of secular societies where, through lectures and the like, the working classes could find the means of moral improvement.

Alternatives to Religion?

A question that will be discussed in detail later is the extent to which atheists try to find a substitute for conventional religion and to which they simply try to eliminate conventional religion. The answer, of course, is that there are both kinds. Holyoake is more the former kind. The same is true of the followers of Comte, who set up a full-blown religion with its own saints. This "religion of humanity"—which had its Anglophone equivalents like the American ethical societies—finds echoes today in so-called humanism, something also to be discussed later in this book. It is hard at times not to smile at the earnestness of some of these movements and the almost pompous silliness with which they performed rituals intended to substitute for traditional religious practices.

Always good with a phrase, Thomas Henry Huxley spoke of the positivists as having Catholicism without Christianity! But one should never underestimate the lasting effects. John Stuart Mill spent some time under the influence of positivism, and to the end of his life, he promoted a kind of secular alternative to Christianity—anticipating another eminent Victorian we shall meet later in wanting a "real, though purely human, religion, which sometimes calls itself the Religion of Humanity, and sometimes that of Duty" (Mill 1985, 10: 486–487). Mill's thinking, far more than that of Karl Marx (1818–1883), had incredible influence on the distinctively British form of socialism—a kind of liberal democracy—that played such an important role in the twentieth century. Likewise, the Co-op played a major role in British lower-middle-class and working-class life. Somewhat amusingly, it became the largest chain of undertakers (funeral directors) in the country—actually, not so surprising when you reflect on the obsession of the decent poor not to fall on the parish and end in a pauper's grave, an emotion captured brilliantly by Charles Dickens (1812–1870) in his portrayal of Betty Higden in *Our Mutual Friend*. My grandmother found it very comforting that she had made full arrangements with the Co-op to do the honors at her death. And it did, at a fair price, with much dignity. The Vicar of Walsall (in Staffordshire) read the funeral service. You did not have to be a nonbeliever to benefit.

Who Were the Militant Atheists?

What about representatives of those whose main motivation was to eliminate conventional religion? There were well-known, notorious examples, although one should note that they had much in common with the more accommodating atheists, particularly inasmuch as everyone was driven by moral and social urges. In England, the key figure was Charles Bradlaugh (1833–1891). Helped on his way by Holyoake, Bradlaugh got himself in hot water for publishing in England the American pamphlet *The Fruits of Philosophy, or the Private Companion of Young Married People*. Philosophy, Socrates would have told us, has many fruits, but one doubts that even he thought they extended to birth control, the subject of the pamphlet. It is interesting although expectable that the very respectable Charles Darwin, who was now openly admitting to being an agnostic, refused to testify on behalf of such a scandalous cause. Saved from prison on a technicality and elected as member of Parliament for Northampton, Bradlaugh then pursued a decade-long, ultimately successful attempt to take his seat without taking a religious oath of allegiance. Probably for reasons of style as much as substance, the Holyoake wing of the secularists did not always favorably view Bradlaugh's open defiance of established authority.

In America, the point man was Colonel (he served in the Civil War) Robert Ingersoll (1833–1899). Like Bradlaugh, he was much given to turning to the law to promote his causes. He called himself "agnostic," but when it came to Christianity, there was not much skepticism or profession of ignorance. "The doctrine that future happiness depends upon belief is monstrous. It is the infamy of infamies. The notion that faith in Christ is to be rewarded by an eternity of bliss, while a dependence upon reason, observation and experience merits everlasting pain, is too absurd for refutation, and can be relieved only by that unhappy mixture of insanity and ignorance, called 'faith'" (Ingersoll 1874). The dilemma is stark. Either we go the way of the heart, of blind faith and conviction, or we go the way of the head, of reason and evidence. "Our ignorance is God; what we know is science." And so on and so forth—at great length.

What Did the Philosophers Say?

As we move into the twentieth century, we prepare ourselves for some of the biggest and worst conflicts the world has ever known. At the same time, there is the rise of godless societies like the Soviet Union and the People's Republic of China (Communist China). The roots of these and much else in the century lie in the nineteenth century and particularly in the writings of Marx. Notoriously, he was against religion, thinking it a tool of oppression by those in charge over those beneath and powerless. Much influenced by the thinking of the philosopher Ludwig Feuerbach (1804–1872), who saw God as something made by humans in their own image, Marx located the problem in the socioeconomic conditions in which most people find themselves. "Religious suffering is, at one and the same time, the expression of real suffering and a protest against real suffering. Religion is the sigh of the oppressed creature, the heart of a heartless world, and the soul of soulless conditions. It is the opium of the people" (Marx 1844). Human beings are thus "alienated" from their true nature, and hence religion is an illusion to be cast off as people become more self-aware and conscious that their very existence is chained by illusions—illusions designed to profit others, not the deluded. This was written in 1843, and that Marx in significant respects spoke truly is underlined by the popular children's hymn written in 1848 by Mrs. Cecil F. Alexander (1823–1895). It is explicit in its use of Christianity to support the status quo, with those in control staying that way.

> The rich man in his castle,
> The poor man at his gate,
> God made them high and lowly,
> And ordered their estate.

Later in the century, there was the ever-polemical Friedrich Nietzsche (1844–1900). Raging against everything, not the least of which was Charles Darwin and his ideas—a critique that Nietzsche managed to extract from a general hostility to anything British—he balanced Marx's cracks about religion and its opiate qualities with his own declaration that God is dead.

Noteworthy is how Nietzsche echoes Feuerbach's claim that God is our construction, as well as the way Nietzsche seems to regard the prospect with existential angst and despair, as contrasted to the nigh sunny prospects of nonbelief for people like Huxley. For them, it was simply a matter of relief to have rid themselves of that dreadful stone around their necks. Not so the tortured author of the *Gay Science*: "God is dead. God remains dead. And we have killed him" (Nietzsche 1974, section 125; the title has nothing to do with happiness or sexual orientation, being the translation of a Provençal term referring to the art of poetry).

Was the Twentieth Century More of the Same?

Well, yes, in one sense—much of the century does seem to have been unpacking and consolidating the moves of the years before—but no in another sense, given the social movements of the era. One thinks of the just-mentioned regimes of Stalin and Mao and, of course, of Hitler and National Socialism. In fact, although atheism in one sense was set to flourish as never before, things are a little more complex than you might think. The figures to be given in the next chapter suggest that it is one thing for a state like Russia (the USSR) or China to declare itself atheist; it is quite another to get people in their hearts to go along with this, especially in vast countries like Russia and China with so many different ethnic groups and different religions or variants, and where religion plays so great a social and cultural role apart from any theological implications.

Mao Zedong (1893–1976) had no love of religion, remarking to the Dalai Lama in 1959 that "religion is poison." During the Cultural Revolution (1966–1976), the Red Guards smashed up or took over religious buildings. The Constitution of 1978, however, guarantees freedom of religion—within limits, for instance Catholics cannot acknowledge the suzerainty of Rome—although Communist party members are not permitted religious belief. Overall, Joseph Stalin (1878–1953) was extremely hostile to religion: church property was expropriated, seminaries closed, writings suppressed and forbidden, and many priests suffered and died, especially in the brutal purges of the second half of the 1930s. A psychoanalyst might seize on the fact that Stalin was raised in a Georgian Orthodox seminary, no less, and ran into enough trouble with the authorities to be expelled. It wouldn't be the first time that the sins of the fathers have been visited on the unfortunate children. Yet it is clear that there was an element of pragmatism in Stalin's attitude toward religion. During the Second World War, he mobilized the Russian Orthodox Church in support of the struggle. Today this pragmatism continues. The authorities are more than happy to encourage nationalistic branches of religion, such as one finds in the Orthodox Church, and to permit (as in China with restrictions) other religions. Matters are made complex by the fact that independence movements are frequently closely linked to regional religious traditions (like Islam) and so it is often difficult to separate hostility to religion from fear of rebellion. As so often, Jews particularly have suffered since the coming of the Soviets.

As always, in a repellent sort of way, Hitler (1889–1945) is really interesting (Kershaw 1999; Evans 2005). He was raised a Catholic, and in his public pronouncements after he seized power, one finds statements clearly supportive of religion. On February 1, 1933 (two days after being named chancellor), he said: "The National Government will regard it as its first and foremost duty to revive in the nation the spirit of unity and co-operation. It will preserve and defend those basic principles on which our nation has been built. It regards Christianity as the foundation of our national morality, and the family as the basis of national life" (Hitler 1941, 144). Privately, however, things were otherwise. Goebbels described Hitler as "deeply religious but entirely anti-Christian." He was much given to critical comments about Christianity, he thought it condoned weakness and regarded it with contempt, and his scorn extended to rival belief systems like the neopagan religions that some leading Nazis favored. However, Hitler certainly believed in some form of Providence, a force guiding him to his destiny—the leadership of the Thousand Year Reich. By the middle of 1940, with France conquered, he truly thought he was "sleepwalking" to destiny (Evans 2005). It was this that led him to the reckless and ultimately catastrophic attack on Russia in 1941. It would therefore be very misleading to suggest that Hitler was an atheist or even an agnostic. With some plausibility, Hitler identified atheism with the hated Bolshevism, and with rather less plausibility, he identified atheism with the even-more-hated Judaism. Later in this book, I shall touch again on National Socialism and Christianity. What is clear is that, as in Russia and China, whatever the beliefs of the leaders and the rules they enforced, most people continued in Nazi Germany as committed Christians, although many would argue that unlike Russia and China there were strong causal links between the ideology of the state and the religious beliefs of the people.

What about More Stable Societies?

What of England and America? Both countries were much influenced by ideas coming from Vienna—especially as Jewish intellectuals fled the oppression of National Socialism. There was the father of psychoanalysis, Sigmund Freud (1856–1939), busily labeling religion an illusion. Although controversial, his ideas spread widely in both Anglophone countries, especially among his fellow Jews. Toward the end of his life, he escaped to London. And in philosophical circles, there were various forms or schools of neopositivism, no friendlier to religion than the nineteenth-century versions. Very important was the Vienna Circle, a group of "logical positivists" who declared "meaningless" anything beyond logic and mathematics and claims about matters of empirical fact. That rather did away with God by definition. At the other pole was existentialism, which generally hewed to the Nietzsche line about the death (or irrelevance) of the deity and the need to make decisions for oneself, not dictated by an imaginary being long ago and far away. Both of these movements found their ways to Britain and America. At mid-century, the most famous nonbeliever of the twentieth century in the English-speaking world was the mathematician and philosopher Bertrand Russell (1872–1970). Thanks particularly to the radio and his attractive quick wit in debate—most notably against the Jesuit historian of philosophy, Father Frederick Copleston (1907–1994)—Russell's nonbelief became almost a matter of national pride. That he was an aristocrat didn't hurt, of course. When you look at his arguments, however, you are struck again and again by the continuity with the past and the extent to which his nonbelief is a moral issue much more than simply one of epistemology—how one should think rather than how one must think. In a well-known talk, "Why I Am Not a Christian," all of the usual objections are trotted out. Hellfire got a special mention. "You will find that in the Gospels Christ said, 'Ye serpents, ye generation of vipers, how can ye escape the damnation of Hell.' That was said to people who did not like His preaching. It is not really to my mind quite the best tone, and there are a great many of these things about Hell" (lecture presented in London to the National Secular Society, March 6, 1927; reprinted in Russell 1927). Repeating a sentiment of Thomas Henry Huxley, who said in debate with Prime Minister Gladstone (1809–1898) that putting devils into the Gadarene swine (who promptly rushed down to the sea and drowned) was a shocking abuse of someone else's property, Russell wondered why Jesus had felt it necessary to inflict such troubles on innocent mammals. And more generally, religion leads to unhappiness and despair rather than anything else. What else can one say of an institution that forces a young, inexperienced girl married to a syphilitic husband to stay with him and, if they have sex, refuses to allow her to practice any kind of disease protection on the grounds that one is also thereby preventing conception?

Were the Nonbelievers Ignored?

The $64,000 question is whether any of this had any effect whatsoever. Have we just been talking about a bunch of out-of-touch intellectuals doing their thing? Obviously not entirely, because we have been talking of major social upheavals in the nineteenth century due to the Industrial Revolution and about people like Marx, who, responding to these upheavals, did have such an influence on the twentieth century. But there is still a sneaking suspicion that really not much of this had a major effect. I can remember going to a state school in England in the late 1940s, where we roared out Mrs. Alexander's hymn with all of the force of our infant lungs. It was Archbishop Geoffrey Fisher who crowned the queen in 1953, not Bertrand Russell. And indeed, Russell, for all of his popularity, was not exactly appearing at the Palladium. The Russell-Copleston debate was on the Third Program of the BBC, where typical fare was a reading of T. S. Eliot's *Murder in the Cathedral*, followed by a relaxing composition of twelve-tone music by Arnold Schoenberg. I am sure my father was not alone in pretending to listen in and then switching to another channel when we left the house. I don't think my father was alone, either, at that time in finding religion a rather comforting cultural bulwark against the godless and dangerous societies that had then swallowed so much of the globe. Like Eliot and Schoenberg, Russell was obviously important but not that emotionally engaging, if one knows what is meant. The future archbishop of Canterbury, Michael Ramsey (1904–1988), had a much-admired, brilliant older brother, Frank (1903–1930), a philosopher and ardent atheist, whose life was cut short by illness. Although very high church, Michael Ramsey always regarded English atheism as really part of the family, a bit naughty but not that threatening.

What Happened Later in the Century?

In fact, speaking mainly of Christianity but also with a nod to Judaism, some good sociological evidence is pertinent to this question. (See chapter 3 for full details and references.) Excluding the United States, of which more in a moment, up until the middle of the twentieth century, religious beliefs held pretty solid and unmoving. Most people were at least nominally Christian, and depending on where you looked, relatively large numbers went to church. In urban Britain admittedly, many spent Sunday morning reading the *News of the World* to learn surprising things about vicars, rather than going to see them doing unsurprising things in the pulpit—although Sunday school in the afternoons was much encouraged so Mum and Dad could get a bit of a break. More than one little Brit got a start in life thanks to enforced sabbatarian Bible study. In Canada, however, an amazing 65% of people went to church, and if one confines oneself to the province of Quebec—different from the rest of the country in being mainly Catholic rather than mainly Protestant—a truly stupendous 90% went to church (Brown 2013; Pew Research Religion and Public Life Project 2013). Then the numbers started to collapse dramatically. Church attendance fell like a stone. In 1960, the percentage of those identifying as people of no religion was minuscule, less than 1%. In a quarter century in Quebec, attendance numbers fell below 30%. A dramatic decline could also be seen in the rest of Canada—leading to non-stop, agonizing op-ed pieces in the Toronto *Globe and Mail* and a 1965 smash-hit bestseller (for Canada!), *The Comfortable Pew: A Critical Look at Christianity and the Religious Establishment in the New Age* by Pierre Berton (1920–2004), a popular journalist and a former Anglican.

Similar tales could be told in Britain and Australasia, and on the continent also, in both Protestant and Catholic countries. *Honest to God* (published in 1963) by the Anglican Bishop of Southwark, John A. T. Robinson (1919–1983), had a huge popular impact, both by showing how far liberal Christians had felt obliged to come in the light of the assaults of the nineteenth century and because it came from a source right in the heart of the established Church of England. Much of the decline, as Berton noted presciently, and as hinted in the prologue, was reinforced by so many churches showing themselves firmly out of step over such issues as contraception, abortion, homosexuality, and the role and rights of women. The pill became readily available by the mid-1960s, one might have thought not the best of all possible times for Pope Paul VI to issue *Humanae Vitae* (in 1968) condemning all artificial forms of birth control. The 1980 novel *How Far Can You Go?* by the English novelist David Lodge (b. 1935), who describes himself as an "agnostic Catholic," tells sympathetically but chillingly how our abilities to fiddle with the chemistry of the body simply rolled over theological issues. What was an issue of agonizing religious importance in 1960 was two decades later a question of baffling irrelevance. Some may have felt an emptiness, a sense that important struggles are now gone, but more and more people were like my Canadian wife (born in 1961), for whom no rejection was necessary. Religion was simply not part of their culture.

What about the United States?

The United States was and still is different. In 1850, it was a Protestant country. In 1950, it was not. Huge numbers of immigrants, mainly Catholic or Jewish, came flowing through Ellis Island, and the religious composition of the country changed. Not the religiosity, though, because as is well known, especially for Catholics, the church became more than just a faith system and very much part of the whole social structure of many American lives. For someone growing up Boston Irish, being a positive nonbeliever was as unthinkable as it might have been for someone growing up in medieval Europe. Jews—especially American Jews—have always had more of a place for intellectual and religious diversity, but even nonbelievers often combine this with complex feelings about race, especially during those troubled times of European persecution and the fraught, if uplifting, era of the founding of the state of Israel. American Protestants continued with more of the same, or rather more of the same intensified. Mainline churches responded in ways similar to their European counterparts, but evangelicals became, if possible, even more hard-line. At the beginning of the century, the big moral force was toward prohibition of alcohol, a campaign that ended in success—if so disastrous a result can be called a success—with the passing of the Eighteenth Amendment. Then the attention was turned full blast toward evolution, culminating in the Scopes Monkey Trial of 1925, when a young Tennessee schoolteacher was prosecuted for teaching his pupils about evolution (Larson 1997). Although his conviction was overturned on a technicality and never appealed, the event had a chilling effect on science education in America, reinforcing an already existing trend with evolution effectively removed from the classrooms—until in 1957 the Russian success with Sputnik led to a revamping of American science education (Numbers 2006; Shapiro 2013).

Was everything frozen? Did none of the changes that occurred in Europe have an American counterpart? In parts of America, they did, of course. Most prominent was the organization American Atheists founded by Madalyn Murray O'Hair (1919–1995) in 1963. Dedicated to the separation of church and state—a wall between the two, as Jefferson called it, often more honored in the breach than the observance—her group won a significant victory when the Supreme Court ruled that state-mandated Bible readings and prayers in public schools are, thanks to the First Amendment, unconstitutional. Redolent of atheists of the nineteenth century, O'Hair was a woman with a nose for the flamboyant, and she was a regular on talk shows and in magazines like *Playboy*. Characteristically, she acted as a speechwriter for Larry Flynt, the publisher of *Hustler*, in his 1984 campaign for the presidency. She was not much of a team player, and the organization dwindled and grew ever less effective. In her defense, she faced and fought ongoing harassment by those opposed to her ideas—feces through the letterbox, pets killed, death threats. O'Hair's struggle on behalf of atheism came to an abrupt end in 1995, when she was murdered by a former employee. The crime was solved and the culprit convicted only thanks to the efforts of supporters and federal authorities, working to fill in for the apathy of the local police department.

The closest counterpart to Bishop Robinson was Episcopalian Bishop John Spong (b. 1931). In declarations (that very much upset the Archbishop of Canterbury), Spong claimed that God talk is impossible, Jesus cannot be considered the son of God, and that there was no virgin birth, or miracles, or Resurrection, for that matter. And that is just a start before we get to the afterlife, to morality, and to the place of humans in the creation. In the more secular realm, no account of religious belief or nonbelief in America in the second half of the last century would be complete without mention and appreciation of Paul Kurtz (1925–2012), a professor of philosophy at the State University of New York at Buffalo. A man of incredible energy and enthusiasm, he founded a publishing house (Prometheus) and several journals and magazines, including the leading organ for modern skeptics, *Free Inquiry*. Ardent in his philosophy—"No deity will save us; we must save ourselves"—Kurtz was always keen to avoid falling into the trap of making a secular religion of his beliefs and practices. As a young man in the US military, he was moved and marked both by firsthand experience of the concentration camps and of Russian prisoners of war who were loath to be repatriated to their communist homeland. He always hated ideologies and absolutes, at both ends of the spectrum, especially those that became hidebound. It is perhaps for this reason that near the end of his life Kurtz broke from organizations that he had been instrumental in founding and maintaining, feeling that the dogmatism of antireligion that had now infused them was akin to the dogmatism of the religion he had long combated.

But there were also strong currents going the other way. The reintroduction of evolution into classrooms in the early 1960s (in response to the perceived Soviet superiority in science) soon brought a counterreaction. *Genesis Flood*, appearing in 1961 and authored by biblical scholar John C. Whitcomb (b. 1924) and hydraulic engineer Henry M. Morris (1918–2006), argued for a short Earth time span (about 6,000 years), a miraculous origin for all organisms including humans, and a universal deluge sometime thereafter. It was a great success, sparking a full-blooded Creationism movement, which in recent years has been transformed into the somewhat smoother Intelligent Design movement, where natural origins are eschewed and a more biblically based world history is endorsed. Attempts formally to introduce Creationism into the science classes of publicly funded schools have (like prayer and Bible reading) run afoul of the First Amendment separation of church and state—first in a court case in Arkansas in 1981 and then in another case in Pennsylvania in 2005—but there is little question that informally Genesis-based accounts of origins is standard fare in many schools, especially in the South and Midwest (Pennock and Ruse 2008). This is but the tip of an iceberg of strong religious belief that motivates and informs the lives of countless Americans.

Are the New Atheists Saying Anything New?

It is really not to their discredit to say that it would be hard for anyone to say anything new, and in truth, there is little if anything in their writings that is completely fresh. If Sextus Empiricus did not say it, then you can bet that David Hume slid it in somewhere. The passion is hardly new either. D'Holbach, Ingersoll, Russell—all of these men were fueled by righteous indignation. But there is a freshness to the writings of the New Atheists, and so bringing our history to an end, let us turn to them. The uniting theme is a detestation of religion, all religion. Start off with Judaism. Richard Dawkins (b. 1941) is eloquent: "The God of the Old Testament is arguably the most unpleasant character in all fiction: jealous and proud of it; a petty, unjust, unforgiving control-freak; a vindictive, bloodthirsty ethnic cleanser; a misogynistic, homophobic, racist, infanticidal, genocidal, filicidal, pestilential, megalomaniacal, sadomasochistic, capriciously malevolent bully" (Dawkins 2006, 31). Dawkins quotes the novelist Evelyn Waugh's report of the reaction of Winston Churchill's son Randolph on first reading the Bible: "God, isn't God a shit!" Christopher Hitchens (1949–2011) also wades into the subject, although he does have more fun, especially with the "demented pronouncements" of Moses: "He that is wounded in the stones, or has his privy member cut off, shall not enter into the congregation of the Lord" (Deuteronomy 23: 1).

Moving to the New Testament and Christianity, everyone is appalled at the violence to which it leads. Sam Harris (b. 1967) spends time with the Inquisition and the persecution of witches and then turns (as do so many works of this ilk) to the Nazis and the Holocaust. The thesis of Daniel Goldhagen (1996) that Nazi anti-Semitism is rooted in Christianity is given full and basically uncritical approval. "And while the hatred of Jews in Germany [under the Nazis] expressed itself in a predominantly secular way, it was a direct inheritance from medieval Christianity" (Harris 2004, 101). In these sorts of discussions, it is usually Martin Luther who is demonized for his table talk, but Harris seems to have a particular animus against Roman Catholics, from their complicity in getting the Nazi leaders safely off to South America when things started to go wrong to putting Descartes's *Meditations* on the index of forbidden books. Not that Protestants escape censure. There is room for condemnation of all for "the terrible consequences that have arisen, logically and inevitably, out of Christian faith" (106). Harris concludes his look at Christianity gloomily: "Unfortunately, this catalog of horrors could be elaborated upon indefinitely. Auschwitz, the Cathar heresy, the witch hunts—these phrases signify depths of human depravity and human suffering that would surely elude description were a writer to set himself no other task" (106).

Hitchens likewise worries about the propensity of all religions, including Christianity, to turn its practitioners to violence. Suppose you met a bunch of fellows and learned that they were just back from a prayer meeting. Would this make you feel safe? Not on your life, literally! Just take cities beginning with a *B*—Belfast, Beirut, Bombay, Belgrade, Bethlehem, and Baghdad. In each of these cities you would do well to avoid the prayer group. Can you imagine being a Protestant in Northern Ireland if a group of hyped-up Catholics approached you, or conversely? And it is no good pretending to be an atheist. In that benighted country, even atheists are either Protestant or Catholic! All of which leads the New Atheists to wonder if, given the way it makes decent people misbehave, religion isn't a form of madness. Harris is particularly ecumenical in his loathing of anything that depends on faith, something that functions entirely without evidence, and that repeatedly he likens to a form of insanity. It gets a pass only because it is so common in so many societies. "And yet, it is merely an accident of history that it is considered normal in our society to believe that the Creator of the universe can hear your thoughts, while it is even more demonstrative of mental illness to believe that he is communicating with you by having the rain tap in Morse code on your bedroom window" (Hitchens 2007, 72).

Richard Dawkins agrees with Harris that there is madness lurking here. He is "inclined to follow" the author of *Zen and the Art of Motorcycle Maintenance* (Robert Pirsig) when he says: "When one person suffers from a delusion, it is called insanity. When many people suffer from a delusion, it is called religion" (Dawkins 2006, 5). But it is no harmless delusion. It is positively evil. For Dawkins, as for Harris, the Catholic Church is a particular focus of loathing. The gloomy superstition, the sexual repression, the knee bending before false authority—nothing can equal the wrong in making another human being cowed in this way. In significant respects, beyond sexual abuse, Dawkins thinks even greater harm is done by bringing a child up Catholic in the first place.

Hitchens chimes in here also, holding forth on the "positively immoral" aspects of religions. Particular hatred is reserved for the Christian views on sexuality. At least the Buddhist leader, the Dalai Lama, tells you that it is okay to visit a prostitute so long as someone else pays. Not even that is an option for the Christian.

Expectedly, Islam comes in for harsh words. Everyone is happy to indulge in a little Muslim bashing. Sam Harris makes it a trademark. *The End of Faith: Religion, Terror, and the Future of Reason* opens with a fictional suicide bomber and the challenging question—why is it that you might know so little about this man and yet have no doubts whatsoever about his religion? Clearly, he is (or was) Muslim. This sets up the tone of the book, for overall it is deeply hostile to Islam, a religion described as fanatical through and through, a danger to its practitioners and a danger to all others. "Any systematic approach to ethics, or to understand the necessary underpinnings of a civil society, will find many Muslims standing eye deep in the red barbarity of the fourteenth century" (Harris 2004, 145). In the same vein, Dawkins approvingly quotes one critic of Islam who writes about British Muslim suicide bombers, asking whether they "were neither on the fringes of Muslim society in Britain, nor following an eccentric and extremist interpretation of their faith, but rather that they came from the very core of the Muslim community and were motivated by a mainstream interpretation of Islam?" (Dawkins 2006, 307).

Perhaps expectedly, as the one with scientific training, Dawkins brings out most clearly the extent to which he thinks that the days of religion are over and the days of science have arrived. Particular attention is paid to Charles Darwin's theory of evolution through natural selection, and it is argued that this theory is nigh to definitive on the God question. Some twenty years earlier, in the *Blind Watchmaker*, Dawkins had merely claimed: "Although atheism might have been logically tenable before Darwin, Darwin made it possible to be an intellectually fulfilled atheist" (Dawkins 1986, 6). Now we have a chapter titled "Why There Almost Certainly Is No God." One should note that, along with the scientific arguments, Dawkins thinks he has some devastating philosophical objections—he is staggered at the thought of the complexity demanded of any god capable of creating such a world as ours. As a professional philosopher, Daniel Dennett (b. 1942) really wades in here. He is particularly scathing about the idea that morality might be in need of religion to articulate and support it. In many respects, this is as far from the truth as it is possible to be. A well-known quote by the physics Nobel Laureate Steven Weinberg (1999) makes its appearance. "Good people will do good things, and bad people will do bad things. But for good people to do bad things—that takes religion." Empirical evidence suggests that nonbelievers do good and harm at about the same rates as believers. Prisons are not stocked by nonbelievers. Indeed, they contain the same ratios of believers to nonbelievers as does the general public. And interestingly, the divorce rates among nonbelievers are significantly lower than among believers, especially those at the Evangelical end of the spectrum.

Thus the New Atheists. As with fervent evangelicals, there is a moral seriousness about their writings that at times begs for a little teasing. This we must resist, or at least try to. They are hectoring and arrogant; they are unfair to and belittling of others; they are ignorant of anything outside their disciplines to an extent remarkable even among modern academics. They also have an earnestness unknown outside the pages of the Old Testament. These are people who feel that we are in desperate times facing great evils. Something must be said and done. For this call, whether we think it well taken or not, we can forgive much. They matter, and they and those who went before deserve a response more measured and thoughtful than they themselves are able to give. Are their concerns well taken or do they misfire? As a start, let us begin with some facts and figures. What do the sociologists and the survey takers have to tell us about the state of play today?

3

STATISTICS

How Many Atheists Are There?

Let's plunge right into the key questions. Start with the most obvious and pressing. How common is atheism today? The world population is around 7 billion. One rough count put the number of atheists as around 2.5%, which means that there are about 160 million atheists. Another estimate, after a meta-analysis of several studies, suggested that with agnostics counted in, one gets around 500 to 750 million nonbelievers. In other words, absolutely quite a few but comparatively not that many. A good source of information is the International Social Survey Programme (ISSP) that does surveys annually and in some years focuses on a special topic like religion (1991, 1998, 2008). The questions asked are a fairly straightforward and sensible range, including "I don't know whether there is a God and I don't believe there is any way to find out" and "I know God really exists and I have no doubts about it." One immediate caveat is that only some countries (North America, Western Europe, and the like) open themselves up to surveying, and other countries (much of Asia and Africa) do not. This means for a start that you are going to get much more information on countries where Christianity is the dominant religion than countries where Islam or other religions dominate. In making our main focus precisely on countries with

Christianity dominant, it seems that we can make a virtue from necessity. (The discussion in this chapter relies heavily on Keysar and Navarro-Rivera 2013, Lee 2013, and Cragun, Hammer, and Smith 2013. The information gathered is given in tables 3.1 through 3.4.)

What does one make of the information? Well, in absolute terms, if you want to find atheists, go to Germany and France, and if you want to find agnostics, go to Japan! Although remember, countries like Japan probably reflect the non-theistic nature of their religions. Percentages are obviously more revealing, although surely not that surprising. Very religious countries like the Philippines, Poland, and Ireland have few atheists or agnostics and don't show much sign of change. (One wonders now about Ireland, given the appalling revelations of priestly sexual abuse.) Secular countries like many of those of Western Europe have much larger numbers of atheists and agnostics, and the numbers (especially of atheists) do seem to be going up. There are a number of theories about what makes for atheism, or nonbelief more generally. Obviously, historical factors are going to be important. The Catholic Church in Poland has always had a major social role in integrating the country through many rough periods when outside forces imposed their wills on their smaller neighbor. There are some popular theories linking religiosity or the lack thereof to various social factors. One possibility is the extent to which a society promotes social welfare and works to eliminate vast income and wealth distributions. The countries with high rates of nonbelief tend to be those where the gap between rich and poor is less pronounced. There is simply less tension in these countries and hence less need to ameliorate it with the comforts of religion. Anecdotally, as one who started life in England, moved to Canada, and now lives in the American South, this seems very plausible. (I will return to these issues in a later chapter.)

Note, however, with the exception of the Czech Republic, the combined atheist and agnostic percentage is still a minority position, and often a significantly minority position. There are two major exceptions or anomalies: Russia and the United

Table 3.1 Number of adult atheists (positive atheists, agnostics, and combined) by country 2008 (weighted data)

Country	Positive Atheists (age 18+)	Agnostics (age 18+)	Combined Atheistic Pop. (age 18+)
Australia	2,642,884	2,415,888	5,058,772
Austria	616,035	682,995	1,299,030
Belgium	1,499,328	1,357,725	2,857,053
Chile	222,164	152,007	374,171
Croatia	191,987	152,140	344,127
Cyprus	15,788	28,252	44,040
Czech Republic	3,400,720	1,248,900	4,649,620
Denmark	785,016	584,496	1,369,512
Dominican Republic	72,289	114,457	186,746
Finland	534,049	638,355	1,172,404
France	11,750,346	8,215,284	19,965,630
Germany	16,103,215	8,461,011	24,564,226
Hungary	1,248,927	1,005,629	2,254,556
Ireland	179,587	190,362	369,949
Israel	291,014	233,766	524,780
Italy	2,949,114	3,698,889	6,648,003
Japan	9,248,832	20,517,524	29,766,356
Korea, South	6,782,398	3,637,487	10,419,885
Latvia	339,427	174,350	513,777
Mexico	2,480,660	1,204,892	3,685,552
Netherlands	2,563,829	1,739,281	4,303,110
New Zealand	404,964	461,036	866,000
Norway	634,138	512,326	1,146,464
Philippines	392,154	896,353	1,288,507
Poland	1,026,315	1,772,725	2,799,040
Portugal	436,379	367,927	804,306
Russia	7,818,446	11,152,783	18,971,229

(Continued)

Table 3.1 *(Continued)*

Country	Positive Atheists (age 18+)	Agnostics (age 18+)	Combined Atheistic Pop. (age 18+)
Slovakia	522,438	269,926	792,364
Slovenia	227,301	95,266	322,527
South Africa	1,408,873	626,166	2,035,039
Spain	3,665,924	3,968,268	7,633,561
Sweden	1,407,293	1,392,859	2,800,152
Switzerland	579,157	621,832	1,200,989
Taiwan	1,170,522	1,494,666	2,665,188
Turkey	965,303	406,443	1,371,746
Ukraine	2,308,949	1,816,878	4,125,827
United Kingdom	6,829,830	7,750,162	14,579,992
United States	7,128,299	11,497,257	18,625,556
Uruguay	203,214	106,333	309,547
Venezuela	116,009	116,009	232,018
TOTAL	**101,163,116**	**101,778,908**	**202,942,024**

Source: ISSP 2008. From Keysar and Navarro-Rivera 2013, 556.

States. In Russia, atheism has been dropping away pretty rapidly. One presumes that this does not call for a major effort to explain. With the end of the Soviet system and state-mandated atheism and hostility toward churches, many people have found Christianity (especially given the way that Russian Christianity has always been so bound up with Russian nationalism and pride) or are now open about beliefs that they had all along. The United States also does not call for major explanatory effort. We have already sampled some of the reasons for the country's extreme religiosity. We will talk more about the United States in a moment.

Table 3.2a Percentage of positive atheists in selected countries (1998 and 2008)

Country	% Positive Atheist 1998	% Positive Atheist 2008	Difference 1998–2008
Philippines	1%	1%	0
Chile	2%	2%	0
Cyprus	2%	2%	0
United States	3%	3%	0
Poland	2%	3%	+1
Ireland	2%	5%	+3
Portugal	2%	5%	+3
Italy	4%	6%	+2
Israel	8%	6%	−2
Russia	20%	7%	−13
Japan	11%	9%	−2
Austria	7%	9%	+2
Switzerland	4%	10%	+6
Spain	9%	10%	+1
Slovakia	11%	12%	+1
New Zealand	8%	13%	+5
Slovenia	14%	14%	0
Hungary	13%	15%	+2
Australia	10%	16%	+6
Norway	12%	18%	+6
Latvia	9%	18%	+9
Denmark	15%	18%	+3
Sweden	17%	20%	+3
Netherlands	17%	20%	+3
France	19%	24%	+5
Czech Republic	20%	40%	+20

Source: ISSP 2008. In Keysar and Navarro-Rivera 2913, 561.

Table 3.2b Percentage of agnostics in selected countries (1998 and 2008)

Country	% Agnostic 1998	% Agnostic 2008	Difference 1998–2008
Chile	1%	1%	0
Philippines	1%	2%	+1
Cyprus	3%	3%	0
Portugal	4%	4%	0
Ireland	5%	5%	0
United States	5%	5%	0
Israel	6%	5%	−1
Slovakia	10%	6%	−4
Poland	4%	6%	+2
Slovenia	9%	6%	−3
Italy	5%	7%	+2
Latvia	11%	9%	−2
Australia	14%	10%	−4
Switzerland	13%	10%	−3
Russia	11%	10%	−1
Spain	7%	11%	+4
Hungary	12%	12%	0
Norway	12%	14%	+2
Denmark	16%	14%	−2
Netherlands	12%	14%	+2
Austria	10%	15%	+5
Czech Republic	14%	15%	+1
New Zealand	12%	15%	+3
France	17%	17%	0
Japan	21%	19%	−2
Sweden	18%	19%	+1

Source: ISSP. In Keysar and Navarro-Rivera 2013, 562.

Table 3.3 Total atheist population (i.e., positive atheists and agnostics combined) in selected countries (2008)

Country	% Positive Atheist 2008	% Agnostic 2008	% Combined Atheist Population
Venezuela	1%	1%	2%
Philippines	1%	2%	3%
Dominican Republic	1%	2%	3%
Chile	2%	1%	3%
Turkey	2%	1%	3%
Cyprus	2%	3%	5%
Mexico	4%	2%	6%
South Africa	5%	2%	7%
United States	3%	5%	8%
Poland	3%	6%	9%
Portugal	5%	4%	9%
Croatia	5%	4%	9%
Ireland	5%	5%	10%
Israel	6%	5%	11%
Ukraine	6%	5%	11%
Italy	6%	7%	13%
Uruguay	9%	5%	14%
Taiwan	7%	8%	15%
Russia	7%	10%	17%
Slovakia	12%	6%	18%
Switzerland	10%	10%	20%
Slovenia	14%	6%	20%
Spain	10%	11%	21%
Austria	9%	15%	24%
Australia	16%	10%	26%
Hungary	15%	12%	27%
Latvia	18%	9%	27%
Japan	9%	19%	28%

(Continued)

Table 3.3   *(Continued)*

Country	% Positive Atheist 2008	% Agnostic 2008	% Combined Atheist Population
Finland	13%	15%	28%
New Zealand	13%	15%	28%
South Korea	18%	10%	28%
United Kingdom	14%	16%	30%
Norway	18%	14%	32%
Denmark	18%	14%	32%
Belgium	18%	16%	34%
Netherlands	20%	14%	34%
Germany	24%	12%	36%
Sweden	20%	19%	39%
France	24%	17%	41%
Czech Republic	40%	15%	55%

Source: ISSP 2008. In Keysar and Navarro-Rivera 2013, 563.

Table 3.4 Estimated number of atheists in selected highly populated countries (2006–2008)

Country	Percent "Convinced Atheist"	Number of Atheists
China	17.9%	234,595,000
India	2.5%	27,691,000
Indonesia	0.3%	695,000
Brazil	1.2%	2,298,000
Total		265,000,000

Source: WVS [World Values Survey] 2006–2008. In Keysar and Navarro-Rivera 2013, 582.

Are Atheists Different?

Kinder, Küche, Kirche—children, kitchen, church—a phrase we associate with the Nazis, although it was around even at the end of the nineteenth century. With good reason, it is a target of scorn by feminists of both sexes, but there is nevertheless some evidence that atheism is more a male than female phenomenon. No doubt, in the past it was true that church was culturally more significant for women, a place where they could find meaning and comfort. But the divisions persist. In Ukraine, 77% of atheists are male; in France and Germany 57%. There is a rough correlation between prevalence of atheism in a society and gender gap—more atheists, less disparity between males and females. But this is very rough, and significant upheavals can change the picture. Probably reflecting its past when much of the country was under communist rule, there exists less of a gender gap in Germany than in Sweden, although overall the latter has more atheists. One suspects that the shrinking of the gap generally has at least something to do with the ways in which parts of Christianity persist in promoting positions hard on women—opposition to contraception being something that springs at once to mind.

Probably expectedly, there is also a gap between ages, with young people more likely to be nonbelievers than older folk. Perhaps also expectedly, the higher the percentages of nonbelievers, the greater the age gaps. This correlation is not inevitable. For instance, as opposed to Spain, Israel sees little or no difference in belief as a function of age. One suspects that in cases like this, the different histories of the two countries have a role to play. Israel has been around in one form or another for a hundred years, and the country was founded in large part by secular Jews who were deeply committed to Zionism as a nonreligious phenomenon. Why should they or their children or grandchildren change? (Obviously, the rapid rise of orthodox Jews needs now to be taken into account, although probably it leads to the same conclusion.) Spain was long under fascist rule, where Catholicism was the norm and very much part of the state. Younger people have grown up free of this, and so whereas the older people are still much into religion, the younger generation feels far less attachment. At a personal level, my father, who died about twenty years ago at about age eighty (and who lived in England), shows that nonbelief is not the exclusive property of the young. His life was a religious journey. He started as a child singing in the choir of the town's main Anglican church. Then, as a young man, he turned to Marxism and went to fight in Spain. The Second World War found him a conscientious objector, he fell among the Quakers, and he and my mother joined the Society of Friends and were deeply committed. After my mother died, my German stepmother brought Rudolf Steiner (1861–1925), the founder of Waldorf Schools, into the family, and he followed this belief system for many years. Finally, in my father's last decade—after dabbling in a range from Scientology to the teachings of Jiddu Krishnamurti—it all fell away, and he found great comfort in a gentle agnosticism. For some reason, the God of the Ruses has always been Randolph Churchill's God—a stern Presbyterian who instantly regretted creating humans once the week of creation was finished. As I said, in the tense years after the Second World War, my father rather needed such a God to make sense of the awful state of the world. Later, things became more relaxed. A man who had had to leave school at the age of fourteen, he was a true autodidact and spent forty years as a school bursar. He felt a great deal of satisfaction in having helped many children and their families, and it gave this modest man a sense of self-worth he did not have in earlier years. God's nonexistence was a great comfort in my father's final years. Apparently, my father is not unique (James and Wells 2002).

There are more nonbelievers among people who have never married or who live together without the bonds of matrimony. This is no great surprise. First, the unmarried tend to be younger and so fit in with the age differential. Second, those who live together outside marriage seem already to have shown that they are not under the suzerainty of religion. Third, it does not seem too outlandish or prejudicial to suggest that older unmarried people are more likely to have minority sexual orientations and feel alienated from systems that seem to go out of their way to make as them feel uncomfortable and unwelcome. People who have more education also tend to be at the nonbelief end of the spectrum. It seems to be the case that being an agnostic is far less education dependent, although there are notable exceptions, like Germany and the United States. Without being condescending, and realizing that such speculations could get me into hot water on the home front, could it be that going all the way to atheism requires a certain book learning to realize exactly what is entailed, whereas being an agnostic can be basically a matter of indifference? One does not need education for this.

How Many Atheists Are There in the United States?

There is some good information on North America, comparing the United States with Mexico and Canada. There are expected differences, and there is much already found true of the rest of the world. The percentage of people in North America who do not think of themselves as religious is quite high, about 30%, although those who think of themselves as atheist is much lower, about 4%. Note that the United States is much below Canada in this respect, the United States under 4% and Canada about 10%. As intimated earlier, Canada here, as so often, is in many respects far more like Europe—as with respect to socialized medicine and the absence of capital punishment—than it is like the United States. As in Europe, atheists are more likely to be male, young, and unmarried or living without the ties of matrimony—although this last figure is less so in the United States. Expectedly, therefore, atheists tend to have fewer children than theists—in the United States, this is quite marked, 0.93 to 1.94. Atheists are more likely to be working—an interesting statistic given the parable of the talents—and much less likely to be stay-at-home moms. They are slightly higher class than theists—although this is not significant in the United States—and as in Europe, they tend to have had more education. Atheists are more likely to live in cities, although again, as with sexual orientation, one wonders which is cause and which effect. It is a lot more fun being gay in downtown Toronto than it is in rural Manitoba, and one suspects the same for nonbelief. Atheists tend to be more liberal than theists but not by very much. This is less pronounced in Canada and more pronounced in Mexico than in the United States. Atheists (and again this seems to fit Europe) seem to be more favorable to government intervention in society. Atheists tend to think about the meaning of life less than do theists. Interestingly and perhaps not immediately expected, atheists tend to report lower satisfaction of life than theists. Not by much, but significantly so. Could this be connected with societal attitudes? More on this in a moment. Finally, and this surely is expected, atheists tend to breed atheists, and theists tend to breed theists. This is not always so, but there are strong patterns. For instance, in the United States, 57% of atheists were raised nonreligious, whereas only 16% of theists were raised nonreligious.

Is There Prejudice against Atheists?

In some respects, this is a funny question to ask. After fifty years as a professional philosopher, I am quite convinced that being a practicing Christian is not a good career move. Philosophers rather pride themselves among the humanities as being the most sciencelike (starting with superior IQs), and while there certainly are Christian philosophers (most obviously in the many Catholic institutions of higher learning), generally someone who has religious yearnings is thought needy or some such thing. Logical positivism left its mark. (In European universities, one could say the same of the influence of existentialism.) I suspect that there would be questions about a candidate for the Royal Society or the National Academy of Sciences who was known to be Evangelical or Pentecostal. But that is academia. What about the real world, where the numbers are reversed and atheists are in the minority? One doubts that being a nonbeliever makes much difference in much of Europe or places like New Zealand. In Canada, for instance, the most flamboyant and successful prime minister of the past half century was Pierre Trudeau (1919–2000). He was at least nominally a Catholic, but, given that he had a ferocious intellect, the general assumption was that *nominal* was the keyword. There was surprise and in some quarters almost distress when it was revealed after his death that he was deeply committed to the faith. Likewise in Britain. Tony Blair (b. 1953) took pains not to convert to Catholicism while still in power. His spin doctor notoriously interrupted him when he was about to discuss his faith in public, saying, "We don't do God."

Things are very different in the United States. Atheism is certainly not a good strategic move if you are running for president! In recent history, much of this clearly goes back to the Cold War of the 1950s. The United States and Soviet Russia were squaring off against each other, and there was a big tendency—think of the witch hunts of Senator Joe McCarthy (1908–1957)—to treat anyone who fell outside the norm, especially outside the norm and perceived to be moving toward the other side, as not merely wrong but traitorous and dangerous. Atheists to society then were what pedophiles are to society now. It just isn't an option for decent folk. This kind of thinking certainly persisted to the 1980s. The soon-to-be president George H. W. Bush said in 1987 that he didn't think that atheists "should be regarded as citizens." This has certainly changed. In his inaugural address in 2008, Barack Obama included nonbelievers within the net. Obviously the writings of the New Atheists have made a difference. One can at least talk sensibly about these things. One suspects, however, that in matters of prejudice, the change is relative and still doesn't compare too well with other countries. Where you live in the United States can be a major factor. Florida State University, where I work, is in northern Florida, still very much part of the South. (We joke that we really should be considered southern Georgia.) For several years in the first decade of this century, we Ruses hosted the neighborhood potluck Christmas party. Then it came out that I write extensively on evolution and have been involved in fighting Creationists. That was the end of the Ruses as hosts, despite the fact that I have written a book with the title *Can a Darwinian Be a Christian?* (Answer: Yes, but you have to work at it!)

We should keep things in perspective. Being an atheist in the American South today is not like being, say, an African American in Mississippi in 1930 or a Jew in Germany in 1938. But as my own experience shows, there is prejudice—and note that I was shunned because as an evolutionist, it was concluded that I must be a nonbeliever and hence immoral or otherwise undesirable. I cannot say that the Ruses felt particularly upset, but one can imagine that it could be a burden. If, say, one wanted to run for office, then one might feel the need to conceal one's beliefs. I have friends who are absolutely convinced that President Obama could never have been a genuine Christian. I think they are wrong, but I understand their thinking. There are certainly systematic patterns of discrimination—jobs denied, relationships fractured, invitations not issued—and they can hurt. There is a reason that atheists might report less life satisfaction than theists, although these things do cut both ways. Atheism, unlike skin color or ethnic origin, is something freely chosen, and many atheists report strong feelings of satisfaction and self-worth in making the commitment and then telling others with pride.

All of which, of course, assumes that atheists have something of which to be proud. Let us now therefore change direction a little and turn to the intellectual content of the debate. Is it reasonable, is it compelling, is it silly, to be an atheist?

4

GOD AND HUMANS

Who Is God?

Hold on, you might say. Before we start to talk about God, tell us why we should talk about God. This is supposed to be a book on atheism. Shouldn't we start there, and bring in God only as needed? The trouble with this approach is that atheism is, as it were, the default position. Atheism says that there isn't a God. So why argue about that? I don't think there is an invisible giraffe in the middle of my sitting room, but I am not going to bother to mount an argument unless and until someone starts to claim that there is one and that it matters. If someone tells me that I am going to go to everlasting hell and damnation unless I believe in the giraffe, then I am certainly going to get on the job! I don't think it is irreverent—and if it is, I will chance it—to suggest God is a bit like that giraffe. Until I have heard about God and why I should take him seriously, I will remain silent and untroubled. The burden of proof is on those who believe. So first let us make the pro-God case. Then we can turn to the anti-God case. (I rely heavily on McGrath 1995, 1997; Gunton 1997; and, above all, on Taliaferro and Meister 2010.)

Given that Christianity—and Judaism and Islam, for that matter—is a religion that makes God absolutely central to its world picture, you might think that it would at least be clear on the notion or concept of God. Boy, would you ever be making a big mistake. As soon as you start to ask, you find two thousand years of unbroken debate and that is still going on. As the Skeptics realized very early on in the game, the problem for Christianity is that it suffers from divided loyalties. It looks to two very different traditions for guidance and understanding—Athens and Jerusalem, the Greek tradition and the Jewish tradition. The question is whether these can be brought together in a harmonious fashion. Christians generally say that they can, but this is for us to decide. And this we can do only when everything is out on the table. Because in a way it is the more basic, and it is certainly the earlier, let us start with the God of the Jewish tradition—the God of the patriarchs and the prophets and (later) the evangelists—and then move to the God of the Greek tradition—the God of the philosophers.

Who Is the God of the Jewish Tradition?

This is the God of the all-defining and all-important work for Christians, the Holy Bible. This work falls into two parts: the Old Testament and the New Testament. What is taken by Christians as foundational is that the God of the Old Testament—the Jewish Bible—is also the God of the New Testament—the exclusively Christian part of the Bible. Nothing makes sense if these are not the same deity, and there are repeated passages in the New Testament, from the mouths of Jesus and others, affirming the identity and continuity. Marcion of Sinope (85–160) argued that there are two Gods, one for each testament, and for his pains, he was excommunicated. One asks, therefore, whether there is a thread that runs through the Bible, linking the various conceptions of God, and the answer seems to be that there is. We find a story of God, of humans, and of the relationship between the two. Humans are persons, that is to say, beings with feelings, thoughts, and a sense of identity. This is true also of the deity. God is above all an intensely personal being. He is not a being like a human with a physical form, although sometimes in the Old Testament he is portrayed that way; he is a person like you and me. He is not a rock or a plant or even an animal. We humans are made in the image of God, and as persons we reflect God.

God is creator, absolutely and completely. He made the universe out of nothing. He is not the Platonic Demiurge who shapes the materials he finds. He is a creator who cares for his creations—for the physical world, for the world of animals and plants, and, above all, for us humans, male and female. "Happy are those whose help is the God of Jacob, whose hope is in the LORD their God, who made heaven and earth, the sea, and all that is in them" (Psalm 146: 5–6). Interestingly, although God is usually referred to by the masculine pronoun and in the New Testament frequently referred to as "Father," it is an important part of the Christian conception of God that he has no sex; in some sense, he is beyond or without it. What is important, whatever the language, God is Father not just in the sense of creator, but also in the sense of ongoing care and concern. God loves his children and wants the best for them.

Not that God is soft. We learn in Proverbs: "Those who spare the rod hate their children, but those who love them are diligent to discipline them" (13: 24). This may not be one of the Ten Commandments, but it is certainly a rule God follows. When humans transgress, they must be punished. Adam and Eve sinned, so they were cast out of Eden. God found that the world was given over to wickedness, so, except for Noah and his family, he drowned the lot. Dazzled by the beauty of Bathsheba, David sent her husband Uriah the Hittite to his death so he could have the woman for himself. God punished him by killing their firstborn. This said, God is amenable to reason and to the possibility of changing his mind. Abraham argues with God over Sodom and Gomorrah, hoping to find just a few righteous people and thus saving the cities. It is not God's fault that he fails to find even a few.

All of this emphasizes the personhood of God and of his being in time and, in a sense, in space—he is arguing with

Abraham in the Middle East and not in Australia. One could go on cataloguing the emotions and feelings of God, including the fact that he does play favorites. By any measure, David is one of them. Although this hero is a murderer and is punished, Bathsheba then gives birth to Solomon, and he, too, is blessed. He had seven hundred wives for a start and three hundred concubines, although when he got old, things got out of hand and he caused no end of trouble. The converse seems also true of God. Although Isaac, the child in old age of Abraham and Sarah, was undoubtedly very special, one never really gets the feeling that God cares too much for Isaac in himself. First, he orders Abraham to sacrifice Isaac. It is true that this is averted at the last moment, but not before Isaac is all trussed up. And then later, God lets Jacob steal the blessing from Isaac, a blessing that should rightfully have gone to Esau. Important for the story, no doubt, but a bit rough on Isaac—although not as rough as it was on that total nonfavorite, Esau.

Of course, none of the favoritism compares to that shown to Abraham and his descendants. God makes a deal with him. Make me your God, and I will shower blessings on you, most importantly making you the father of a great nation. For all that the Genesis story implies that there is one God and he did all of the creating, at this somewhat later point, as already noted, there is no implication that God—Yahweh—is the only God. But he is going to be the God of Israel and anathema to those who stand in his way. This does not mean that the "chosen people" never suffer—one thinks of the agonies in Egypt, for instance—but it does mean that God, the Lord, is ever mindful of their fate and their needs, and that when the time comes, he will deliver.

What about the God of the New Testament?

No one reading the Bible can miss how the picture of God changes through the various books. Not only is there a move to God being the only God but also a more refined and concerned being starts to come into view. The picture of a tribal God starts to fade, and God is seen with more overreaching feelings for the whole of his creation. Moreover, as we move through the Old Testament toward the New Testament, the thinking gets (shall we say) more sophisticated, as God (through the prophets especially) makes it very clear that we are not to think of ourselves as in any sense in the same league as God. In the book of Job, God reproves Job for pretending to understanding on a par with his. "Where were you when I laid the foundation of the earth? Tell me, if you have understanding" (38: 4). Again in Isaiah: "For my thoughts are not your thoughts, nor are your ways my ways, says the LORD. For as the heavens are higher than the earth, so are my ways higher than your ways and my thoughts than your thoughts" (Isaiah 55: 8-9). Saint Paul echoes this: "But we speak God's wisdom, secret and hidden, which God decreed before the ages for our glory" (1 Corinthians 2: 7).

Nevertheless, the personhood of God remains central, and this holds true through the New Testament, although obviously with the appearance of Jesus and then the increasing role of the Holy Spirit (or Holy Ghost), things do get more complex. God gets less and less focused on the Jews exclusively and starts to extend his care and compassion to all peoples. Perhaps relatedly, he does start to do things more at a distance, through Jesus particularly. But it is the same God, and it is a personal God. The parables of Jesus make no sense unless we assume this. The father in the parable of the prodigal son, for instance, cares very much for his lost son and rejoices on his return. At the same time, he is sensitive to the worries and needs of the older son, who behaved and yet apparently gets no real affection. More than this, although he is now preaching a doctrine of love and compassion, God is still fully prepared to show his wrath when he is crossed or otherwise upset. Think of the parable of the fig tree. "A man had a fig tree planted in his vineyard, and he came seeking fruit on it and found none. And he said to the vinedresser, 'Look, for three years now I have come seeking fruit on this fig tree, and I find none. Cut it down. Why should it use up the ground?' And he answered him, 'Sir, let it alone this year also, until I dig around it and put on manure. Then if it should bear fruit next year, well and good; but if not, you can cut it down'" (Luke 13: 6-9). Is this really any different from a modern-day televangelist saying to God: "Give them another chance, Lord, and then if they refuse to come to you, strike them down with hellfire and destruction"? The God of the New Testament is a father, but like real-life fathers, there is not only unconditional love but also serious expectations and obligations. If you really love your father, then you had better show it. Dad is picking up the tab for your college fees. Don't spend four years drinking and playing video games.

Who Is the Philosophers' God?

It would be an unfair caricature to suggest that the God of the Jewish tradition is that grandfatherly fellow in the Michelangelo painting of the creation of Adam. But it wouldn't be quite that unfair, because the emphasis is totally on the personhood of God. He is an individual who creates and who relates to his creation in an almost physical way. We turn now to a very different picture of God, a God who, one can state with some authority, does not have a beard. The trouble is that he is not clean-shaven either, and therein lies the start of our difficulties. God on the classic theistic position of the philosophers is not one of the chaps at all. God is not a person, like Michael Ruse or Richard Dawkins or Queen Elizabeth the Second—or like the God sketched in the passages just given (Davies 2004).

The problems start with the Greeks, although one should not really blame them because the answers come from the Greeks also. The difficulty is that when Jesus died on the cross, when Jesus went up to heaven, there was no religion of Christianity. Those who came after, first Peter and Paul, and then the great theologians—the Church Fathers and their successors—had to develop and articulate the faith. Agreed that God was the creator out of nothing, a being that had started everything simply because he wanted to—a being, therefore, that is worthy and demanding of worship by us— the question now is how to flesh this out, and it is here that the philosophers and the theologians turned to the Greeks, initially Plato via the Neo-Platonists (particularly for Augustine) and later Aristotle (particularly for Aquinas). Plato's theory of Forms is the crucial model, the theory that shapes, infuses, drenches classical theistic views of God—although often as filtered or modified by later philosophers, Aristotle and the Neo-Platonists, Plotinus (204–270) in particular. Remember that we have this supersensible world—ideal but in a way far more real than our physical world—filled with eternal entities, all bound together and getting their being from the supreme entity, the Form of the Good. In Plotinus's language: "a nobler principle than anything we know as Being; fuller and greater; above reason, mind and feeling; conferring these powers, not to be confounded with them" (*Ennead* V 3, 14, in Plotinus [250] 1992). The classical theistic view of God takes in all of this and ends with an entity that is eternal, in some sense self-sufficient, perfect, and sustaining everything else. Plato's Form of the Good may not be a creator out of nothing, but it is very much a sustainer in the sense that everything else gets its being from Good. For Plotinus, it is the eternal soul "attached to the Supreme and yet reaching down to this sphere, like a radius from a centre" (IV 1, 1).

It is like geometry—more than just a loose analogy because it is clear that Plato's thinking is deeply informed by geometry—where the initial axioms don't make the later theorems, but in an important way guarantee their truth. Pythagoras's theorem could not exist without the axioms, things one should note that are eternal and necessary. They don't come into being, they don't go out of being, they just are. It is the same with the philosopher's God—he doesn't come into being, he doesn't go out of being, he just is, and he is the source and reason for the existence of everything else. He uniquely exists necessarily; all else is contingent. Hence, this is not the God of deism, where God stands back after he has finished his job. The work is never over—although in a paradoxical sort of way, it never began either. Note that this does not mean that God is identical with his creation (pantheism) any more than Pythagoras's theorem is identical with Euclid's axioms, but it does mean that God—although himself outside time—is there for all of material existence, and that without him, all would collapse into nothingness. He is immanent.

Is the God of the Philosophers the God of the Bible?

Did the Gospel stories just get lost in the mix? Well, no, although one has to say that there are times when the sense is that the Bible is playing catch-up, with the quest for passages that apparently confirm what has been determined on philosophical grounds. Thus, on the tricky question of God's eternal nature, Psalm 90—with its claim that "Lord, you have been our dwelling place in all generations. Before the mountains were brought forth, or ever you had formed the earth and the world, from everlasting to everlasting you are God" (1-2)—was much appreciated. Malachi 3: 6 was a good backup: "For I the LORD do not change; therefore you, O children of Jacob, have not perished." As was John 8: 58: "Jesus said to them, 'Very truly, I tell you, before Abraham was, I am.'" And James 1: 17: "Every generous act of giving, with every perfect gift, is from above, coming down from the Father of lights, with whom there is no variation or shadow due to change."

God is loving; in fact, he is all loving. He is as well all powerful (omnipotent) and all knowing (omniscient), although God doesn't so much *have* the properties as that he himself *is* the properties (Wainwright 2010). Plato, again, argued that things of this world have their properties because of the Forms, because, remember, they "participate" in the Forms. The Forms are the properties, and God is love and power and knowledge. This leads to one of the more puzzling aspects of classical Christian theology. You might think (with Richard Dawkins) that with everything he has to do, God is pretty complex. This is to misconceive the kind of thought pattern followed here. God is not like a member of Mensa, with an IQ of 170. God is not a person. The traditional position is that God is the ultimate simple! He is the properties, but in an important sense, the properties are all one. In the words of St. Anselm: "God is life, wisdom, eternity, and every true good.—Whatever is composed of parts is not wholly one; it is capable, either in fact or in concept, of dissolution. In God wisdom, eternity, etc., are not parts, but one, and the very whole which God is, or unity itself, not even in concept divisible" (Anselm 2008, *Proslogium* chapter 8). I hardly need say that in some respect this makes sense only by thinking of Plato and the Good. It is the One from which all else stems or flows. Simple, therefore, is not opposed to complex, in the sense that "the instructions for putting together this bookshelf are unnecessarily complex." It is more an ontological claim about the nature of God being the ultimate, on which all else depends (Davies 2010).

How Can We Know God?

All of this is starting to sound pretty remote. How on earth can we be expected to relate to—let alone worship—a being who is so very different from us? We may not always approve, but we know what worship is about when we are talking about persons, about humans. It was one of the great tragedies of the twentieth century that so many Germans worshiped Adolf Hitler, and we know it was one of the great tragedies precisely because we know what it is to worship—to adore, to venerate, to put our trust in. But how can we worship something that is not a person, that is eternal and unchanging, that has (or rather is) all of the properties rolled into one? It is a question not of being willing but of being able.

It is at this point that, through his theory of analogy, Aquinas made one of his great contributions to theology (Davies and Stump 2012). Let's distinguish three senses in which we might use words. First up is "equivocal," where the meanings are quite different. Compare "John is a naturalist," meaning John doesn't believe in miracles, with "Mary is a naturalist," meaning Mary is a nudist. Not the same thing at all! Next is "univocal," where the meanings are the same. Compare "John is a naturalist" with "Fred is a naturalist," meaning Fred doesn't believe in miracles, either. The same word with the same meaning. And finally "analogical," meaning similar in respects but not all respects. Compare "John is a naturalist" with "Alice is a naturalist," where in her case it means, inasmuch as she is doing science, she doesn't allow miracles, but that as a Christian, she doesn't rule out a priori the possibility of miracles. Not the same, but an overlap. Aquinas applied this trichotomy to the problem of speaking of and understanding God. When we say that God is love or God loves us, we are clearly not using the word in the same way as when we say that Romeo and Juliet were lovers, Romeo loved Juliet, and Juliet loved Romeo. Apart from anything else, not to put too fine a point on it, God does not want to have sexual intercourse with us. So God's love and human love are not univocal. But neither are they equivocal. If I had a hobby of stomping on small babies just for laughs, I don't think I would be very loving. But when I say that God is love, I am ruling that out for him, also. God doesn't do that sort of thing for laughs. God is love. At which point you might be inclined to throw up your hands and declare defeat. The best we can do is say what God is not—he is not a baby stomper. God is ineffable. The Jewish philosopher Maimonides (1135–1204) argued this way, going so far as to say that negation was positively better than alternatives: "I do not merely declare that he who affirms attributes of God has not sufficient knowledge concerning the Creator. . . but I say that he unconsciously loses his belief in God" (Maimonides 1936, 87). However, Aquinas thought there was a better option, namely, the middle way of analogy. God's love is not identical, but we can still see that God merits worship. Human love and God's love are analogical. "In this way some words are used neither *univocally* nor purely *equivocally* of God and creatures, but *analogically*, for we cannot speak of God at all except in the language we use of creatures, and so whatever is said both of God and creatures is said in virtue of the order that creatures have to God as to their source and cause in which all perfections of things pre-exist transcendently" (Aquinas 1952, Ia, 13, 5).

What Do Christians Believe about Jesus?

Where does Jesus Christ fit into all of this? Not easily. Judaism may have begun in polytheism, but it became increasingly and stridently monotheistic. "Hear, O Israel: The LORD is our God, the LORD alone" (Deuteronomy 6: 4). Christianity, on the other hand, seemed to split not just into two but into three: "The grace of the Lord Jesus Christ, the love of God, and the communion of the Holy Spirit be with all of you" (2 Corinthians 13: 13). We can say two things with confidence about the second figure in the Trinity (McGrath 1997; Rogers 2010). On the one hand, Jesus is purely human. He had a mother; he ate and drank like the rest of us—seems to have been quite approving of a glass of wine—he had friends and loved some more than others; he got mad at times; as far as we know, he never had sex, but he had close relations and friendships with women, and much more. He was also mortal in the sense that he could be and was killed. He was the "son of man." On the other hand, Jesus is God. He did not just turn up happenstance. He came for a purpose, to redeem us. There is the aura of miracle about him, from having no physical father, through being able to perform quite domestic miracles like turning water into wine at a wedding feast, to truly stupendous ones like raising Lazarus from the dead, and finally coming back to life himself. He was anticipated and had a preordained role to play. He was a great teacher, but more than that, he spoke with the authority of God about what we should think and how we should behave. He was kind and loving beyond normal human abilities, and in the end was prepared to make the supreme sacrifice for others—for us—when he could quite well have kept his mouth shut and stayed out of harm's way. He was the "son of God."

The Holy Spirit is a little trickier and has rather amusingly been described as the Cinderella left behind when the other two sisters had gone to the theological ball, although whether one wants to describe either God or Jesus as "ugly" is another matter (Feenstra 2010). It is that which Jesus left behind to be with us always, helping and guiding. However, general Christian tradition is that it was around before the coming of Jesus and is often associated with breath, as when God breathed life into Adam and Eve. Early Christians were not always entirely sure that the Holy Spirit was indeed God or just an emanation of God, but opinion swung to its divinity. Very influential (as so often) was Augustine, who identified the Holy Spirit with love: "Scripture teaches us that he is the Spirit neither of the Father alone nor of the Son alone, but of both; and this suggests to us the mutual love by which the Father and Son love one another" (McGrath 1995, 8, quoting *De Trinitate*).

What Is the Status of Humans?

We are pretty important. One hesitates to say that we are all-important, because it seems that God is aware of every sparrow that falls to the ground, but it is hard to escape the conclusion that we are the real point of the creation. However you read the creation stories of Genesis, they lead up to the appearance of humans, and then we uniquely are the beings made in the "image of God" (Vanhoozer 1997). Expectedly, there has been a lot of discussion about precisely what this means, but Augustine (again!) is definitive in saying that we humans uniquely are rational beings, able to enter into a relationship with God. The influence of Plato is the key here, because the Greek's psychology (especially in the *Republic*) makes rationality not just one of the parts of the soul but the key, dominant part. Englishmen like me spend a lot of time discussing whether there is a place for dogs in heaven—could it be heaven without dogs?—but even if there is a divine hound lying at the foot of the creator, it will not have quite the same relationship with God as every one of us humans has or has the potential to have.

With rationality goes morality. Indeed, it seems fair to say that without rationality, you cannot have morality. Someone with a damaged brain who is not thinking properly may do horrendous damage to people or to property, but, because such people are not in control of their senses, we do not judge them culpable. Likewise, in civilized countries at least, we do not judge children by the same standards we apply to adults because we realize that they are not fully formed human beings—in an important sense, they are not fully rational. Note, then, that this all rather presupposes that humans have free will. A falling rock may do terrible things to those in its path, but we do not blame the rock. Once released, it had no choice about the path it was taking. However, if *I* am bashing you and not the rock, I am to blame. I did have a choice about whether to harm you. We shall have to dig into the notion of freedom, but for now, we can leave it at the level of the ability to make choices and also the possibility of carrying out those choices. I may want to kill you, but if I am in chains, I am not free to carry out my desires.

What Is Original Sin?

If we are free, then we are free to do the right thing, to be good, or to do the wrong thing, to be bad or sinful or evil (Moser 2010). Later, we shall have more to say about right and wrong, good and evil—that is, about morality. For now, let us simply ask why on earth we would ever do wrong, be sinful? If we are the special creation of a good God, then surely, above all else, we ourselves are going to be good. We would never sin. To do so would imply that somehow God has opened the door to ill behavior, to evil. And that is simply impossible. The Christian has a ready answer to this paradox. It was better that God gave humans freedom than that he made humans like clockwork automata, going through the motions without any choice (Meister 2010). God himself is obviously free. What constraints could there be on him? Hence, here is a major instance of how and why we are made in his image, thinking now of the features we share with God (like rationality) rather than just the functional side, of being set over the creatures of creation as he is over us. But being free means that we could do wrong; otherwise, it is a chimerical form of freedom, like the freedom possessed by a hypnotized person who then goes through certain absurd motions on stage. Unfortunately, we humans did do wrong—Adam and Eve disobeyed the direct orders of God—and so sin entered the world. From then on, humans were in some sense tainted. We are born free but with a disposition to do bad things. Not all of the time obviously, but much of the time and many times. "Therefore, just as sin came into the world through one man, and death came through sin, and so death spread to all because all have sinned" (Romans 5: 12).

This, I should say, is the Augustinian line on original sin—one that obviously owes much to Paul—and it has been incredibly influential in the West, not the least because the great Reformers—Martin Luther (1483–1546) and John Calvin (1509–1564)—were both much influenced by Augustine and bought into this perspective entirely. It reached its apotheosis in the famous sermon "Sinners in the Hands of an Angry God," preached in 1741 by the Puritan minister Jonathan Edwards (1703–1758): "The God that holds you over the pit of hell, much as one holds a spider, or some loathsome insect over the fire, abhors you, and is dreadfully provoked: his wrath towards you burns like fire; he looks upon you as worthy of nothing else, but to be cast into the fire; he is of purer eyes than to bear to have you in his sight; you are ten thousand times more abominable in his eyes, than the most hateful venomous serpent is in ours" (Edwards 2005, 178). Later, we shall encounter other positions on the topic. One thing that this Augustinian viewpoint does is give an immediate reason for the coming of Jesus. He died on the cross for our salvation (Graham 2010). Through his suffering, he took on our sins and hence made possible our eternal happiness. "And now you have an extraordinary opportunity, a day wherein Christ has thrown the door of mercy wide open, and stands in calling and crying with a loud voice to poor sinners; a day wherein many are flocking to him, and pressing into the kingdom of God" (Edwards 2005, 183). It is not really necessary here to go into the many convoluted explanations as to how this all could be or what eternal salvation might mean exactly—although if I were asked, it would be having a new Mozart opera every night of the week and lots of fish and chips at the intermission. (Coupled, I might say, with never, ever, having to grade a student paper again.) The point is that Jesus suffered on our behalf, vicariously as one might say, and this opens up the prospect of never-ending bliss with our creator.

Of course, this all comes at a price. Although there have been universalists, believing that eventually all humans will be saved, generally there is agreement that even Jesus dying on the cross is not going to do much for the eternal prospects of Adolf Hitler. Humans can never be worthy of salvation, but we can do our bit. Unfortunately, there is considerable controversy over what doing our bit might entail. As noted in our history of atheism, the Catholic position has always stressed good works—helping the poor and so forth. These can never be enough, but they are a good start. " 'Come, you that are blessed by my Father, inherit the kingdom prepared for you from the foundation of the world; for I was hungry and you gave me food, I was thirsty and you gave me something to drink, I was a stranger and you welcomed me, I was naked and you gave me clothing, I was sick and you took care of me, I was in prison and you visited me'" (Matthew 25: 34–36). Protestants, on the other hand, as we also noted, have tended to put belief above works. Perhaps reflecting his own history of persecuting Christians and yet being saved, Paul put a big emphasis on commitment: "We hold that a person is justified by faith apart from works prescribed by the law" (Romans 3, 28). This does not mean that Protestants have no obligations to help others, but such help is done in gratitude for mercies shown rather than as a down payment on a ticket into heaven. (To think otherwise is known as the Pelagian heresy.)

Christians have had two thousand years to work on their religion. In discussing it, if one is not careful, one runs the risk of giving the unfortunate reader a lesson in the meaning of eternity. There are those who would say that that is precisely what is done by the great theologians, from Augustine through Aquinas and on to the greatest theologian of the twentieth century, Swiss thinker Karl Barth (1886–1968). Let us pause now, and turn from exposition of the claims to the matter of belief.

5

BELIEF

Why Should We Believe Any of the Claims of Christianity?

Traditionally, philosophers and theologians make a distinction between beliefs based on revelation (revealed theology or religion) and beliefs based on reason and evidence (natural religion or theology). Starting with the former, this is all about the kinds of beliefs that you get from reading the Bible or from listening to the pope (at least when he is speaking authoritatively or ex cathedra). But more basic in a way than even the Bible or the pope is the ground of your conviction that these are the places to go for information. One speaks now of the medium or power of faith. So let's ask about that, for whatever the significance of faith in the ultimate scheme of things, Catholics and Protestants agree that it is central in the life of the Christian.

What Is Faith?

It has many dimensions. Some are psychological, involving commitment. We shall look at those later. Others, those on which we focus here, are more to do with belief, for essentially faith is the means by which we come to knowledge of God and of his ways, inasmuch as this is possible. In a sense, therefore, faith is like a telephone line to the divine, or to update things a bit, the theological equivalent of Skype. On September 18, 1998, Pope John Paul II, writing an encyclical letter to his bishops, *Fides et Ratio* ("Faith and Reason"), laid it out. "Underlying all the Church's thinking is the awareness that she is the bearer of a message which has its origin in God himself (cf. 2 Corinthians 4: 1-2). The knowledge which the Church offers to man has its origin not in any speculation of her own, however sublime, but in the word of God which she has received in faith (cf. 1 Thessalonians 2: 13)." This is something given to humans by God, revealing the essential truths about God, his nature, his purpose for us, and how this is to be achieved. "As the source of love, God desires to make himself known; and the knowledge which the human being has of God perfects all that the human mind can know of the meaning of life."

From the Protestant corner, John Calvin is pretty good on these matters. How do we know God exists? Because God put within all of us an awareness of his existence. "To prevent anyone from taking refuge in the pretense of ignorance, God himself has implanted in all men a certain understanding of his divine majesty. . . . Therefore, since from the beginning of the world there has been no region, no city, in short, no household, that could do without religion, there lies in this a tacit confession of a sense of deity inscribed in the hearts of all" (Calvin 1960, 43–46). If faith is such a natural instinct put there by God, how then do you explain those without faith, like Baron d'Holbach or Bertrand Russell? Obviously, through original sin. Their vile nature leads them to distort or ignore the avenue to God. For the rest of us, though, faith is self-sufficient.

What about Reason and Evidence?

Belief in God through faith is what the Calvinist philosopher Alvin Plantinga (b. 1932), following the Dutch theologian Herman Bavinck (1854–1921), calls "properly basic": "the believer is entirely within his intellectual rights in believing as he does even if he doesn't know of any good theistic argument (deductive or inductive), even if he believes there isn't any such argument, and even if in fact no such argument exists" (Plantinga 1981, 42; see also Bavinck 1951). What is perhaps not the contradictory but more the complement to faith? It is knowledge obtained through reason and the senses, in the area we are discussing as the subject matter of natural theology. Aquinas (1952, 2, 1, 1) puts faith somewhere between knowledge, where we deal with what he characterizes as "something which is self evidently true" (or derivable from self-evident truth), and opinion. This rather implies that faith is not up to the same high standard as knowledge, but such an inference is a bit misleading. Famously, Aquinas believed that we can get knowledge of God and his attributes through a number of arguments (of which more in a moment), but he didn't believe that this made faith superfluous. It was much more a matter of showing that faith could be given a rational basis. Anselm (2008) put the point well when he said, "*Credo ut intelligam*" ("I believe so that I may understand") and when he spoke of "*fides quaerens intellectum*" ("faith seeking understanding"). (No prizes for guessing that these phrases go back to Augustine.) The point is that no one thought that the arguments were uniquely going to lead you to belief or that they would be the basis of one's belief. It was more that they fleshed out the beliefs given through faith.

Aren't we letting the believer get away with too much here? Faith trumps everything, and reason and evidence just play catch-up? So much for being made in God's image! Hardly. Whatever the actual position of Aquinas on the faith and reason issue, he and his fellow philosophers did the heavy lifting on the God and reason and evidence front. And this is very much the Catholic tradition to this day—a tradition that has stimulated responses part in rejection and part in parallel, for Protestants have been somewhat divided on the issue of natural theology. Perhaps because of the emphasis on justification by faith, there has long been a thread of Protestant suspicion about the whole appeal to reason and evidence. Influenced by

Calvin, the most noted recent representative being Karl Barth, these skeptics reject natural theology with distaste and scorn. They go so far as to say that natural theology is not just wrong, but somehow demeaning of God, because it elevates reason above him. The Danish writer Søren Kierkegaard (1813–1855) argued that faith backed with reason is faith emasculated. Faith is genuine only when it carries a whiff of risk, a "leap into the absurd." Countering this, however, for many Protestants, natural theology is a vital part of their belief system. Since the Reformation, for historical as much as theological reasons, this has been very much an English tradition (Ruse 2003). Elizabeth the First (1533–1603), known still as "Good Queen Bess," was faced with a division between the would-be Catholics (backed by powerful Spain), focusing on the authority of the church, and the Calvinist Protestants just back from exile on the Continent during the short but awful reign of Catholic "Bloody Mary" (1516–1558). These latter focused on the unadorned Word of God as found in the Bible. The queen and her church forged a path down the middle—the Elizabethan Compromise—and one of its distinctive features was an emphasis on natural theology, something that obviously meshed nicely with the growing importance of science in that period. The great empiricist philosopher John Locke (1632–1704), writing in the years after the English Civil War and concerned about all of the new rival sects that showed undue "enthusiasm," made the definitive case for reason measuring faith: "Nothing that is contrary to, and inconsistent with, the clear and self-evident dictates of reason, has a right to be urged or assented to as a matter of faith, wherein reason hath nothing to do" (Locke 1959, XVIII, 10). This opened the way for a succession of English philosophers and theologians down to the present to proclaim the glories of their Lord through reason and evidence. Best known was Archdeacon William Paley (1743–1805), who wrote a series of texts, used not just by the young Charles Darwin but by undergraduates at his alma mater (Cambridge) even into the twentieth century.

What are the fruits of all of this effort? What are the various arguments that have been made for the existence of God? Let us find out. (Davies 2004 gives a good overview of the arguments; Re Manning 2013 puts natural theology in historical and theological context.)

What Is the Ontological Argument?

The ontological argument is not the earliest of the arguments—that honor probably goes to the argument from design, to be found in the thinking of Socrates—but it is the one that usually comes first. It strikes almost everyone as irritating, altogether too clever by half, and frankly not very convincing at all. After that, people divide. For most folk, that is enough. Richard Dawkins (2006) is scathing, not just about the argument but about the foolishness of those who take it seriously. It is not worth wasting the time. For a minority, the irritation is more a matter of knowing that something important is being said, of knowing that it is almost certainly not the conclusion to which the argument points and that it is going to be the very devil to dig out precisely what is of value. I won't say that belonging to this second group is a necessary and sufficient condition of being a philosopher, but it helps. For all that he rejects it, it is interesting to note the respect with which Dennett treats the argument, as opposed to Dawkins's contemptuous dismissal.

There are two standard versions of the argument. The first is by Anselm (2008), who takes as his starting point the quotation from the Psalms: "The fool hath said in his heart there is no God." Although almost surely the psalmist is saying that there are people who ignore God and his commands, Anselm takes him literally as saying that some people deny the existence of God. By a reductio ad absurdum argument, Anselm sets out to show that this cannot be. We start with a definition: God is that than which no greater can be thought. The question now is whether God exists. Deny that he does and assert that he is just a mental fiction. Then think of another entity, like the first entity, but with the attribute of existence. Clearly, this second entity is better than the first entity. But this cannot be because the first entity is greater than anything else. Hence we have a contradiction, so it must be the case that God exists!

The second version comes some several hundred years later from Descartes in his *Meditations*. "Certainly, the idea of God, or a supremely perfect being, is one that I find within me just as surely as the idea of any shape or number. And my understanding that it belongs to his nature that he always exists is no less clear and distinct than is the case when I prove of any shape or number that some property belongs to its nature" (Descartes 1964, 63). What's he saying here? Basically that I have the idea of God as a being with all perfections. Existence is a perfection. Therefore, God exists!

What Is the Causal or Cosmological Argument?

Now there are obviously some differences between the two versions of the ontological argument, but not so much that it is confusing to take them together. What I want to point out here is how the argument is deeply embedded in (what we saw in the last chapter was) the classical (philosophers') theistic conception of God. One cannot overemphasize—and here the ontological argument is a most valuable guide—how fundamental to the classical conception is the notion of God as a necessary being (Leftow 2010). What Anselm and Descartes are saying is that God doesn't just exist. By his very nature, he had to exist. This point is crucial to understanding the next argument to which we turn, the causal or cosmological argument, one that goes back to the Greeks, Plato and Aristotle, and played a major role in medieval thought, particularly that of St. Thomas Aquinas (Ruse 2003). Again we find an argument with somewhat different forms, but for our purposes, it is enough to focus on the central inference. Everything has a cause. There must therefore be a cause of the world. This is, or call this, God. It is either that or we cannot break or stop the chain of causation, which seems to imply that it is infinite, which simply doesn't make sense. "But if the chain were to go back infinitely, there would be no first cause, and thus no ultimate effect, nor middle causes, which is admittedly false. Hence we must presuppose some first efficient cause—which all call God" (Aquinas 1952, 1a, 2, 3).

Proceed with caution here. Prima facie, you can drive a horse and carriage through the cosmological argument. If everything has a cause, then what caused God? What caused that "first efficient cause"? Actually, if we are going to take science seriously, we know that what caused everything was the Big Bang. This may be many things, but it is certainly not God. No one is about to worship an explosion. However, if you start to dig into Aquinas's writings, as well as those of others who have supported the argument, you soon see that they are ahead of you here. For a start, they are not really thinking of a cause that just so happens to come at the beginning of a chain. Aquinas, as a Christian, thought that revelation shows that the universe has a beginning. But as a good Aristotelian, he was quite prepared on philosophical grounds to accept the possibility of an infinitely old universe. It is more a cause in the sense of what keeps everything going, sort of orthogonal to the chain of time. It is the answer to what has been called the fundamental question of philosophy: "Why is there something rather than nothing?" So all of the talk about the Big Bang is irrelevant. For a follow-up, everybody knew that you had to stop the chain with God, or you are stuck with an infinite chain of causes. The claim is that God is something that doesn't need a cause. He stops the chain dead.

Now you might say that this is all very well, but why should God stop the chain? Isn't this just the assumption that you are trying to prove? Not quite. The real assumption is that the fundamental question is a genuine question and that it has an answer (Ruse 2010). Moreover, that the only satisfactory answer is a being that needs no cause. Let's assume that it is indeed God, because there don't seem to be any other candidates for the job. Moreover, it does seem to mesh nicely with the biblical claims. "In the beginning when God created the heavens and the earth" (Genesis 1: 1). How then can God need no cause? It is here that the insight of the ontological argument is crucial. Clearly, God needs no cause because he is in some sense necessary. He doesn't need a cause any more than 2 + 2 = 4 needs a cause. He just is. In the language of the philosophers, God has a mode of existence that is entire unto himself, to which they give the name *aseity* (Hick 1961). Perhaps it is no surprise that Anselm gives one of the clearest characterizations: "The supreme Substance, then, does not exist through any efficient agent, and does not derive existence from any matter, and was not aided in being brought into existence by any external causes. Nevertheless, it by no means exists through nothing, or derives existence from nothing; since, through itself and from itself, it is what it is" (Anselm 1903, 48–49, *Monologium* 6).

Note that this is all part and parcel of the classical theistic conception of God. Such a being is going to be out of space and time, eternal, and so forth. Saint Augustine in his *Confessions* is definitive: "Your years neither go nor come, but our years pass and others come after them, so that they all may come in their turn. Your years are completely present to you all at once, because they are at a permanent standstill. They do not move on, forced to give way before the advance of others, because they never pass at all. But our years will all be complete only when they have moved into the past. Your years are one day, yet your day does not come daily but is always today, because your today does not give place to any tomorrow nor does it take the place of any yesterday. Your today is eternity" (Augustine 1961, 263).

Would this being be good? Well, that presumably depends at least in part on the quality of what it has produced. And that is the topic of the next argument on our list.

What Is the Teleological Argument?

Better known as the argument from design, we have encountered it already in earlier chapters, both its place in the thinking of people like Robert Boyle and the debunking (if that is the right word for someone who continued to believe in a designer God) thinking of Charles Darwin. The argument, as Boyle stressed, focuses on Aristotelian (1984) final causes, the ends that seem to control and explain so many features, especially so many biological features. The existence and nature of the hand, for instance, is clearly a matter of embryology—first, there were buds, and then there were fingers and thumbs—but it does not seem to be simply a matter of embryology. To understand the hand fully, we need to know what it is for—what is it intended to do? What is its purpose? To which the answer comes that it serves the end of grasping, as the nose serves the end of smelling, and the teeth of biting and chewing. Note that in a sense there is a forward reference—the teeth exist to chew, even if I live off fluids all of my life—but there is nothing spooky here, with little men in the future pulling strings affecting my present. *Intention* is the keyword, meaning that this is what hands and noses and teeth are for, even if they never actually get used. Brushed aside is Lamy's suggestion that features might first appear without design and only then find their function. How could something as intricate as the eye, something that is so good for seeing, just appear by chance?

Intention implies a consciousness. I intend to write three thousand words today. My computer and its software intend nothing at all. This is the key to the teleological argument. Final causes seem to imply that someone intended them to work, someone designed the system, and in the case of the physical world, that someone was God. Paley's exposition is the classic. The eye is like a telescope. Telescopes have telescope designers and makers. Therefore, the eye must have a designer and maker. God, the supreme optician. Moreover, you can make an inference about the nature of the designer. "For instance, these laws require, in order to produce the same effect, that the rays of light, in passing from water into the eye, should be refracted by a more convex surface than when it passes out of air into the eye. Accordingly we find that the eye of a fish, in that part of it called the crystalline lens, is much rounder than the eye of terrestrial animals" (Paley 1819). How can you doubt God's intelligence and concern? Denial of this kind of reasoning? "This is atheism."

What Is the Anthropic Principle?

An argument that in respects seems to be a corollary of the argument from design is the argument from law. Here one suggests that the very existence of the laws of nature points to the deity, and if one can bring in the nature of these laws, one has a correspondingly stronger argument. One enthusiast for this position starts with the (somewhat tenuous) biblical evidence: "As long as the earth endures, seedtime and harvest, cold and heat, summer and winter, day and night, shall not cease" (Poythress 2006, quoting Genesis 8: 22). He then makes the key abduction: "Law implies a lawgiver. Someone must think the law and enforce it, if it is to be effective" (20). He adds an elaboration about the nature of law and hence of the lawgiver: "Scientific laws, especially 'deep' laws, are beautiful. Scientists have long sifted through possible hypotheses and models partly on the basis of the criteria of beauty and simplicity. For example, Newton's law of gravitation and Maxwell's laws of electromagnetism are mathematically simple and beautiful. And scientists clearly *expect* new laws, as well as the old ones, to show beauty and simplicity. Why? The beauty of scientific laws shows the beauty of God himself" (23). And he wraps it all up with a bit of a threat. "People can try to disobey physical laws, and when they do they often suffer for it. If one attempts to defy the law of gravity by jumping off a tall building, he will suffer consequences. There is a kind of built-in righteousness in the way in which laws lead to consequences" (24). "God's rectitude," this is called.

A variant on this kind of thinking has become very popular in recent years, particularly among believers from a physics background. It centers on the anthropic principle (Barrow and Tipler 1986). This comes in a number of variants, with the extremes being the most interesting. The Weak Anthropic Principle (WAP) makes the fairly benign observation that since humans exist and flourish, the universe must be of a kind that allows humans to exist and flourish. The basic constants embedded in the laws of nature come together to allow the existence of humans. The Strong Anthropic Principle (SAP, known in skeptical quarters as the Completely Ridiculous Anthropic Principle) claims that had the laws of nature been even a fraction different from what they are, humans would not have been able to flourish. Indeed, some doubt that the universe could have gotten off the ground in the first place. For instance, if the strong nuclear force were 2% stronger than it is, diprotons would never be stable (this is a form of helium that in this universe is generally very unstable), and deuterium and regular helium would not be formed. Stars would be very different from what they at present are, and it is highly unlikely that life could have gotten started. In other words, the universe as it is can be thought of as fine-tuned. This cannot be chance, and so the reasonable inference is that there is an intelligence behind it all.

What Are Miracles?

Perhaps a little confusingly, another argument for the existence of God seizes on the fact that the world is not entirely law-bound! Suppose one were invited to an undergraduate B and B party. (B and B parties are, or at least were around 1960 when I was a student, parties to which one was encouraged to bring a bottle and a bird or a bottle and a bloke. I am not sure that one would dare offer such an invitation today.) Suppose, as tends to happen at such parties, before the end, the second set of Bs have consumed everything in the first set of Bs. Suppose, then, that a rather shaggy guest of the host—no problem at these events in finding such guests—asked us to fill up our bottles with tap water, and lo and behold, they are now filled, not with cheap Spanish plonk, but with finest Bordeaux. A bit of a waste, you might think, magical pearls before all-too-real swine, but impressive nonetheless. Perhaps so much so that one would feel compelled to accept that there was some intervention from without, an intervention that points to the existence of God. It just couldn't have been natural. It's a miracle!

Of course, a lot depends here on what you mean by *miracle* (Swinburne 1970; Sullivan and Menssen 2010). The fairly standard notion is an intervention, a breaking or suspension, of the laws of nature. When Lazarus was raised from the dead, one assumes that, as is customary after death, his body had started to break down. He was not in some kind of trance or whatever. "Jesus said, 'Take away the stone.' Martha, the sister of the dead man, said to him, 'Lord, already there is a stench because he has been dead four days'" (John 11: 39). The processes were reversed, and he came back to life. Often, though, we find that people extend the notion of miracle to cover events that were surely law-bound. When I grew up in England after the Second World War, almost everyone was convinced that the evacuation of Dunkirk in 1940 was a miracle. The remnants of the British army crossed the channel back to England and thus formed the basis of a new, bigger, better army that could continue the fight against the Nazis. That weekend, the often-rough channel was like a millpond, and even the smallest ship could and did cross and pick up troops. Everyone thought that this was God's work to enable the British to continue the struggle against the forces of evil.

But if you had asked people if God actually got involved in the meteorology of the weekend, I suspect most people would have thought you were at best making a bad joke. It was the meaning that counted, and frankly, how it happened was totally irrelevant. If it was done through unbroken law, then so be it. That is God's business, not ours.

What Is the Moral Argument?

If you go to Wikipedia and check the entry on "Arguments for the existence of God," you will find more than twenty contenders. Expectedly, many of these are variations on a theme, but still there are enough to keep one going for a much longer book than this. There is no need for panic, for with one more argument we will have covered the basic claims one finds made in the name of theism, including the central tenets of natural theology. The now-to-be-discussed argument was made popular by the great eighteenth-century German philosopher Immanuel Kant (1898), and it appeals to the moral world.

Humans are social animals, and much of our thought and behavior is dedicated to getting along with our fellows—finding partners, having children, making friends and enemies, getting a job, playing a role in the civic arena, and much, much more. A lot of what we do starts with some fairly basic or gut emotions. I work hard to send my kids to college because I love them. I pay my taxes because I am scared of what would happen if I didn't. I join the army during a war because I love my country and I don't want to be judged a coward by my friends. But there is more to all of this than just emotions. There is reasoning—I start a plan to pay college tuition, I work out exactly how much I owe the government, I decide which branch of the military I want to join—and entering into this reasoning there is morality, our sense of right and wrong. I care for my kids because having brought them into the world, I have obligations to them. It is my duty to ensure that they get as good a start in life as it is possible for me to give them. I don't pay my taxes just because I am scared. I do so because as a member of society I realize that we all benefit when we pull together, and so I ought to do my share. I join up at a time of war because I should defend my country against aggressors. I should fight, even unto death, because of what I think is valuable and worth preserving.

Of course, there is a lot of complexity about the exact nature of morality—the calls of obligation—and sometimes over such things as abortion, there are major differences between people. But whatever the exact nature of moral dictates (philosophers call this part of the business substantive or normative ethics), apart from psychopaths and like misfits, no one denies the existence of morality. And this point is not denied by the fact that from Friedrich Nietzsche on, many continental thinkers have been much given to pronouncing on its end. It does not take much digging to show that they are not denying morality as such, but more the hypocrisy that infects so many contemporary claims about moral behavior. Most of the naysayers would be very uncomfortable roommates, because every little peccadillo would be subjected to endless critical analysis.

Is Morality Objective?

The big question, then, is where does morality come from and what is its status? (Philosophers call this part of the business metaethics because it is about morality, substantive morality, that is.) It seems to be a generally accepted aspect of what we might call the phenomenology of morality that it doesn't just seem to be a matter of opinion or of how people may sometimes behave. Take rape, sexual intercourse with another person against that person's will. We can all agree unambiguously that rape is wrong. You might argue about whether this is a basic statement in its own right or whether it derives from something else. A Kantian, for instance, argues that the supreme moral norm is treating others as ends in themselves and not means to ends, and hence rape is immoral because one is using another person for one's own gratification and not for the benefit of the person being raped. But either way, rape is wrong. Think of the situation in East Prussia toward the end of the Second World War (Beevor 2003). Russian soldiers raped the womenfolk repeatedly and indiscriminately, with the permission if not outright approval of their superiors. "The Germans had it coming to them." It may or may not have been understandable and predictable—I'll leave that to others—but it was still morally wrong.

The point being made is that somehow morality seems to be objective (Mackie 1977; Ruse 1986). "Rape is wrong" is not up for grabs in the way that "I don't much care for broccoli" and "I'd rather be a philosopher than a sociologist" are matters of taste—although, as it happens, even the most atheistic of philosophers think of their calling as divine destiny. "Rape is wrong" is binding on all of us, even if, like the Russian soldiers, we can get away with it and no one is going to condemn us. I can make a judgment of you on this, in a way I cannot if you say that you prefer George Eliot to Charles Dickens, to take a matter over which I, as an ardent Dickensian, have had some long and bitter arguments with good friends. Morality is a bit like the laws of nature in that it exists outside me and I am subject to it. (Of course, it isn't always the case that I follow it, but that is another matter.) Or in a stronger way, morality is a bit like the laws of mathematics, because morality seems to be about the world, not of it. David Hume ([1739–1740] 2000) made this point very clearly. The world is about matters of empirical fact. Morality is about matters of obligation. You cannot deduce the latter simply from the former. Logically, they are chalk and cheese. So here, then, is the conundrum. Morality is objective. In the lingo of philosophers, apparently one ought to be a moral realist, meaning one ought to believe that moral claims (substantive ethics) really exist as things in their own right. Morality is binding on us humans. And yet, morality is not simply a matter of the way that (empirical) things are. It has its own being.

Some people have thought—Plato obviously—that the analogy between mathematics and morality strikes deep. They both refer to entities in the supersensible world of pure rationality. Unfortunately, even if this is so, mathematics doesn't have the sense of obligation that morality has. So where does morality come from, and what is the authority behind its binding nature? The obvious answer is that it is to be found in the will of God. Morality is what God wants of us. Conversely, this gives us an inference-to-the-best-explanation proof for the existence of God. Morality must have a cause or foundation. It is not to be found in this world. It is not to be found in the world of the Forms. Hence, the most reasonable explanation is that it is the will of God. Hence, God must exist.

John Henry Newman in his *A Grammar of Assent* makes the case powerfully: "If, as is the case, we feel responsibility, are ashamed, are frightened, at transgressing the voice of conscience, this implies that there is one to whom we are responsible, before whom we are ashamed, whose claims upon us we fear" (Newman 1870, 109). The only being who would fit this bill is God. Anything less will not do. "These feelings in us are such as require for their exciting cause an intelligent being; we are not affectionate towards a stone; we do not feel shame before a horse or dog; we have no remorse or compunction on breaking merely human law; yet so it is, conscience excites all these painful emotions: confusion, foreboding, self-condemnation; and on the other hand it sheds upon us a deep peace, a sense of security, a resignation and a hope, which there is no sensible, no earthly, object to elicit" (110).

Is That Everything?

I quote Newman—the greatest theologian in Britain since St. Anselm—because, on leaving this and the preceding chapter,

I want the reader to take away a sense of the deep existential seriousness of religious commitment. However we end up, we do no one—believer or nonbeliever—any favor by trivializing this sincerity, one that Newman himself shows characterizes some of the most powerful of intellects as well as the simplest. This is not a call to suspend critical judgment. It is a call for respect, at least until it is seen no longer to be warranted. And with this we can move on. The time has come to hear the case for the other side.

6

THE MATTER OF SCIENCE

How Religious are Scientists?

Let us open the batting with science. Our history has primed us for this charge: Modern science basically and thoroughly makes religious belief untenable, or, if not untenable, then at least implausible and unneeded. It is the cry of the New Atheists, but it is far from new. Its seeds are in the Scientific Revolution, and it has grown and intensified (Taylor 2007). In Britain in the middle of the twentieth century, there were often bitter disputes between people like the geneticist J. B. S. Haldane (1892–1964), backed by general man of science and television personality Jacob Bronowski (1908–1974), and people like the fantasy Christian novelists C. S. Lewis (1898–1963) and J. R. R. Tolkien (1892–1973) about whether a new paradigm was now in order, with scientific materialism replacing Christian idealism (Bud 2013). This echoed the nineteenth-century clash between T. H. Huxley, representing agnostic science, and Prime Minister William Gladstone, defender of the Anglican faith. Certainly, if you look at the empirical data about beliefs, these arguments are a peephole into general sentiments. Start with top-rank British scientists, that is to say, fellows of the Royal Society. (The data is taken with permission from Stirrat and Cornwell 2013.) About ten years ago, they were asked about their religious beliefs. (Of 1,074 asked, 253 responded. Of the respondents,

243 were male and 10 were female.) About half of the respondents came from the physical sciences and about half from the biological sciences. They were asked about the following four assertions:

1. I believe that there is a strong likelihood that a supernatural being such as God exists or has existed.
2. I believe in a personal God, that is one who takes interests in individuals, hears and answers prayers, is concerned with sin and transgressions, and passes judgment.
3. I believe that science and religion occupy non-overlapping domains of discourse and can peacefully co-exist.
4. I believe that when we physically die, our subjective consciousness, or some part of it, survives.

Scoring was from 1 to 7, with the lower scores representing disagreement and the higher scores agreement. As you can see in figures 6.1 through 6.4, God does not come off very well! We are looking at about 80% who don't believe in a God of any kind, let alone a personal God, and about the same number who don't believe in immortality. What is

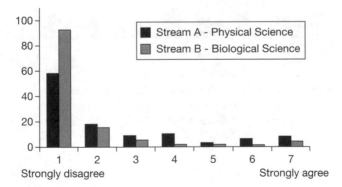

Figure 6.1 I believe that there is a strong likelihood that a supernatural being such as God exists or has existed. Stirrat, M., and R. E. Cornwell. 2013. Eminent scientists reject the supernatural: A survey of the fellows of the Royal Society. *Evolution: Education and Outreach* 6(33), doi:10.1186/1936-6434-6-33

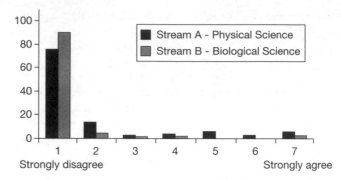

Figure 6.2 I believe in a personal God, that is one who takes interests in individuals, hears and answers prayers, is concerned with sin and transgressions, and passes judgment. Stirrat, M., and R. E. Cornwell. 2013. Eminent scientists reject the supernatural: A survey of the fellows of the Royal Society. *Evolution: Education and Outreach* 6(33), doi:10.1186/1936-6434-6-33

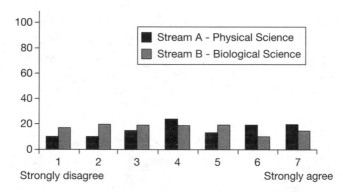

Figure 6.3 I believe that science and religion occupy non-overlapping domains of discourse and can peacefully co-exist. Stirrat, M., and R. E. Cornwell. 2013. Eminent scientists reject the supernatural: A survey of the fellows of the Royal Society. *Evolution: Education and Outreach* 6(33), doi:10.1186/1936-6434-6-33

interesting is that biologists seem to be less religious than physicists. In the past century, they have been on the front line more or less.

Turning to America, there was a detailed study done about ten years previous to this one, in other words, about twenty

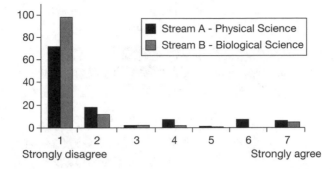

Figure 6.4 I believe that when we physically die, our subjective consciousness, or some part of it, survives. Stirrat, M., and R. E. Cornwell. 2013. Eminent scientists reject the supernatural: A survey of the fellows of the Royal Society. *Evolution: Education and Outreach* 6(33), doi:10.1186/1936-6434-6-33

years ago. (See figures 6.5 and 6.6. Taken with permission from Larson and Witham 1997 and Larson and Witham 1998, respectively.) It was somewhat richer than the English study, first in that it compared views now (1996) with recorded views earlier in the century, and second in that it compared regular scientists with elite scientists, this time using as the criterion membership in the National Academy of Sciences. With respect to the God question, there is not a huge difference across the century. Large numbers do believe in God, although still at only about half of the rate of the general public. Interestingly, belief in or desire for immortality seems to have dropped precipitously. Is life so much more awful later in the century that no one wants to extend it beyond this existence? When we turn to the elite scientists, we can see that they were always less God-believing than regular scientists, but by the end of the century, their belief had shrunk to vanishingly small numbers, very much on a par with the figures recorded for England ten years later.

Which came first, the chicken or the egg? Is it that the better you are as a scientist—assuming that successful and recognized equates with better—the more likely you are to drop the God hypothesis? You follow Laplace's quip to Napoleon.

Survey Results: Belief in God

ALL RESPONDENTS

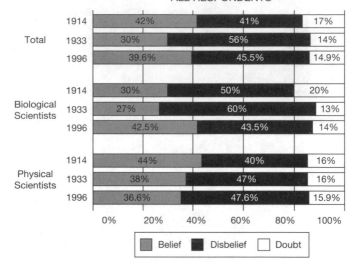

RESPONSES OF "GREATER" SCIENTISTS

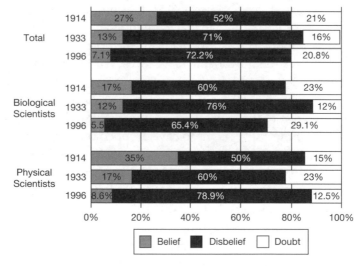

Figure 6.5 Larson, E. J., and L. Witham. 1997. Scientists are still keeping the faith. *Nature* 386: 435–436

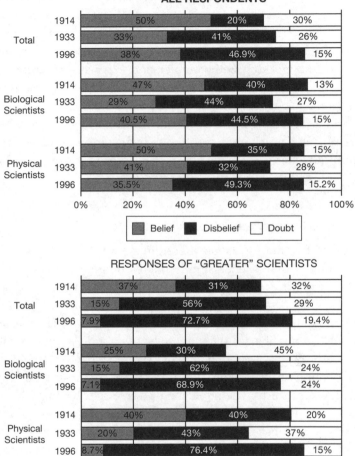

Figure 6.6 Larson, E. J., and L. Witham. 1998. Leading scientists still reject God. *Nature* 394: 313

"Sire, I have no need of that hypothesis." Or is it that having dropped the God hypothesis, you go into science, and the more the dropping, the more you bury yourself in your work? The nineteenth century suggests the latter, but one suspects that there must be elements of both. Certainly, the life of an elite scientist today is going to be quite different from that of a regular scientist. One is going to be in a large metropolitan area, in a big research-oriented university, looking for huge grants and working with complex and expensive machinery, surrounded by postdocs and graduate students. Life is simply going to be more secular and sophisticated than for people working at land grant institutions, places where instructors are probably much more oriented to their communities—communities where God plays a large part. In America, one should never forget the social role that religion plays.

Why Does Science Push Out Religion?

We find two main reasons offered in answer to this question. The first is that science simply makes religion unnecessary. The Nobel Prize winner Steven Weinberg (b. 1933) says: "One of the great achievements of science has been, if not to make it impossible for intelligent people to be religious, then at least to make it possible for them not to be religious. We should not retreat from this accomplishment" (Weinberg 1999). Actually, that sounds a little more accommodating than he really is. He has also said: "The more the universe seems comprehensible, the more it also seems pointless," and this, as is so often the case in these sorts of discussions, opens the way to the moral judgment. Remember how Weinberg claims that to get good people to do bad things, you need religion. Expectedly, given that several of them have backgrounds in science, this kind of sentiment finds favor with the New Atheists. Richard Dawkins drums in the redundancy of religion. In the *God Delusion*, he identifies complexity as a major reason that people demand religious explanations and then goes over the scientific explanations for this complexity—natural selection for organisms and modern physics for the rest. This leads to the expected conclusion: "The factual premise of religion—the God Hypothesis—is untenable. God almost certainly does not exist" (Dawkins 2006, 158).

Of course, Dawkins and the other critics do not rest with redundancy. They think that science—evolutionary biology particularly—gives good reasons why the Good God of Christianity does not exist and why the whole religion comes tumbling down. Chemist Peter Atkins (b. 1940) is eloquent on the subject. "Science and religion cannot be reconciled, and humanity should begin to recognize the power of its child and beat off all attempts at compromise." He goes on to say: "Religion has failed and its failures should stand exposed. Science, with its currently successful pursuit of universal competence through the identification of the minimal, the supreme delight of the intellect, should be acknowledged king" (Atkins 1995, 132).

At some level, people like Dawkins and Atkins are absolutely right. Start right in on the early chapters of Genesis. If you are an American evangelical—these days not just American and not just Christian—the odds are you believe that every word of the Good Book is true, literally, as it was written. To use language introduced already, you are what used to be known as a Fundamentalist and more recently as a Creationist (Numbers 2006). You think the world was made in six days, probably within the last ten thousand years. You think that organisms were created miraculously, with humans coming last. Whether you think that Adam and Eve came together or that Eve was something of an afterthought to keep Adam occupied is a matter of opinion. There are two versions from which you can choose. You think that sometime after God created everything, he got mad at humankind and that he wiped out almost everybody and everything with a worldwide flood—the Deluge. Note that this was not some restricted event somewhere in the Middle East. It covered the whole globe. You think that God gave Joshua a helping hand by fiddling with the motions of the heavens. You think that Jonah was swallowed by a whale, except you know better and that it was truly a fish. "But the LORD provided a large fish to swallow up Jonah; and Jonah was in the belly of the fish three days and three nights" (Jonah 1: 17). Then, after the appropriate prayers, Jonah was thrown up: " 'I with the voice of thanksgiving will sacrifice to you; what I have vowed I will pay. Deliverance belongs to the LORD!' Then the LORD spoke to the fish, and it spewed Jonah out upon the dry land" (Jonah 2: 9-10).

There is a lot more that you believe, and in the eyes of modern science, every one of these beliefs is absolutely dead wrong. False, false, false! The earth is more than 4 billion years old, and the universe is nearly four times that amount. Organisms were not created miraculously at the end of one week, but have evolved slowly for almost 4 billion years. That is true of humans, as well as of all other organisms, so don't lose sleep over whether Adam and Eve came together or in succession. Noah's flood is fiction. Don't waste your time calculating how much food the animals needed on the ark or how the waste was going to be managed. There was no hippopotamus-poo problem. There was no flood, and there was no ark. The sun did not stop for Joshua, and neither did the moon. Who knows what would have happened to the Earth and its denizens if they had done so. And whale or fish, Jonah did not spend three days inside it. If you believe that, then you will believe that Pinocchio was turned into a real boy after he, too, spent time in a whale. You will believe anything.

Is That the End of Religion?

Of course not! American Evangelicalism is an idiosyncratic form of Protestantism that took shape in the first part of the nineteenth century, very much in response to the country's needs as it built itself into the great nation that it is today.

Many of these needs were far less theological than social and cultural. This was no less true a century later. *The Genesis Flood* was published in 1961. The bible of Young Earth Creationism (YEC), it would have come as a surprise to traditional literalists like William Jennings Bryan (1860–1925), the "Great Commoner," three times a presidential candidate and prosecutor at the Monkey Trial. He thought the Earth was very old, believing that since "a thousand years are but as a day in the eye of the Lord," there might be long periods of time unrecorded in the Bible or that the six days were themselves long periods of time. Whitcomb and Morris, influenced by the YEC of the Seventh-day Adventists, were writing in the depths of the Cold War. Apocalyptic scenarios were a dime a dozen, and Whitcomb and Morris used their literalism about the creation to segue straight into literalism about what their title shows was the real focus of their interest: the flood. This was taken as a harbinger of the worldwide destruction, Armageddon, we are about to experience. "But the day of the Lord will come like a thief, and then the heavens will pass away with a loud noise, and the elements will be dissolved with fire, and the earth and everything that is done on it will be disclosed" (2 Peter 3: 10).

Science clashes with biblical literalism. But literalism is not traditional or genuine Christianity. If it were, then neither Augustine nor Calvin could be considered traditional or genuine Christians! They were deeply into metaphorical or allegorical readings of the Bible. Augustine in particular worked on this problem, arguing that we really should not expect God to speak literally all of the time to a tribe of uneducated, illiterate people. He had to speak in metaphor or allegory. For sophisticated people like us—Roman citizens at the end of the fourth century—there has to be a more careful, subtler approach. The rule should be that we work with the literal until we find that the knowledge of today renders it unacceptable. Then we must switch to the allegorical. Thus in the context of Genesis, it is "too disgraceful and ruinous, though, and greatly to be avoided, that he [the non-Christian] should hear a Christian speaking so idiotically on these matters, and as if in accord with Christian writings, that he might say that he could scarcely keep from laughing when he saw how totally in error they are" (Augustine 1982, 1, 19–20). Of course, so often the problem is where, exactly, you are supposed to draw the line between greatest certainty and not. The crucifixion is on one side of the line, but what of six days of creation? Augustine argued for an instantaneous creation and then a gradual unfurling and actualization of the already potential. This did not make him into an evolutionist, although there are those who think that he offered a theological underpinning to evolution (McMullin 1985). Be this as it may, and recognizing that there are still going to be significant issues, we can defend traditional Christianity against some of the cruder attacks on the literalism matter. The question is not where did Augustine himself stand on something like the Flood, but where would he stand today on the Flood. Quite a different matter.

What Are the Nonnegotiable Claims of the Christian?

Grant, then, the importance of interpretation. So where do we go from here? Let's start with the essentials, expecting later to pry into the more baroque details. What is the fundamental core of Christian belief? We have just spent two chapters going over it, but what is the absolute minimum—no equivocations, no metaphors, no behind the veil? Obviously, that there is a god, or God, and that he is creator of heaven and earth. Perhaps as obviously, that there are human beings and that we have a special place in the creation, whatever that might mean. It may not mean that we are the only ones with such a place, but that we have it is a bottom-line demand. From this it surely follows that God has a purpose and destiny for us. It is not likely that he would create us, have a special place for us, and then, with a celestial laugh, blow us into nonbeing as if we were cartoon characters. I would not say that the God of the Christians is necessarily without humor, but he is certainly not one just to do things for a couple of giggles. And bound up with this is the thought that we ourselves must do something to earn this destiny. If we are nothing but God's playthings, then the whole Christian story does get rather trivialized.

There is a lot more about Jesus and everything, and we have been dealing with that and will again deal with that. But let us take these four demands as basic:

1. A creator God exists.
2. There is a purpose to it all.
3. We humans are special.
4. We have obligations.

The question we must now ask is: Does science block or deny these claims? It is not whether they are true, but whether science shows them untrue.

What Are Magisteria?

There are ways you can get answers to these questions fairly easily and readily. My fellow expert witness in the (earlier, Arkansas) Creationism trial, the late Stephen Jay Gould— paleontologist, baseball lover, and the only science writer with claim to Dawkins's justified fame at his craft—thought the answer could be given fairly readily so long as we see that science and religion basically are trying to answer different sorts of questions and hence cannot clash (Gould 1999). Science is trying to answer factual questions. Religion is trying to answer meaning or moral questions. Thus, suppose you ask Lizzie, my wife, what she did yesterday. One answer would be that she went in the car with the family to a park, where we had a picnic, and then drove home and got caught in traffic. Another answer would be that she celebrated her birthday, her husband and kids fixed a picnic, and we had a great day at the park, where she was surrounded by love and gratitude.

Two answers, both right, about different things, and unable to conflict. Invoking the notion of what he called a *magisterium*, a kind of worldview or way of looking at things, Gould argued that science and religion are different magisteria and hence cannot conflict. Science is about the way things are, religion is about morals and spirituality, and the two are in different domains. Not incompatible but not competing either.

Theologically, this kind of position is known as neo-orthodoxy, embraced earlier in the century by Karl Barth. Of course, in the light of what has already been said in this chapter, we know that it cannot be strictly true—science, modern science, and religion (at least some versions of Christianity) can and do come into conflict. But with respect to the basic claims just given, the question is still open. Unfortunately, though, Gould's treatment of the problem is hardly adequate. Obviously, religious people do want to make factual claims. God exists and is creator. The universe has a purpose. We are special. We have distinctive abilities. Morality may be involved—it is involved—but Christianity goes beyond this. Simply labeling things different magisteria and leaving the discussion at that is not adequate.

Should We Think about Metaphor?

We need to look at the nature of science and, instead of making it all up as we go along, find out what others would say. What would be generally accepted truths about science? One answer we have been primed for already: Science is deeply metaphorical (Hesse 1966; Kuhn 1962, 1977; Lakoff and Johnson 1980). Science is not just a matter of observing and describing absolute reality: "Just the facts, ma'am, just the facts." Rather, it is what I like to call the police photographer's view of science, although in truth police photographers are probably just as much into interpretation as Van Gogh painting a wheatfield. Science is a matter of conceptualizing reality, and here metaphor is crucial. This is a linguistic device where we look at one thing, the *tenor*, in the light of, through the lens of, another thing, the *vehicle*. "A mighty fortress is our God." By doing so, we bring out aspects of the thing being discussed, we look at it in a new light, we stimulate fresh questions. This is the way of science—force, field, work, attraction, repulsion, struggle, selection, genetic code, selfish gene, arms race, landscape, Oedipus complex—the list is endless. Moreover, metaphors don't just come isolated. They tend to be embedded in others. Take health or goodness and the metaphor of up and down: Stand up, stand up for Jesus! I am feeling a bit down today. This will get you up and about. You are the lowest of the low. A man never stands as tall as when he bends to help a child. Or argument as warfare: I beat him down. I countered his thrust. I came up with a new strategy. I won! He lost!

These big metaphors are known as root metaphors, and we have already encountered the root metaphor of modern science. It is the machine. The world is seen as a contraption, as a mechanism. In the vision of Robert Boyle, the world is like the clock at Strasbourg, doing all sorts of wonderful things—it shows the motions of the heavens and much more—all entirely automatically. You wind it up, and off it goes. It has taken four hundred years for this metaphor to work itself out, and in respects it is still doing so, and scientists much hope that this will continue. In physics, from the late seventeenth century onward, the science has shown nigh unto unbroken success. Of course, there were changes and advances and modifications—the coming of electrical theory demanded changes in our thinking about the nature of machines, and obviously the physics of the twentieth century set major challenges. But note that it was quantum *mechanics* and not some other metaphor.

Biology was a real challenge. Yet, thanks to the physiologists of the nineteenth century who started to break down the components of life and show them to be merely chemicals in motion, and then most particularly Charles Darwin and his theory of evolution through natural selection, the metaphor moved right in and conquered (Ruse 1979). In the words of Richard Dawkins: "We are survival machines, but 'we' does not mean just people. It embraces all animals, plants, bacteria, and viruses." He continues: "We are all survival machines for the same kind of replicator—molecules called DNA—but there are many different ways of making a living in the world, and the replicators have built a vast range of machines to exploit them. A monkey is a machine which preserves genes up trees, a fish is a machine which preserves genes in the water; there is even a small worm which preserves genes in German beer mats. DNA works in mysterious ways" (Dawkins 1976, 22). Most recently, the metaphor has been extended to the human brain. That is the underlying premise of so-called cognitive science. The brain is a computer. "With regard to the very special class of machines known as computers, the claim is that the brain (and, by not unproblematic extension, the mind) actually *is* some such device. It is not that the brain is somehow *like* a computer: everything is like something else in some respect or other. It is that neural tissues, synapses, cell assemblies, and all the rest are just nature's rather wet and sticky way of building a hunk of honest-to-God computing machinery" (Clark 2000, 7–8).

Is There a Downside to Metaphor?

Well, not exactly, but as Thomas Kuhn (1922–1996) pointed out, metaphors are successful in major part because of what they do not set out to do rather than what they do set out to do. A good metaphor—and the machine metaphor is a good metaphor—succeeds because it pushes inquiry forward. Thinking of the brain as a computer, for instance, spurs you to look at what computers do and how they do what they do and then turn to the brain and see if there are comparable phenomena and processes. But a good metaphor succeeds also because it stops you from wasting time on unnecessary procedures and asking unnecessary questions. Or at least, because in the broader view, these procedures and questions may be far from unnecessary; they restrict you in the field in which you are working and free you to get on with what you can do. Take a metaphor like my love is a flower, she is a rose. It summons up all sorts of pictures: My love is young and fresh. She is beautiful and vibrant and living. And so forth. If you are joking a bit, you might also be hinting that your love is capable of being a little prickly. What you are not doing is talking about your love's mathematical abilities or her religious affiliation. She may be a whiz at sums or she may be hopeless. She may be a devout Anglican or she may be a New Atheist. The metaphor says nothing about them and doesn't encourage you to ask about them. As I said, this isn't a weakness. This is how metaphors—good metaphors—work.

Unasked Questions?

So what questions go unasked, given the machine metaphor? Let me suggest the following four. I am not saying that these questions are written in stone or that they are the only questions. Perhaps time will bring them into the metaphor, but for now they stand without (Ruse 2010).

The first question is what, for obvious reasons, we have seen characterized as the fundamental question of philosophy: Why is there something rather than nothing? Now notice this is not a question about how things came from other things. It is about why there are things at all (Heidegger 1959). In other words, although it may be the case that the universe started with the Big Bang, making reference to this—or to possible states before this—is not the answer. It is rather a question of ontology, about the very state of being. And obviously the machine metaphor is silent. An automobile is made of metal and plastics and so forth, and you can ask where the iron ore came from and even how the iron formed in the first place. But you are saying nothing about the ultimate origin of the substance as such.

The second question is about purpose. What is the meaning of it all? Now you might say that the whole point about machines is that they are into purposes, meanings. They promote questions about final causes. A clock is for telling time. A pump is for getting water out of mines. An automobile is for going from A to B. However, as we know, as soon as the machine metaphor came on board, scientists realized that purpose questions simply didn't help. Nobody could answer them, and in any case no one was really sure what they were supposed to be. Questions about final causes got pushed out of science, and God, as we remember, became a retired engineer. It is true that organisms posed problems for two hundred years after physics expelled final causes, but eventually Darwin did the job (Ruse 2003). Steve Weinberg finds no purpose because there are no purposes within the system he embraces.

What about the special nature of humans? Obviously, we think here of consciousness. Not just brains, but sentience—self-awareness and so forth. Without getting into arguments about how conscious some other animals are—many dog and cat owners would emphatically assert that there is consciousness beyond humankind—it is certainly true that this ability to think and to know that we are thinking is pretty special. Let us grant that cognitive science and related disciplines have thrown a lot of light on what is going on in the brain, but it is far from obvious that this explains consciousness as such. Descartes, remember, thought that material objects and thinking objects are different substances—*res extensa* and *res cogitans*—and while this is probably too great a separation, brains are not minds and conversely. Leibniz put his finger on it. If you go in with the machine metaphor, you are going to come out with the machine metaphor, and you are not going to find consciousness along the way. "One is obliged to admit that perception and what depends upon it is inexplicable on mechanical principles, that is, by figures and motions." With a machine, all you are going to get is matter in motion, not consciousness awareness. "In imagining that there is a machine whose construction would enable it to think, to sense, and to have perception, one could conceive it enlarged while retaining the same proportions, so that one could enter into it, just like into a windmill. Supposing this, one should, when visiting within it, find only parts pushing one another, and never anything by which to explain a perception" (Leibniz 1965, section 17). Machines cannot think. Hence, within a science that is machine-metaphor-based, consciousness is an insoluble given.

Finally, what about obligations, morality? I see no reason we shouldn't have a moral sense, just as much as we have perceptual senses, and, without anticipating discussion, I see no reason these should not have come about naturally. People without moral senses are psychopaths, just as people without visual senses are blind. But morality itself, assuming that it exists (and I will have more to say about this later), is not something captured by the machine metaphor. We noted in the last chapter that David Hume stressed this. You cannot get an *ought* from an *is*. Unfortunately, Hume noted, people slide without comment from talking about the way things are to talking about the way things should or ought to be. "This change is imperceptible; but is, however, of the last consequence. For as this ought, or ought not, expresses some new relation or affirmation, it is necessary that it should be observed and explained; and at the same time that a reason should be given, for what seems altogether inconceivable, how this new relation can be a deduction from others, which are entirely different from it" (Hume [1739–1740] 2000, 302). Of course, a guillotine is made for chopping off heads, just as a vibrator is made for toning up muscle, but whether either or both are morally good things, I will leave for the reader. Science isn't going to tell you.

Scientism, Skepticism, or What?

Modern science is incredibly powerful, and only the foolish or the blind would say otherwise. It throws light on huge areas formerly given over to religion or philosophy or simply

so-called common sense. But if our discussion in the last section or two has shown anything, *scientism*, meaning science
has all of the answers, is a fool's game. It simply doesn't and
couldn't. Of course, you might respond that science has all of
the answers that matter, but that is a matter of judgment, and
frankly the judgment that is so is as much a fool's game. It
is true that there has been endless discussion over the fundamental question and whether it is genuine, but even those
who think that it is not will usually conclude that their doubt
is based on the fact that they cannot imagine what a genuine
answer would look like! The same is true of the other questions. There are those like Paul Churchland (1995), Patricia
Churchland (1986), and Daniel Dennett (1992) who think that
the body-mind problem has been solved in favor of materialism. The brain is a computer, and that is all there is to it.
Most of us don't agree, but even if we did agree, the claims
about what science can or cannot do—cognitive science tells
us all we need to know about the brain, and this includes consciousness—would not themselves be scientific. So there is no
escape there. Morality likewise. We shall see shortly that there
is much debate about the nature of morality and that science is
deeply involved in this debate. But in the end, claims about the
powers and limits of science are going to be about science and
not themselves scientific. Scientism is a false god.

One can say this even though in the end one might have to
admit ignorance. I don't find that prospect particularly scary.
Our thinking apparatuses were forged by natural selection to
get us out of the jungles and onto the savanna. I don't see why
they should guarantee the ability to answer everything, even
if there are answers. J. B. S. Haldane thought about this: "My
own suspicion is that the universe is not only queerer than
we suppose, but queerer than we *can* suppose" (Haldane
1927, 286). Recently, Richard Dawkins has raised the same
point: "Modern physics teaches us that there is more to truth
than meets the eye; or than meets the all too limited human
mind, evolved as it was to cope with medium-sized objects

moving at medium speeds through medium distances in Africa" (Dawkins 2003, 19).

Why is there something rather than nothing? I confess that I do not know. I think it is a real question, and it is one that puzzles me, but in the end I have no answer. Perhaps there is no answer. Perhaps things always did exist, and that is an end to it. The Greeks thought this. As we shall see, Buddhists think this. Because science cannot give an answer, it does not follow that something else must give an answer or we must go back to science. The same is true of the other questions. Recently, a school of thought has sprung up suggesting that the nature and existence of sentience can never be explained (McGinn 2000). Because of the way of our minds, it may forever be beyond our ken. Not everyone agrees with the new mysterians, but it seems to me plausible. Indeed, it seems to me to be more than this. The problem of the origin of life has not yet been solved, but I can see it being solved, and I know what a solution would be like (Ruse 2006). I just don't know what a solution to the body-mind problem would be like. Surprise me! Until then, skepticism.

Can Religion Step in?

And so we reach the final stage of the argument. What if the religious person says: I can give you answers. These answers are the ones listed earlier—a creator God, a purposeful universe, humans special, obligations to be fulfilled. I really don't see that one can or should stop the argument at this point. If the Christian wants to answer the unanswered questions of science, that is his or her right. As always, note carefully what is being said and what is not being said. No one is saying that you should be a Christian. I have just made a case for skepticism, whether you think this implies agnosticism or atheism or whatever. Certainly, no one is now saying that Christianity is beyond critique. Flip through the next few chapters if you think that. It may well be that science will go after particular (non-Fundamentalist) claims over and above the four main question-answers, for instance, claims about Jesus and his status. What is being said is that modern science as such cannot stop the Christian from offering answers. Although note that the Christian must not cheat. The answers given cannot be scientific answers. Six days of creation are ruled out, and so is the move made by one of the popes who thought that the Big Bang supported Genesis. This is not on.

Within the context, however, the Christian can and does give answers beyond science, this is legitimate, and—pace Gould—these can and do go beyond sentiment and feeling. They can be about reality. They can be ontological. Thus we have seen the claims about God as creator, especially about God as necessary being as creator. Does this make sense? We shall see. Here, it is enough that it can be made and it is not a scientific claim. We have the claim about purpose. It answers a meaningful question, it is about the way the world is—the eye really is for seeing, the world really is the place for humans to work out their destiny with God—and it certainly is not scientific. Humans are made in the image of God and as such are sentient beings with intellectual and moral capacities. This is not a claim about evolution. We could have been created by a magician and taken from his hat. It is a claim that Christians are allowed to make. And finally, morality. Again, I promise that we shall say much more about morality, but for now it is enough that whatever it may be, it is not something justified by science.

Has the Family Silver Been Sold?

As too often happens in these sorts of family squabbles—Freud spoke of the "narcissism of small differences"—there is a lot of bitterness by the New Atheists over those they feel are letting down the side. As he has made very clear, Richard Dawkins (2006) would far rather have dealings with an honest-to-God Fundamentalist than with anyone who would make an argument for the accommodation of religion by science lovers. There is a particular place in his hell for those like Stephen Jay Gould and Michael Ruse who give any ground to the enemy. We are charter members of the Neville Chamberlain school of thinkers, so named after the pusillanimous British prime minister who tried to do business with Adolf Hitler. We are kidding ourselves. At best, we are dupes. At worst, we are dangerous. Throughout, we are contemptible.

Now that he has crossed the Rainbow Bridge, whether he is singing hymns—he was very fond of performing in oratorios— or shoveling coal, I am sure Gould will speak for himself. For myself, I am happy to let the arguments fall as they may. No one could ever doubt my love of science. More important, you have seen only part of the argument. Science does not preclude religion. This does not make religion right, nor does it stop science from going after specific claims made by religion. It does not stop the critic from going after religion on other grounds, theological or philosophical, for example. It is to that side of the argument that we turn now.

7

QUESTIONS FOR THE CHRISTIAN

Is God an Ethnic Cleanser?

Let's start right in with the God of the Bible. Literal, allegorical, whatever. One thing is crystal clear. If you take a disinterested view of the God of the Jewish tradition, the God of the Old Testament—Yahweh—and don't read his acts and his nature through preconceived rosy glasses, Richard Dawkins is absolutely right. He is a tyrant and a bully and a murderer of the very worst order. Think of what happened to the people who were not on the ark. Or Sodom and Gomorrah. Not one healer or teacher was worthy of saving? Not one little child who suckled at the breast was to escape? When God tested Abraham's faith by demanding his son as a sacrifice, consider the psychological damage that must have been done to Isaac. These sorts of comparisons can easily descend into the facile, but truly by any objective measure, he is at one with Hitler or Stalin or Mao or Pol Pot or any of the other vile monsters of the twentieth century or earlier. It is true that God on a good day can be warm and friendly—although often this warmth and friendship manifests itself as grotesque favoritism, as with the promises to Moses of a land of milk and honey, which will come at the expense of the Canaanites, the Hittites, the Amorites, the Perizzites, the Hivites, and the Jebusites (Exodus 3: 8). But Hitler was fond of dogs. Overall, the God of the Jews was a vile being and in no sense worthy of worship. At most you can say we have a tribal God of a formerly nomadic people who fought their way into some real estate between the Mediterranean and the River Jordan. At first, he wasn't even the only god in the business. Now it would be positively immoral to have anything to do with him.

Isn't This All Very Unfair on Christians?

Isn't this a very one-sided view of Yahweh? He is far more multifaceted, with many fine and loving qualities. Remember the God of the Twenty-Third Psalm that David hymns. He is a shepherd. He cares for my well-being. He looks after my needs. He comforts me. He is by my side at the very worst of times. This is a God of love and concern as well as wrath and judgment. And you have taken stories like that of Abraham and Isaac out of context. The story is not about Isaac but about Abraham and about his relationship to God. It is to point out his fidelity and to praise it, offering it as a model for others. One might even say that the story points to God's good side. Child sacrifice was commonplace in the Middle East at that time. The whole point of the story is that God shows that he does not need such offerings and is content with an animal substitute.

Well, yes, although in the end, it is going to leave you with a pretty complex figure. The Jewish God is at best like Peter the Great, who did some truly dreadful things to a lot of people but who nevertheless built St. Petersburg. But before we go further, let us introduce the follow-up protest that all of this is essentially irrelevant because when Jesus arrived, the game plan was changed and the clock was put back to start. The behavior of Yahweh is not relevant. It is the thought and behavior of the Christian God that counts, and he is very different. He is the God of the Sermon on the Mount. "You have heard that it was said, 'You shall love your neighbor and hate your enemy.' But I say to you, Love your enemies and pray for those who persecute you" (Matthew 5: 43–44). He is the God of the Good Samaritan. Here, remember, we have a man—from a group that was hated by the Jews and that returned the animosity tenfold—who crosses the barriers and gives help and friendship to a person in need, no matter who they are or what they do or where they belong. This is indeed a God worthy of worship.

The problem with this response is the Christian insistence that the two Gods—the God of the Old Testament and the God of the New Testament—are one and the same. The God who drowned everyone except Noah and family is the God who preaches: "Truly I tell you, just as you did it to one of the least of these who are members of my family, you did it to me" (Matthew 25: 40). The God who said "Let the little children come to me; do not stop them; for it is to such as these that the kingdom of God belongs" (Mark 10: 14) is also the God who wiped out wholesale the infants and children of the enemies of the Israelites. Moreover, just as you might say that there is prejudice shown by the person who seizes on the violent passages of the Old Testament and ignores the ameliorating passages, so might one say that there is distortion in just seizing on the nice parts of the New Testament and ignoring the less wholesome comments. Jesus tells us to leave our families. Is that really what God wants? "Whoever comes to me and does not hate father and mother, wife and children, brothers and sisters, yes, and even life itself, cannot be my disciple" (Luke 14, 26). Or what about the views of St. Paul on women? Since God went out of his way to make Paul his apostle, surely this is authentic? "Women should be silent in the churches. For they are not permitted to speak, but should be subordinate, as the law also says. If there is anything they desire to know, let them ask their husbands at home. For it is shameful for a woman to speak in church" (1 Corinthians 14: 34–35). What makes this so tragic is that it comes right after 1 Corinthians 13, surely the most moving and beautiful plea for love and kindness ever penned. And above all, there is the slavery problem. Those antebellum Americans who turned to the Bible for support of slavery knew what they were about. Onesimus, an escaped slave, is sent back home. "I am appealing to you for my child, Onesimus, whose father I have become during my imprisonment. Formerly he was useless to you, but now he is indeed useful both to you and to me. I am sending him, that is, my own heart, back to you" (Philemon 10–12). It is true that Paul was walking on thin ice, for slaves were happily signing up to Christianity, given its promise that all were equal before God, but still!

What about Interpretation and Context?

Are we not still being unfair? Why should we not agree that we start the Bible with a tribal God, one who in the early years incidentally shares many characteristics with other local tribal gods, the nature of whom is more and more refined as the years go by, until when we get to Christianity, fashioned to fulfill all sorts of prophecies made in the Old Testament, we get the God of the New Testament? All very satisfying, no doubt, but not necessarily a God who is compelling except to those who already believe. Perhaps on balance, though, the good does outweigh the bad. If you think of the Bible not so much as a formal philosophical text, but as the records of a people moving from savagery to civilization, one does see the emergence of a wholesome morality. This is the position of the conservative Anglican philosopher Peter van Inwagen (b. 1942). "Almost every atheist (in Western Europe and the anglophone countries) however committed he or she may be to atheism, accepts some modified version of what Judaeo-Christian morality teaches about how human beings ought to treat other human beings" (Van Inwagen 2011, 81). Van Inwagen invites us to compare our thinking and behavior today with the casual brutality that existed in the Roman Empire. To which one can only respond that there seems a remarkable gap in van

Inwagen's memory about the events in the Soviet Union in the 1930s, in German-occupied Europe in the 1940s, and in the Balkans in the 1990s. Actually, to be fair to van Inwagen, even though the full story is little more comforting to van Inwagen's line of argumentation, it is more complex, and we shall return to this point later, in chapter 11.

None of this, as such, makes the God of the Bible a fictional being, but if (as we are now) you are looking at this from the outside, without faith or some such thing that supposedly guarantees truth, one might be forgiven for suggesting that we have a set of fables like the sagas of the Norse gods, for instance. Because they may be fictional, it doesn't mean that there is nothing of value in them. Even if Ruth and Naomi are totally fictitious, one can surely read the story of Ruth as a powerful tale of love and devotion, one that can inspire no less than the absolutely, completely true story of Anne Frank as given in her diary. But truth is another matter.

Is the God of the Philosophers to Be Preferred?

At this point, the sophisticated theist will rightly point out that we have looked at only one side of the story. The other side is the story of classical theism and its God. It is not that the biblical story and the philosophical story are different—although more on this in a moment—but, because it is not tied directly to writings of Middle Eastern folk, long ago, the philosophical story does speak to some of the worries just expressed, about goodness and so forth. So for the moment, leave the biblical God and turn to the philosophers' God. This is the eternal God, outside space and time, all loving and all powerful and all knowing. Although you are putting things in a Christian context, you are committed to Platonism; to be really historically accurate, you are in the tradition started by the pre-Socratic Parmenides, who stressed the unchanging One. This is true even of people like Aquinas, whose greatest immediate debt was to Aristotle: "God bears a more than passing similarity to a Platonic form or idea" (Davies 2016). Above all else, God is like the Form of the Good, from which all else stems. It is not always easy to grasp the nature of the Form of the Good, but, by analogy, one can say God must exist in some way like the existence of a mathematical object. His existence must be like that of the 3, 4, 5 triangle. And this leads to a big question: Is this really the kind of existence that you want for God? We can say with some confidence that triangles really don't seem very active. It is hard to think that the ideal triangle is in some sense going out and grasping the things of this world. Or, for that matter, that the ideal triangle gives a damn about this world. Ideal triangles just don't seem to be the kinds of things that give a damn about anything.

This is the big problem with the classical God. Once you have made him necessary and given him eternal existence, then it is hard to see how he can do anything at all or care about whether he has done anything at all. He just is, unchanging. For the moment, let's focus on God's engagement with the world. Aquinas says we can think of all of this analogically, but can we? Anticipating the various attributes of God, let us take the all-important one of being loving. Now I know what it is to be loving, and I am sure you do, and it is not very different from my idea. I love Lizzie, my wife. We have been together for thirty years now, and we have built and shared a life together. At first, there was a lot of passion and physical activity. Then the kids came along, and we had a job together. It wasn't always easy, and it was very hard work, but we were in it together, and friendship and commitment were absolutely central—a sense of humor didn't hurt either, together with a lot of other things like responsibility and pride and concern and the rest. Now the children are more or less grown up and leaving home—some days rather less than more—and we are lucky in finding that we do really like each other and have fun doing things together, trying out new recipes, traveling, and so forth. If our relationship has been anything, it has been dynamic, it has been physical as well as emotional, and it has been interactive. Our love has depended all of the time on the response of the other. It has been changing—thank goodness, because as Socrates says in the *Phaedrus*, although first love may be terrific, it is a kind of madness, and no one wants to stay in that state forever. Can any of this apply to a being who is like a 3, 4, 5 triangle? Mathematical objects simply don't come home at the end of the day at work, see your wife frazzled and driven to distraction by toddlers, and say: "Come on kids, let's go out to the park and give your mum a break." They don't, incidentally, have your wife both grateful and cheesed off that you can just walk in, and the kids become instantly happy and agreeable to what you propose! I make this kind of point, not at all in an irreverent way, but to ask bluntly how the classical God can function. Analogy just doesn't seem to do it.

Is God Omniscient and Omnipotent and, If So, What about Free Will?

Push on now to the other attributes of God, starting with being all knowing and all powerful (Wainwright 2010; Hasker 2010). Is God omniscient and omnipotent? It seems sensible, but does it really make sense, particularly of a being supposedly outside time? I take it that we do not want to say that God knows how to make 2 + 2 = 5, although Descartes seems to have thought that a real possibility. Does God know how to make me jump twenty feet into the air? You might say that of course he does, but before you rush in, think about some of the issues. The reason people like me, people like you, cannot jump twenty feet into the air—although a grasshopper can do the equivalent—is basically a matter of physics. Building legs to do this kind of thing is going to require a lot more material. That means you are going to have to scale up the rest of the body to provide the food and so forth. But weight goes up by the cube, and before long you have a body way too big to jump even what we can now, apart from the legs being needed just to keep the body up at all. There is a reason cats can jump and elephants cannot, and why whales live in the sea and not dry land—Archimedes's principle is kicking in and making them comparatively lighter than they would be on land. So already it is starting to look as though there is quite a bit that God cannot do.

Problems really multiply when we get to time. If God is outside time, it is hard to know how he relates to us at all if we are in time. But if we get over that hurdle, there are still massive problems. For a start, what about quantum mechanics? It is built in that you cannot predict events at the individual level. You can do it only across groups. But individual events count. We all know the story about a butterfly's wings flapping in one part of the world and a storm happening in another part of the world. A mutation at one moment might cause massive changes in evolution at later times. The same actually goes for the whole building of the universe. So unless you are prepared to go against the whole of modern physics—which says not that we cannot make the predictions but that the predictions are in principle not possible—God's predictive abilities seem very constrained.

For a second, there is the whole thorny question of free will. Massive amounts have been written on this problem, and one hesitates to plunge in, but essentially there are two solutions (Fischer et al. 2007). One says that there is something radically different about choice, something that puts it outside the normal causal chain. This is known as *libertarianism* and is not to be confused with the political philosophy of that name. No one wants it to be random, obviously, and usually the analysis is in terms of reasons or some such thing. Kant is an exemplar. "Since the conception of causality involves that of laws, according to which, by something that we call cause, something else, namely the effect, must be produced; hence, although freedom is not a property of the will depending on physical laws, yet it is not for that reason lawless; on the contrary it must be a causality acting according to immutable laws, but of a peculiar kind; otherwise a free will would be an absurdity" (Kant 1959, section 3). There are obvious problems here, starting with the fact that many would argue that reasons can be causes. Even if they are not, there are still predictability issues. Even where reasons are in play, a lot of people are pretty predictable. Put me in front of a glass of single malt when I have just spent an hour explaining to a student that I am not going to raise the mark from a B– to an A+. In this case, although I may be autonomous, you might ask about my freedom. But if there is real freedom, then it is very difficult to see how God can know the future. If he is outside time, then past, present, and future are as one to him. But this brings us right back to how God relates to beings who are very much in time.

The other solution, going back at least to Thomas Hobbes (1588–1679) and well discussed by Hume ([1739–1740] 2000), argues that one can (must) keep within the causal chain. It is suggested that freedom consists in a break from constraint and not from determinism. This position is known as *compatibilism*; note that it shares with the libertarian like Kant the belief that the key notion is autonomy. For the Kantian, however, autonomy means being outside the causal chain, whereas for the Humean, autonomy means not subject to external constraint. The free person is not in chains or hypnotized or at the end of a gun. Here, God can certainly know the future, but (as libertarians complain) the whole question of ultimate judgment is thrown into question. If God knows that you are going to sleep with your best friend's wife, then, even though you were free (in the sense that no one made you do it), it seems mean of him to condemn you to everlasting damnation, since he was the being who made the clock and wound it up in the first place. Calvinists like Jonathan Edwards who believe in predestination would accept this consequence, even though they would also argue that you have enough freedom to warrant the punishment. In any case, God is totally sovereign and not to be judged by our standards.

Most of us, I suspect, find this kind of thinking in itself reason enough to reject Calvinism.

Can We Save God from Himself?

Here, of course, we have the $64,000 question. Within the Christian tradition, we have two conceptions of God, and it is far from obvious that they can be reconciled. On the one side, we have those who endorse the God of the philosophers, the philosophers, that is, who created the God of the Greek tradition, often for fairly obvious reasons (simply because it was formulated in the first thousand and more years of Christianity) those in the Catholic tradition. On the other side, we have those who endorse the God of the Bible, the God of the Jewish tradition, often for equally obvious reasons (primarily because they make the Bible paramount) those like Plantinga in the Protestant tradition. And this dispute is part of a bigger quarrel about the personhood of God. For the philosophers, God just isn't a person, one of the gang like the rest of us only more so. For the Protestants, if there is one thing we can say about the God of the Bible, it is that he is a person. "That God is a person, yet without a body, seems the most elementary claim of theism" (Swinburne 1977, 99; see also Plantinga 1980). We humans are persons. We are made in his image. It is this personhood that makes for this connection. God is not a rock or a dog or a mathematical concept. He is a person who lives in time, who has emotions, who cares and hates, who bargains and who feels pride and scorn, who is pleased and disappointed, and who dislikes some and rather plays favorites with others.

Admittedly, it is not always easy to see this. Remember that "my thoughts are not your thoughts, nor are your ways my ways. . . ." Naturally, therefore, "as the heavens are higher than the earth, so are my ways higher than your ways and my thoughts than your thoughts" (Isaiah 55: 8–9). Passages like this led some twentieth-century theologians, notably Karl Barth, to share with Maimonides the doubt that, in a positive way, one can speak meaningfully of God: "to speak of God would be to speak God's word" (Barth 1957). This we cannot do because we are not God. But usually the message of personhood comes through loud and clear. And this is just not the God of the philosophers. Eternal, unchanging beings don't wipe away tears, don't fret when a child goes astray, don't rejoice when a sinner repents, don't weep for the poor and the afflicted and the lonely and the unhappy (Edwards 1978).

By now, with good reason, the traditionalists are starting to get very tense. If you go the personhood route, you bring in a host of problems (Weinandy 2000). Most fundamentally, can such a being really be a necessary existent? It looks very much like you are creating a God in our image, and we are contingent. And this is apart from other issues, like those raised by Sextus Empiricus. If God is a person, does God have the quality of continence? Does this mean that God has sexual passions that he overcomes? Does God, did God, have a bit of a thing about Marilyn Monroe? Or in this day and age, about Cary Grant, or about both? It is starting to look like you are out of the frying pan of Catholicism and into the fire of Protestantism. Or to be a little less flowery with the metaphors, it is starting to look like you have two traditions, that they clash, and that you are left with a hopelessly incoherent notion of God. We have a hybrid—Greek and Jewish—and ultimately they cannot be reconciled.

Can We Reconcile the Two Conceptions of God?

This is such a fundamental criticism that it cannot be left without response. Certainly, Christians are aware of the problem and have spoken to it. The moves to be made are obvious. You start with one side or the other and then try to speak to the issues you are missing. For Protestants, stressing the personhood of God, the usual move is to interpret the unchanging nature of God in moral terms. It is not that God is ontologically unchanging but that he is ethically unchanging. When God says: "For I the LORD do not change" (Malachi 3: 6), what he means is that he doesn't change in his love and affection for us. That is steady. Of course, this doesn't let you off the hook with other problems, about the nature of eternity, for instance, but it is a start.

The other side, the classical side, is a bit trickier. One move is to think of God in more Aristotelian than Platonic terms. Aristotle's God, the Unmoved Mover, is to be thought of as the ultimate final cause, somehow the perfection that all of life is directed toward. In a sense, although unmoving, this makes God dynamic in a way that Plato's Good is not, or at least not obviously. It may just exist, but somehow its very existence reaches out to you and has effects, just as that cherished grant-ing of tenure governs the life and thought and actions of the young assistant professor. You have to modify the Aristotelian God, because, remember, it contemplates only the perfect— namely, itself—and has no knowledge of others, including humans. The Christian God is directed toward us. Still, there are issues about how this God can relate to things like human pain and distress—the youth strangling slowly and painfully at the end of a rope in Auschwitz. God cannot himself suffer, because this is dynamic and also in some sense a bad thing— suffering is painful—and the completely good cannot go there. (He is impassible.) A certain amount of psychological soft-shoe shuffling is needed here. Apparently we can reach out in love to the sufferer, and the pain we feel is a distraction, not some-thing good. "Suffering is an evil even when attached to the good of love, for love rightly cries out at the absence or loss of some good, and seeks, if possible, to restore it. The reasons human beings suffer is for the good of love and so the suffering entailed in love is seen as good, but it is precisely the love that is good and not the suffering in itself" (Weinandy 2000, 160). Rubbing it in: "What human beings cry out for in their suffer-ing is not a God who suffers, but a God who loves wholly and completely, something a suffering God would not do" (164).

A lot of people, including a lot of Protestants, don't find this adequate. They recoil with horror when Anselm draws this line of thinking to its conclusion: "For when thou beholdest us in our wretchedness, we experience the effect of compassion, but thou dost not experience the feeling" (Anselm 1903, 13). Or when Aquinas says: "To sorrow, therefore, over the misery of others does not belong to God" (Aquinas 1952, I, 21, 3). To the critics, any answer that does not have God at Auschwitz suffering with his people fails to show a God worthy of worship. We shall return to this question in the next chapter, when we turn to the problem of evil. And to be fair, we have not yet taken up the Jesus factor, which we shall do next in this chapter. For the rest, defenders of the philosophers' God, as do all Christians in various respects, pull back and acknowledge mystery. "For now we see in a mirror, dimly, but then we will see face to face. Now I know only in part; then I will know fully" (1 Corinthians 13: 12). Is this enough?

What about Jesus?

We haven't had much luck with the father. What about the son? I don't think you can take the easy way out by denying that Jesus ever existed (Ehrman 2012). There is a highly vocal group of deniers of the existence of Jesus. But frankly, they come across like most conspiracy theorists, overpassionate in their cause, unwilling to compromise, and (a sure sign) very touchy when you question their credentials. It is true that the extrabiblical evidence is vanishingly minimal and that the Gospels are pretty confusing on what Jesus did or did not say. It is true also that the Synoptic Gospels (Matthew, Mark, and Luke) date from about forty years after Jesus' supposed death, and John is at least twenty years later. But they are clearly (at least some of them) using earlier writings (about twenty years after Jesus' death) and also an oral tradition of people who certainly had the chance to see and hear Jesus. The Acts and the Epistles of Paul are somewhat earlier than the Gospels. Paul claims to have spent time with both Peter and a brother of Jesus, who presumably would know. (Protestants tend to think that the brother really was a brother. Catholics who believe in the perpetual virginity of Mary tend to think that the brother was either a relative like a cousin or a close acquaintance.) And before you go off on flights of fantasy inspired by *The Golden Bough* (1890) by Sir James G. Frazer—about gods being sacrificed and eaten and resurrecting, and so the Jesus story is just a reflection of a common archetype—note that anthropologists these days are not that impressed by Frazer's conclusions and think he jumbled together a lot of very different stories and patterns. In short, we can almost certainly let Christian theists have Jesus. There is really not much reason to doubt that Jesus really did exist, that he lived near the Sea of Galilee, that he preached, and that he went up to Jerusalem and, running afoul of the authorities, got himself crucified by the Romans, the occupying power. They certainly wouldn't have had much hesitation in putting down a rabble rouser.

The problem is where you go from there. A huge amount written into the Gospels is based on expectations, on prophecies from the Old Testament, on borrowings, on hearsay, on the dictates of telling a good story from a point of view, and much more (Ehrman 2001). You don't need atheists to tell you this. Christians have done it for you! Start right off with the conception of Jesus. It is pretty important to many Christians that his mother, Mary, was a virgin. But the physical facts aside (we will take up the question of miracles later) and apart from the fact that only two of the Gospels (Matthew and Luke, both of which are thought to draw on a now-lost common source Q) mention this—you might think that something as major as this would get full billing—there is the fact that this is explicitly said to be the fulfillment of a prophecy. "Therefore the Lord himself will give you a sign. Look, the young woman is with child and shall bear a son, and shall name him Immanuel" (Isaiah 7: 14). At once, you start to wonder if the Jesus event is being enhanced (as one might say) to fit the prophecy. And it doesn't help matters much to learn that there is some significant ambiguity about the passage from the Hebrew (of Isaiah) to the Greek (of the Gospels). Although the Greek uses the word *parthenos*, meaning "virgin," the Hebrew uses the word *almah*, which can mean virgin but can also be used generically for any young woman. Then apparently Joseph and Mary set off from Nazareth, where they live in the north, down to Bethlehem in the south. Why? Because the Romans were doing a census connected with their need for efficient taxation. Unfortunately, according to the Jewish historian Josephus, the most likely date for any such census was about 6/7 AD, whereas Herod the King, who was supposed to be around (he was about to order the murder of newborns, fearing the threat of the new King Jesus), died around 4 BC. In addition, Roman censuses covered only Roman citizens, and the very last thing the Romans wanted was wholesale movements of people journeying to their ancestral homes. And all of this is just the beginning! Next up, we have the wise men, the shepherds, the murder of the innocents, and the flight to Egypt.

The fact of the matter is, since the beginning of the nineteenth century, when serious biblical scholarship got underway, there has been a veritable plethora of different interpretations of the life of Jesus: where he lived, what he said, what he did, what others thought of him, and so forth. About the best you can say is that the Bible is not always tremendously helpful about many of the major claims of Christianity—the exact relationship between Jesus and God and where the Holy Ghost fits into the picture, for example. And when it comes to some of the distinctive claims that are made in the name of Christianity, the Bible is often tremendously unhelpful. Take, for instance, family life. Focus on the Family was founded in 1977 by the evangelical psychologist James Dobson. Its mission statement is: "To cooperate with the Holy Spirit in sharing the Gospel of Jesus Christ with as many people as possible by nurturing and defending the God-ordained institution of the family and promoting biblical truths worldwide." This includes the sanctity of marriage, the importance of children, and other aims dear to the hearts of Evangelicals, including the prohibition of abortion and the denigration of homosexuals. Turn to Jesus, however, and you get a rather different story. Earlier in this chapter, we quoted him on the subject of family life and the need to "hate" your parents, your spouse, and your kids. You have to break loose from all of these. In the light of comments like these, it is hard not to be smug when you think of how far so many Christians—especially today's Evangelicals—really have come from their biblical roots.

The problem with getting the Jesus story right has led some scholars to throw up their hands and declare that they were never in that business in the first place! Rudolf Bultmann (1958), for instance, argued that the essential Christian claims about the nature and importance of Jesus (what he called the *kerygma*) really don't rely on historical fact, more than that Jesus died and was crucified. Bultmann wasn't even bothered by the resurrection and whether it was literal (Davis 2010). For him, as a Lutheran, the conviction in his heart that Jesus was his redeemer outweighed any physical evidence. Which is all very well, of course, but for those of us who don't have this kind of faith, he perhaps asks even more than the literalists ask of us to accept the importance of Jesus.

What Is Man That Thou Art Mindful of Him?

Move on to the next key figure in the religious chess game: *Homo sapiens*. The Christian does not claim that the world exists only for humankind. God cares about the fallen sparrow. But it is the claim of the Christian that humans have a special place in the creation. They are the creatures made in his image and the creatures that he so loved that he died in agony on the cross for their salvation. And at once this leads to a major problem, because although humans may not exist necessarily, in the Christian story they are not just a contingent add-on. They had to exist. Let me put this a little more carefully. God did not have to create at all. That was his choice. God did not have to create humans or humanlike creatures. That was his choice. But once he had decided—or if it was always part of his nature that he would create beings that he could love and they in turn could worship him—then you have the problem of how God was going to create humans or humanlike beings. Obviously, this is no big issue if you take literally the story of Genesis. They are the climax of the week of creation. Unfortunately, if you take modern science seriously, then matters are somewhat more complex. Here, for those who worry that I might have given too much to religion in its struggle with science, is a point where the fangs were not drawn. Let me spell things out (Ruse 2001, 2012).

Charles Darwin's theory of evolution, encountered in earlier chapters, argues that all organisms are the end result of a slow, natural process of development, from primitive forms and probably ultimately from the inorganic. The process took almost four billion years, from start to end, and one of the reasons all is so slow is that the course of evolution is meandering (Ruse 1996). There is no direct drive from A to B, and most particularly there is no direct drive from blobs to humans— "monad to man," as they used to say in Victorian times. There are two major reasons for this. One is that the building blocks of evolution, variations or what today are known as mutations, are random. This does not mean that they are uncaused. In fact, today we know a lot about the causes of mutation. It does mean they appear without any connection to the needs of their possessors. A small mammal, thanks to climate change, might find itself in an environment where its previous camouflage no longer protects it from predators. There is no reason at all to think that the mammal will get mutations providing it with new and effective camouflage. The mutations could cause virtually anything. And that means you cannot expect the course of evolution always to be in one, the best or right, direction. It is a crapshoot.

A second reason for this lack of a firm purpose in Darwinian evolution is that the key mechanism of Darwinian evolution is natural selection. Analogous to the selection that breeders exercise in making bigger and better cows and sheep, Darwin argued that population pressures lead to a natural equivalent of breeders' selection, with some surviving to reproduce and others falling by the wayside. Over time, this differential reproduction, as today's biologists term it, leads to significant change. However, note that natural selection is relativistic. If food supplies are abundant, then being big and strong might be favored by selection. If food supplies are scarce, then being small and inconspicuous might be favored by selection. There are no absolutes and no necessary direction that all must take. And this at once gives you reason to doubt that evolution will— must—produce humans or humanlike beings. You might think that things like intelligence, something clearly important in the human case, will always beat out other features, but this is not necessarily so. Intelligence requires big brains, and big brains require lots of protein, generally chunks of other animals. If prey is scarce but low-grade fuels like grass are abundant, then, in the immortal words of the paleontologist Jack Sepkoski: "I see intelligence as just one of a variety of adaptations among tetrapods for survival. Running fast in a herd while being as dumb as shit, I think, is a very good adaptation for survival" (Ruse 1996, 486). Cows might be the highest point in evolution.

The end story is that Darwinian evolutionary theory poses a major problem for Christianity. For the Christians, in the sense I have specified, humans must exist. I suppose they could be green and with six fingers, but beings with intelligence and a moral sense are not one option among several. They are essential. But Darwinism cannot guarantee their appearance.

Can You Solve This Problem?

A number of solutions have been proffered, none of which is entirely satisfactory. You can take the problem out of the range of science, suggesting that every now and then God gives the new variations a shove in the needed direction and thus ensures that humans arrive on the scene. This, for instance, was the solution of Darwin's American supporter, the botanist Asa Gray (1876). An updated version slips the directed changes in at the quantum level (Russell 2008). The trouble is that there is no evidence that this happens, much evidence that it does not happen, and the massive theological problems created along the way. For instance, if God is prepared to get involved in his creation in this way, why does he stop where he does? Why doesn't he alter those horrendous new variations that lead to appalling physical and mental deficiencies? Why doesn't he just step in and stop Tay-Sachs disease in its tracks? Once God starts or can start doing this sort of thing, there seems to be no end to it.

Some scientific solutions have been offered. Darwin seemed to think that, for all of the problems, big brains would win out in the end. In a related vein, Richard Dawkins suggests that organisms engage in arms races—as the prey gets faster, the predator gets faster—and he suggests that, as in real-life arms races, electronic equipment has become more and more important, so in nature those organisms with the biggest on-board computers are likely to win out. "Directionalist common sense surely wins on the very long time scale: once there was only blue-green slime and now there are sharp-eyed metazoa" (Dawkins and Krebs 1979, 508). Another solution, mooted by Gould (1985) and taken up by his fellow paleontologist Simon Conway-Morris (2003), focuses on the notion of ecological niches. Different lines of organism seem to converge on the same niches—for instance, both marsupial and placental mammals independently found the niche for sabertooth tigers—big mammals with stabbing weapons. Could not organisms other than humans have found the culture niche? Other solutions drop natural selection entirely. Perhaps life just naturally gets more and more complex, and humans would come almost by chance, as it were (McShea and Brandon 2010). Maybe so.

Gould sometimes suggested that this might be so, if not here on Earth, then on some planet or planets in the universe. Even here I am not sure that humans are bound to appear, at least so long as the number of planets is finite.

Overall, you can see that generally these solutions do not guarantee that humans (or humanlike creatures) absolutely, ironclad, no excuses, must evolve. And if you strengthen them to make the case complete, you are multiplying scientific and probably theological requirements wholesale. Making joking reference to the asteroid that hit Earth 65 million years ago and wiped out the dinosaurs, making possible the age of mammals, Gould wrote: "Since dinosaurs were not moving toward markedly larger brains, and since such a prospect may lie outside the capabilities of reptilian design. . . we must assume that consciousness would not have evolved on our planet if a cosmic catastrophe had not claimed the dinosaurs as victims. In an entirely literal sense, we owe our existence, as large and reasoning mammals, to our lucky stars" (Gould 1989, 318). Amen.

Why Sin?

But once we have humans, we still have problems. Take our sinful nature. If God is so good and we are his special creation, why are we sinners? We know the standard answer, accepted by Protestants as well as Catholics. It is due to Augustine (Moser 2010). Adam sinned and thenceforth humans were tainted. We may not be born actually as sinners and in sin. There is debate about this. But we have a propensity to sin that we are quick to exercise.

There are at least two big problems here. First, modern paleoanthropology—the study of the evolution of humans—absolutely denies that Adam and Eve (meaning a unique first couple) could have existed. All of the genetic and other evidence points to a group of protohumans that never dropped below the tens of thousands in number (Ruse 2012). Even if the group was a lot smaller than this, it was never two. Second is the problem of our sinful nature. No one is going to deny the nature, but that it should all be due to Adam seems a little far-fetched. This is especially so if you are going to put it all in an evolutionary context, for it is unlikely indeed that he was born of parents who never sinned—not if they were the same species as he! Added to this is the free will problem. If you, like most philosophers, are a compatibilist, believing that free will is possible given causal determinism, then, even though you believe that Adam and his successors were free in not being constrained, as God you still have the responsibility for setting the whole process in action in the first place, presumably (being omniscient) knowing what they were going to do in the future. (I am assuming that quantum indeterminacy is not going to get in the way of things here. If it does, then at least God must have recognized the end result as a possibility and moreover we can hardly be blamed if what we do is the result of a random motion of a tiny particle.) If you are not a compatibilist, believing that freedom somehow takes you outside the causal chain, still there is the problem that you, God, put a couple of very inexperienced young folk down in a garden and left them to the seductive wiles of a very clever serpent. At the very least, it seems to me, you are coresponsible, quite apart from the fact that there is something very schoolmasterish about your prohibition. It is a bit like being told, as I was told at school, that you cannot wear blue jeans to class because, well, because the authorities had decided to have some arbitrary rules about clothing. If God had told you not to stomp on babies and you had gone ahead and done that, then perhaps there would be reason for concern. But not to eat a piece of fruit? I don't really think it merited the response it got.

There have been other approaches to the original sin problem. Before Augustine, Irenaeus of Lyons (130–202) made a suggestion that still finds favor in Eastern Christianity, namely, that God planned the whole thing, and the Adam and Eve act is far less significant. God made humans in an incomplete state, and what we have is a process of development toward perfection. The Augustinian position really makes everything that comes afterward Plan B—God playing catch-up and trying to put right the mess made by the first pair. Irenaeus's position has God in control all the way (Schneider 2010). At least part of the problem here, though, is that it is difficult to see the necessity of the crucifixion and resurrection on this alternative view. Although supporters of the philosophical view deny that God suffers, they accept fully that Jesus as man suffers, presumably not only when he sees our hurts but also when he is being hurt. Then the question arises: Why did God have to suffer on the cross to bring to fruition something he had been planning all along? Why not just send Jesus down to give people a bit of moral guidance? Although when you think about it, the Augustinian position is hardly out of the woods on the crucifixion and resurrection (Graham 2010). Why does Jesus suffering a terrible death on the cross wipe out my sins committed two millennia later? My experience is that most people intensely dislike the idea of scapegoats. The troops are acting up, so let's shoot every tenth one. It is even worse than that, really. At least the victims here were probably culpable, just unlucky to be chosen. There has been mass cheating in class. One of the innocent ones says: "Don't worry, fellas, I will take the blame." Where does that leave the rest of us? Blameless? There is something very distasteful about the idea of sacrificial lambs, especially when those lambs are rational bipeds. If I have done something wrong, then I take the blame, not someone else. That is the behavior of a decent person. And if you say, as I think Aquinas would say, that it is not so much a matter of scapegoats, but of paying a debt—righting a wrong—owed to God, and that one person can obviously take over the debts of others (parents paying their kids' college fees), it is still hard to see why someone screaming in pain on the cross is the sort of payment anyone or anything would consider appropriate.

What Is the Soul and Can It Be Saved?

Finally, in dealing with humans, there is the question of our souls and our salvation (Hasker 2010; Moser 2010). Whatever the hereafter may be, it almost certainly will not be of a form imagined by most believers, namely, much the same as life down here but without commuting, Internet spam, and university administrators. Rupert Brooke in his poem "Heaven," imagining piscine paradise, does a pretty good job of poking fun at this kind of thinking:

> We darkly know, by Faith we cry,
> The future is not Wholly Dry.
> Mud unto mud!—Death eddies near—
> Not here the appointed End, not here!
> But somewhere, beyond Space and Time.
> Is wetter water, slimier slime!
> And there (they trust) there swimmeth One
> Who swam ere rivers were begun,
> Immense, of fishy form and mind,
> Squamous, omnipotent, and kind;
> And under that Almighty Fin,
> The littlest fish may enter in.
> Oh! never fly conceals a hook,
> Fish say, in the Eternal Brook. . . .

Sorry, but in the hereafter, there will be no swimming for fish and no opera going for humans. If God is eternal and unchanging, presumably we are going to be the same way, which is perhaps as well (Williams 1973). Even I might find 10 million years of bel canto every night of the week somewhat tedious—although I am prepared to chance it! Yet, whatever salvation may be, it is almost certainly going to involve consciousness (Walls 2010). God's promises are a bit thin if all he intends is that we stay embalmed and unchanging through the ages, with no more interest in ongoing affairs than a lump of clay or a moss-covered rock. Does that mean just disembodied consciousness? Is it the mind alone that will survive death? Is this what we mean when we talk about the soul? This seems to have been the position of Plato, especially in the *Phaedo* that tells of the last day of Socrates. And something of that nature gets transformed into the Christian position by Augustine. However, this was very much not the Jewish position on the matter. Paul assures us that in the afterlife we will have bodies of some kind: "So it is with the resurrection of the dead. What is sown is perishable, what is raised is imperishable. It is sown in dishonor, it is raised in glory. It is sown in weakness, it is raised in power. It is sown a physical body, it is raised a spiritual body. If there is a physical body, there is also a spiritual body" (1 Corinthians 15: 42–44). Aquinas offered something of a compromise, relying as always on the philosophy of Aristotle, who, although unwilling to separate soul and body, thought there were three levels of life or soul—plant, animal, and human—and only the last has consciousness. Aquinas seized on this soul as a life force, without the commitment to body, and used it to spin his theological take on the matter. "Therefore the soul, which is the first principle of life, is not a body, but the act of a body; thus heat, which is the principle of calefaction, is not a body, but an act of a body" (Aquinas 1952, 75, 1). Of course, as for Aristotle, for Aquinas a human soul would come into being only with some development. Mere life alone is not enough. One has to be moving up toward intelligence or some real potential.

If one is considering any of this in the light of modern science, the very idea of life after death is problematic. We don't have disembodied minds—indeed, we don't always have minds when we have bodies, as with the very young and the very old, especially the senile or those with strokes. And modern biological science has turned sharply away from the idea that life is some kind of animating force that informs the body. This kind of Aristotelianism, so-called vitalism, promoted a hundred years ago by the German embryologist

Hans Driesch and the French philosopher Henri Bergson, just doesn't seem to add anything particularly explanatory. One does not have to have the annoying self-confidence of the discoverers of the DNA double helix, James Watson and Francis Crick, to agree (what was mooted before) that two centuries of biochemistry, physiology, and, more recently, molecular biology have shown that however complicated living things may be, ultimately Descartes was right and that it is mechanisms all the way down, or up. Life is no more than molecules in motion. This is true also of consciousness, in the sense that the brain is a machine, even if one wants to argue that sentience somehow supervenes on the material, in ways that we may not ever grasp.

But even if one argues that some notion of extrascientific soul is viable—after all, "in God all things are possible"—there are still some tricky conceptual problems. I go to bed tonight and I have seven or eight hours sleep and then I wake up tomorrow. I have never been very good at the dream-reporting business, and basically there is an eight-hour gap between my drifting off, having just finished a chapter of the detective story I am reading right now, and waking up and the dogs making clear that it is time for their morning walk. Am I the same Michael Ruse? Well, obviously, yes, I am. My poor wife hears me snoring within seconds of putting my head on the pillow, and when one of the dogs barks in the night, she puts out her hand and reassures herself that I am still there and still breathing! Now I die, and presumably at some later point, it is the day of judgment, and I will learn my eternal fate. Am I now the same Michael Ruse? There was a gap until God brought me back. There is not the physical continuity that makes us certain that today's Michael Ruse and tomorrow's Michael Ruse are one and the same person. Presumably, God is going to have to get into the creative business on Judgment Day to get me ready to learn my fate. I have seen it suggested that perhaps we are a bit like a software program, and God keeps us in his files and

then downloads us on the big day. That might give us the continuity needed. But what is to stop God from making two copies of Michael Ruse? Or since you can never have too much of a
good thing, a dozen copies? A million copies? All with exactly
the same thoughts about having been married to Lizzie and
having written a book called *Atheism: What Everyone Needs to
Know*. Is there a true Michael Ruse, and if there is, why should
you pick out that one rather than one of the others? I am not
sure that you get out of trouble if you suggest that from death
to eternal life is but an instant. God is going to have to do
something at that crucial moment. Corpses don't think, nor do
they have spiritual bodies. Again, I don't see any reason that,
after Charon ferries us over the Acheron, two of us should not
step off on the other side. After all, at the beginning of life,
sometimes we split into two and develop from there.

None of this is intended to make fun of Christianity. It is
intended to make sense of what Christians claim and to see if
there is anything compelling for one who comes to the issues
neither committed nor uncommitted, but with an open mind.
And the longer you think about it, surely, the more problematic everything starts to seem.

8

ARE THERE GOOD REASONS TO BELIEVE?

Why Should We Believe?

Turn next to the reasons for belief. What about faith? The nonbeliever is faced with an option. It is genuine, or it is self-deception. I'll leave out options along the lines that no one really believes any of this stuff, because that is simply not true. I am sure that most people who declare themselves believers do so truly. But why shouldn't we simply say that at some deep level people are kidding themselves? They are scared of death or frightened by illness or want to meet again a dearly loved family member or some such thing. At age thirteen, I had just gone off to boarding school when my mother, age thirty-three, died suddenly of yellow jaundice. I have spent my whole life wanting one last hour of conversation with her. Showing her this book and waiting with pride and fear for her response. Don't talk to me about the seductive wiles of life beyond the grave. Presumably, the counterreply comes back that you have to respect the integrity and authenticity of believers, and that counts in their favor. If everyone who claimed to have faith were a shifty, unreliable drunkard, you might with reason doubt their claims. You wouldn't trust someone like that with your car or your daughter, so why should you trust them on the afterlife? But the fact is that there have been and still are many highly educated and deeply moral people who claim to know about God and Jesus Christ because in some sense they have an insight into these matters and their truth status. Take Alvin Plantinga, among today's most distinguished philosophers of religion. He and I have had some fairly sharp differences over evolution, an idea about which he is considerably less enthused than I. But I would never deny his formidable intellect, his deep learning, and his total commitment to a moral, Christian lifestyle. If a man like that believes—and one could mention those who are considerably more science-friendly, like Francis Collins (b. 1950), the head of the National Institutes of Health—then who am I to deny that they really do know?

In the end, then, it all seems to come down to rival authorities. Some say that they have experience of the divine. Others do not. Catholics rely on the tradition of their church to ferret out the details of their faith, whereas Protestants turn to the Bible—*sola scriptura*. But these are not much help here; they are precisely what is at stake. Why should the disinterested observer accept either Catholic or Protestant without some prior sense that they point to the truth? In the end, therefore, we seem to be thrown back on something like Clifford's ethics of belief. If you have revelation, that is enough, but if you don't have it, then you shouldn't pretend to it. Of course, both sides can explain the other's mistaken position. For the Christian, the nonbeliever's judgment is clouded by original sin. For the nonbeliever, the Christian's judgment is clouded by wish fulfillment. Perhaps here the nonbeliever does have the edge, because while only one side accepts original sin, both sides accept the legitimacy of offering naturalistic explanations. One doubts, however, that this will be the end of the discussion, if only because many believers will quite happily accept a naturalistic explanation and then add to it a theological interpretation. Heads, I win; tails, you lose.

Does the Ontological Argument Work?

At the beginning of the next chapter, we will return to faith and another problematic aspect. For now, let's push on to reason and evidence and the arguments for the existence of God, starting as before with the ontological argument. The argument goes from a definition or characterization of God as something as good as it possibly could be (Anselm) or being perfect in every way (Descartes) to something that therefore must exist. Anselm's contemporary Gaunilo of Marmoutiers, who spotted the problems at once, wrote that we can no more deduce God's existence than we can deduce the existence of an island than which none better can be thought. There is something phony about treating existence as just another property like sandy or warm or uninhabited. Somehow you have those properties, and then you need to see if they apply in real life. This act of finding is not another act of property adding. Immanuel Kant (1999) brought this out clearly when he criticized Descartes's version of the argument, where he listed the perfections of God and included existence. Kant pointed out that existence is not a predicate, a property, and so should not be included in the list. It is more that, having listed the properties, you then need to mount a search to see if there is something with the properties. Is there an Englishman with the property of having been named Michael Ruse? Yes, there is, but you or someone needs to go to Tallahassee, Florida, to check. Is there an American with the property of being over ten feet tall? I very much doubt it, but you need to check first or find some proof that humans simply cannot get that tall.

And yet! The argument doesn't work, so the atheist need not worry. But it is saying something. It tells us something about the nature of God's existence if he does exist. If God exists, then he exists necessarily—that is, if God is the sort of being that the argument supposes. If God is just a mountain, then I don't see he has to exist necessarily. But if he has all perfections or is that than which none greater can be thought, then he must exist necessarily. Although this might be a case of being wary of gods bearing gifts. If God's existence must be necessary existence, it is legitimate to ask about this necessary existence. We have seen that the philosophers' position is that this is some kind of factual necessity: God is cause of himself, and all else follows from him. But it seems that the ontological argument proves that God is logically necessary—to deny his existence is contradictory—and it is not at all obvious that logical necessity is the same as factual necessity. Compounding the problem is that although some would argue that logical necessity and mathematical necessity are the same thing— logicists like Bertrand Russell—others would argue that they are different; Kant, for one, argued that although logic is analytically true, mathematics is what he called *synthetic a priori*, and the denial of a mathematical statement, although false, is not contradictory.

Why would anyone worry about any of this? Logical necessity, mathematical necessity, factual necessity—they all point to God's necessary existence. The problem is that many feel that logical necessity and (whether or not they are identical) mathematical necessity do not apply to things as such, but describe relationships between things. Thus if I talk about π, I am talking about the relationship between the circumference and the radius of a circle. I am not talking about a thing, π. This may seem odd, because surely one does talk about the thing π, as in "Someone has now calculated π to a billion decimal places." However, the response is that the true analogy is with "No one runs faster than Achilles." Just as "no one" is not a person but a way of telling you about relationships—Achilles is faster than all of his competitors—so π is not a thing but about relationships. It would seem that if this line of thought is well taken, the validity of the ontological argument implies that the concept of God is incoherent. You might even say that you have a proof for the nonexistence of God (Findlay 1948).

Does the Causal Argument Work?

This discussion points us toward the causal argument, for it works only if you have some way of stopping the infinite regress. And that has to be a necessary being. If logical or mathematical necessity cannot do the trick, what about factual necessity? Does that help? John Hick (1922–2012) has this to say about it: "I suggest, then, that the concept of God as eternal, and as not dependent upon any other reality, but on the contrary as the creator of everything other than himself—which is compendiously expressed by the term (factually) 'necessary being'—is a concept concerning which the factual question can properly be raised: Is there a being or a reality to which this concept applies?" (Hick 1961, 733). Note that you are not now giving up on Platonism and the Form of the Good, but switching the emphasis from necessity in the sense of like mathematics, to necessity in the sense of that which is cause of itself and from which all else stems. But aren't you just now making things up wholesale as you need them? This was Hume's worry. "Whatever we conceive as existent, we can also conceive as non-existent. There is no being, therefore, whose non-existence implies a contradiction. Consequently there is no being, whose existence is demonstrable" (Hume 1947). So much for the general point. Hume now gets specific. "It is pretended that the Deity is a necessarily existent being; and this necessity of his existence is attempted to be explained by asserting, that if we knew his whole essence or nature, we should perceive it to be as impossible for him not to exist, as for twice two not to be four." Nonsense, responds Hume. You are just mouthing meaningless garbage. "The words, therefore, necessary existence, have no meaning; or, which is the same thing, none that is consistent."

This really is the point at which the rubber hits the road. You have two ways to counter Hume. You can opt for a fairly robust version of Platonism, arguing that there is an unseen world of real entities. Logic and mathematics do more than just describe relationships. For what it is worth, you will probably have most mathematicians on your side—they think they are discovering things about a world at least as real as the one in which we live—but even then you have got to go on to say that this world can and does contain God. I suspect few mathematicians today will follow you there. Or you can opt for a factual necessity, one where God is cause unto himself. The trouble here is that even if one does allow that the notion of a factually necessary being makes sense, one no longer (as in the robust Platonic case) has the success of mathematics to give your position plausibility. It is hard to know whether one is proving the existence of such a God or just assuming it. And if this is the case, why should one not simply say, in the sense Hick expounds, that the universe taken as a whole qualifies and does all that is needed? As I argued in the discussion of science and religion, one could allow the possibility that the universe (in the extended sense of physical reality) just exists, always has, always will; that it has no behind-the-scenes reason to exist; and that everything follows from that. I am not saying that this is the case. I am not even saying that there is no God behind it all. What I am saying is that no proof of the God has been given, and that is what we are looking for. We know that this would not worry Aquinas at all. He wasn't looking for a proof in this sense. He knew God existed. He was trying to work out the nature of his God. But if you don't have that prior conviction, then I doubt the causal argument will help.

Does the Argument from Design Work?

To a correspondent, John Henry Newman wrote: "I believe in design because I believe in God; not in a God because I see design" (Newman 1973, 97). Before Darwin, the argument was compelling. After Darwin, well. Or have we been a little too quick in our dismissal? Although like Newman he would probably no longer have thought that organic complexity proves design, Darwin himself continued to believe in design after he discovered natural selection. Today, the already mentioned Intelligent Design theorists would probably insist on even more. They agree that the organic world shows adaptation but argue that not all of the causes can be natural because there is too much to be explained; some phenomena are "irreducibly complex." They conclude that every now and then an intelligence has had to intervene (Behe 1996; Dembski 1998; Dembski and Ruse 2004). Some of these people are not evolutionists at all, although others are close to being what is often known as *theistic evolutionists*—evolution guided by God. Either way, there is not much to worry about because the notion of irreducible complexity simply does not hold water. A mousetrap is supposedly the paradigmatic example of irreducible complexity, with five necessary parts, all of which must be inserted at the same time or nothing works. Also supposedly, no natural process could assemble five parts all at the same time. Alas, however, critics have shown that it is possible to get a gradual stepwise evolution of the mousetrap, because one can make a functioning mousetrap with only one part, as well as traps with two, three, and four parts. Admittedly, a one-part trap is not a very good trap, but it does work, and that is what matters. In addition to these more conceptual points, critics have also shown that the purported empirical examples of irreducible complexity are nothing of the kind. One instance is the so-called blood-clotting cascade. When you cut yourself, blood flows and then clots; there is an underlying, quite involved chemical reaction, in humans requiring more than thirty steps. But it is certainly not irreducibly complex. Researchers have found much simpler cascades in other organisms, leading to the reasonable belief that the human case could have been built up gradually through time under the influence of natural selection. Intelligent Design theory just doesn't work (Miller 1999; Ruse 2003).

Is There Nevertheless Evidence of the Christian Designer?

Even if we agree that the design argument can no longer force belief upon us, surely (in the spirit of Newman) we can allow that it can illustrate the nature and workings of God. Perhaps so, but does the evidence of design point to the kind of God at the center of Christian faith? Hume showed that if we take seriously the claim that the world is evidence of God's handiwork, we multiply paradoxes. For a start, good design usually implies a history of failed attempts and gradual improvement, not to mention the way that big projects usually demand multiple designers, a team in fact. Are we to assume that this is true of God or gods? To argue otherwise starts to sound like circularity, assuming the conclusion one wants. But of course, outweighing everything is the problem of evil. If God is so good and also, as Christians claim, all powerful, why is there so much pain and suffering in the world? Hume writes eloquently about the pain of gout. Darwin worried himself silly about the suffering brought on by the struggle for existence: "I cannot persuade myself that a beneficent & omnipotent God would have designedly created the Ichneumonidæ with the express intention of their feeding within the living bodies of caterpillars, or that a cat should play with mice" (Darwin 1985–, 8: 224).

One can speak readily to some of these concerns. It is hard to imagine that God would not create by law; such a world is nigh unto impossible to conceive, and the kinds of beings we are would be very different from the way we would be if God did not create by law. The nineteenth-century naturalist Philip Gosse (1810–1888) suggested that God could have created giving the illusion of law-bound origins, but that makes him the mass deceiver of all time (Gosse 1857). If law, then perhaps the cost of getting adaptation is the struggle. As Leibniz (1646–1716) pointed out, and as we saw in the discussion of the elephant being unable to jump like a cat, God cannot do the impossible. Richard Dawkins has suggested that natural selection is the only natural way of getting design-like features in the world— every other way presupposes some kind of intention or fails to produce the goods. So perhaps pain and suffering are part of a package deal to get functioning organisms. I am not sure how appreciative Dawkins would be to learn that he did not get to this point first: "lions would not thrive unless asses were killed" (Aquinas 1952, 1a, 25, 6). Some would combine this kind of thinking with the view that this struggle is a good thing, for we come out better in the end. Popular here is the sentiment of the poet John Keats (Hick 1978). "The common cognomen of this world among the misguided and superstitious is 'a vale of tears' from which we are to be redeemed by a certain arbitrary interposition of God and taken to Heaven—What a little circumscribed straightened notion! Call the world if you Please 'The vale of Soul-making'" (Letter to George and Georgiana Keats, April 1819).

What about the Problem of Moral Evil?

I doubt that Keats's hunch is always true. I know some people who have failed to rise above adversity and have become very much embittered by their physical suffering. But all of this surely palls beside the big problem, namely, the pain and suffering caused by humans themselves. Auschwitz. We've already worried about whether a good and loving God would suffer because of this, but we ask now whether a good and loving God would allow this in the first place. The usual response is that this is a function of free will and that it was better that God create free creatures, in his image, than make everyone a robot behaving impeccably. "God therefore neither wills evil to be done, nor wills it not to be done, but he wills to permit evil to be done, and this is good" (Aquinas 1952, 1a, 82, 1). For the sake of argument, let us grant that some dimension of freedom does exist—if anything, evolutionary theory comes to the support of a compatibilist view of things. Humans need to be like those complex organized machines—Mars Rover—that can respond and change direction in the face of challenges (Dennett 1984). They live in too complex a world just to be preprogrammed to do one thing—like simple missiles shot at a target—whatever the challenges. But even if you grant this, it is hard to see how the free will of Adolf Hitler and Heinrich Himmler and Joseph Goebbels outweighs the sadistic, painful deaths of small children, although, admittedly, this has not stopped some from trying. One way is simply to say that God could not prevent the deaths because he is not in fact all powerful. Supporters of this line of thought, generally associated with so-called process theology, a movement based on the thinking of early-twentieth-century philosopher Alfred North Whitehead (1861–1947), argue that God is a kind of co-creator with humans; that he, too, is developing; and that he cannot prevent moral evil. "God is the great companion— the fellow-sufferer who understands" (Whitehead 1929, 351). Often, biblical justification is sought in the notion of kenosis, the idea that God in becoming Christ somehow emptied himself of his powers. "Christ Jesus, who, though he was in the form of God, did not regard equality with God as something to be exploited, but emptied himself, taking the form of a slave, being born in human likeness. And being found in human form, he humbled himself and became obedient to the point of death—even death on a cross" (Philippians 2: 5–8). To which the obvious response is that, apart from the fact that this kind of thinking is totally unacceptable to traditional Catholics and Protestants—"literally impotent and thoroughly impoverished" (Weinandy 2000, 146)—God should not have done this if it was going to lead to such horrendous evil effects on the innocent. No end could justify those means.

Arguing from more traditional premises, faced with the Israelites killing the children of the Canaanites, William Craig (b. 1949) argues that "if we believe, as I do, that God's grace is extended to those who die in infancy or as small children, the death of these children was actually their salvation. We are so wedded to an earthly, naturalistic perspective that we forget that those who die are happy to quit this earth for heaven's incomparable joy. Therefore, God does these children no wrong in taking their lives" (Craig 2013). Since we are his instruments, presumably we do no wrong either in doing the actual killing. I cannot see this as a reasonable defense of the Auschwitz guard who dropped in the Zyklon B. Not much more convincing (or comforting) is the suggestion of Alvin Plantinga (2004), working very much in the Calvinist tradition, that a solution can be found in what is known as *superlapsarianism*—God decided to save some before he decided to let us fall into sin. Perhaps God allows the agonies of evil because then he can save us through (his already intended) incarnation and atonement. The latter, which would be meaningless without our sin, is a so much greater good than any sin that, on balance, God is creating through love a very good world. Plantinga argues that because of God's actions, in thinking of creating a world like ours, "no matter how much evil, no matter how much sin and suffering such a world contains, the aggregated badness would be outweighed by the goodness of incarnation and atonement, outweighed in such a way that the world in question is very good" (Plantinga 2004, 10).

To which one can only say, tell that to Anne Frank as she lay dying in Bergen-Belsen.

What about the Argument from Law?

Laws imply a lawgiver. Even if this argument works, you still run into some of the problems highlighted by Hume. Were there multiple gods at work designing the laws, and are we the end point of a series of less-good worlds, or perhaps the midpoint on the way to better worlds? The argument does rather collapse down into the "why is there something rather than nothing?" discussion. As noted, it is hard to know what a world would be like that was not law-bound. And this being so, the critic can simply say that there is no explanation or need of explanation and that referring to creators who are necessary beings does not help matters. What of the riff on the argument from law centering on what we have seen called the anthropic principle? The laws of nature cannot be due to chance, because if the laws were even fractionally different from the way they actually are, then no life could have been produced, let alone flourish. "If gravity had been stronger or weaker by one part in 10^{40}, then life-sustaining stars like the sun could not exist. This would most likely make life impossible" (Collins 1999, 49). And from this is drawn the inference that the universe is fine-tuned, pointing to something higher. My experience is that, linking with the point made earlier about biologists being more at the nonbelief end of the spectrum than physicists, this argument is greeted by the biological community with emotions ranging from the incredulous to the irritated. Two centuries of beating back Genesis, explaining final causes naturally, unraveling the secrets of life, and now the physicists try to put the clock back to Paley! Is there no end to their ignorant arrogance? Part of the problem here is that one really doesn't know. We have no way of experimenting, and only our universe to judge from. Think of a number, double it, and the answer you want is a half. Although certainly on our planet the only life we know is carbon-based, dare one say—can one offer a kind of ontological argument in reverse—that there is no other possible form of life, a form that could do all that is theologically necessary? Would God love us any less if we were made of silicon rather than carbon? Moreover, what if there are multiverses, that is to say, universes parallel to ours, possibly having all sorts of different laws and constants? In other words, our universe is one of very many. Of course, it is a universe that works, in the sense that it can and did produce life. But this is no big issue, because we wouldn't be in it if it didn't work. Only one person in a million is going to win the lottery, but there is no miracle about the person who is the winner being the winner. Someone had to win. Perhaps no universe had to produce life, but our existence shows that life could be produced, and if you have enough universes and combinations, then our existence seems no more miraculous than that someone won the lottery.

Even if there are no multiverses, one is still working blind. The physics Nobel Laureate Steven Weinberg (1999) is not impressed. He notes that one of the favorite examples of supposed fine-tuning is the carbon atom. This is something that did not occur in the early moments of the universe. Then everything was just hydrogen and helium. It had to be formed, and it seems that for carbon we need three helium nuclei. However, normally this cannot happen because the energy of carbon is way below that of three helium nuclei. Fortuitously, however, there is a radioactive form of carbon that has just the higher energy that is needed, and so everything works out just fine. But before you dash in and say that it is not just fine but fine-tuned, keep digging. The three helium nuclei come together in a two-part process. First, two of them combine to make beryllium, and then the third is added to make carbon. It turns out here that there is significantly more wiggle room, that it is the energy level at this level that is crucial for the production of carbon, and that in fact there is a range of possible energies that would do the job. In short, perhaps the laws we have were not really so tightly designed.

Does the Argument from Miracles Work?

Complementing the argument from law, we have the argument from miracles (Swinburne 1970). These out-of-the-ordinary events, like the raising of Lazarus, point to the existence of a deity and, set within the Christian context, to the Christian deity. It is the miracles that readers of the Gospels would say set the story of Jesus above and beyond that of simply a preacher of two thousand years ago. Because of the miracles, especially the resurrection, we realize that Jesus was something very much more (Davis 2010). But are there miracles? Obviously, if you define miracles simply as unexpected, perhaps meaningful, experiences, there are miracles. I have mentioned the calm sea between England and France at the time of Dunkirk. I grew up with many people who thought it was a miracle. Whether something like this proves the existence of God is another matter. The people I knew thought that Dunkirk did just that. It saved the world from Hitler. What about the plot against Hitler in 1944? From all accounts, he should have been killed. With reason a bulletin went out: "A miracle has worked on the Fuhrer" (Anonymous 1944, 628). Or in the words of his good friend Benito Mussolini: "Heaven has held its protective hand over you." Was God at work here, too? Or is God busy only when it suits us? What about in football games where both sides pray to God for victory? How can he be responsible for the success of one team and not for the loss of the other? Perhaps after all, it is better to leave God entirely out of the discussion, or at least admit that we are using a prior belief in God to make sense of an important event.

The more traditional definition of miracle involves the breaking or suspension of natural laws. In the words of David Hume (2007), a miracle is a "violation of the laws of nature" (83). Do they ever occur? Of course, logically they could. Water could turn into wine, and a dead man could come back to life. The question is whether they ever do, together with the subsidiary question about what it would all mean if they did occur. As far as the second question is concerned, obviously not all (real) miracles would be that meaningful—suppose the chair I am sitting on changed from maple to ash—but let us agree on the fairly uncontroversial claim that if the miracles of the Gospels did occur, then we have some pretty strong evidence for the truth of Christianity. If Jesus was really dead on Friday and really alive on Sunday, then I for one will be satisfied. So let us focus on the first question about whether miracles (with religious meaning) ever do occur. And here obviously we run into a roadblock, because some people think they do occur, and others think they do not occur.

The question we must ask, therefore, is whether it is reasonable to think that miracles occur. At this point, you have to make a distinction between those miracles for which empirical evidence seems pertinent—water into wine—and those where such evidence seems irrelevant. An example of the second I have in mind is the Catholic belief in transubstantiation, where supposedly the bread and the wine are turned into the body and blood of Christ. Even if you think

this is a meaningful notion, no amount of looking or testing is going to prove this right. The whole point is that the
accidents do not change. I take it that the reason one would
accept this doctrine is that one is already committed to the
truth of Christianity, and this comes along as part of the
package deal. So the evidential miracles seem primary, and
expectedly, David Hume had some strong thoughts on the
subject. We must be guided by the following maxim: "That
no testimony is sufficient to establish a miracle, unless the
testimony be of such a kind, that its falsehood would be
more miraculous, than the fact, which it endeavours to establish: And even in that case, there is a mutual destruction of
arguments, and the superior only gives us an assurance suitable to that degree of force, which remains, after deducting
the inferior" (Hume 2007, 83). In other words, to take Hume's
own example, if we have a report of a man rising from the
dead, which is it more reasonable to believe: that he really
did rise from the dead or that his followers lied or fooled
themselves? And put this way, given the near-impossibility
of rising from the dead but the propensity of human beings
to lie to others or to themselves, the resurrection fades from
plausibility.

Obviously in real life, many people do not find Hume's
maxim that convincing because they are happy to go on
believing in miracles, understood as violations of the laws
of nature. One good move Hume does make, though, is to
invite us to think outside the loop. Part of the problem with
miracles is that we so rarely come to the questions without
previous convictions and prejudices, so it is hard for us to
make up our minds. If we are committed Christians because
of our cultural background, we are going to be much easier
on the miracles than otherwise. Therefore, what we should
do is think of miracles in a different, non-Christian context.
Consider for a moment the thinking of Mormons on the subject. (If you are a Mormon, then think of Scientologists. If you
are a Scientologist, then I have not the slightest idea why you

are reading this book.) Around 1820, Joseph Smith, a young man living in western New York State, starts to have visions of Jesus, who tells him that all of his sins are forgiven. He also encounters a prophet warrior Moroni, who tells him that Jesus led people to the New World, where they still live. This is written down on a series of Golden Plates that Smith translates (from "Reformed Egyptian") with the aid of a "seer stone." Apparently Smith had this special stone that he put in a hat and then put his own face in and pulled the rim tightly around. He was then able to see the words on the plates and the translation that he dictated to others, and thus we got the Book of Mormon. This tells you all about Jesus going to North America and why his death and resurrection were important.

Now do you honestly believe that any of this is really true, or is it all just hocus-pocus from a young man and his acquaintances who were living in a part of the world already famous— notorious—for its excessive religious beliefs and tendencies, speaking in tongues and so forth? Do you really believe that there were Golden Plates that Joseph Smith dug up on instructions and translated and then returned to the ground, where they conveniently disappeared? Remember, if you say no, then you are going against what a great many people—including a presidential candidate—take to be absolutely and completely true. But then, of course, many people in the 1930s thought that Hitler was a good thing, and look where that led us. More immediately, if you say no, then why on earth should anyone take seriously the story of Jesus and his miracles? We probably grew up with Jesus and his miracles, so we are more comfortable with them. But this is no argument. Is the story of the loaves and fishes any more convincing than the story of the Golden Plates? Is it not better to say that everything is made up and to leave it at that? Miracles are really just too implausible to be accepted. Certainly people may have had visions, but better to explain it all naturalistically. It was not that Jesus was a high-class caterer—a kind of divine, take-out entrepreneur—but that he so filled people's hearts with love that they shared their food with others.

Does the Argument from Morality Work?

There remains the argument from morality. We all have a moral sense, and it is through this that we become aware of an objective morality, one that exists independently of us individually. The only possible explanation is the Christian God. As "most Christians see things, God himself is the origin of moral constraints. It is his will, his commands or approvals, that determine what is right and wrong, morally acceptable or morally objectionable. Moral obligation is established by his commands to his (morally aware) creatures" (Plantinga 2011, 114). Admittedly, there is the *Euthyphro* problem (named after the Platonic dialogue of that name). Could God ever command what seems to be morally offensive, and, if not, doesn't it follow that he, too, is subject to a prior established system of morality? To his credit, if that is what it is, Plantinga is prepared to grasp this particular nettle. "If God approves, as no doubt he does, of his accepting the sacrifice of his son on the cross as propitiation for human sin, then that arrangement is morally impeccable" (114). Perhaps so, but if nothing else, given that we apparently have a moral system that permits human sacrifice, one would like a bit more on the nature of this objective morality. Christians are not tremendously helpful on this matter, or perhaps one might say that they are altogether too helpful. In the name of the same Lord, some are in favor of military actions, and some are pacifists; some think homosexuality is an abomination, and others think it is just another lifestyle; some favor capital punishment, and some oppose it; some think abortion is always wrong, and others think it a woman's choice; some think that women should know their place, and others agree but think that place is out front; and so the story goes. For the sake of argument, however, let us put these disagreements down to nonmoral factors and perhaps in major part to nonreligious factors. Let us say that they represent cultural and other factors, not the least of which are disagreements about matters of fact. Is capital punishment a good thing or not? The deterrence factor plays a major role in this debate, and there is much discussion about whether capital punishment is indeed a deterrent. Let us agree that it is not so much morality that people disagree over—we all accept "love your neighbor as yourself"—but is all a matter of interpretation of what love is and who my neighbor is.

What then about morality itself? Love your neighbor as yourself. Where does it come from? Let us agree on one thing. Whatever else morality may be, it is not just an emotion or a preference like other emotions and preferences. I like Brussels sprouts; my wife loathes them. End of argument or, rather, beginning of argument! We can both be right in our tastes, and even though we can argue about them—the health-giving benefits or the vile smell while cooking—in the end there is no resolution, no right or wrong. Stomping on little babies for fun is wrong even if the whole world thinks otherwise. Even if you can understand why those Russian soldiers raped German women as they moved across East Prussia—for a start their officers and leaders encouraged it—it was still wrong, absolutely and completely. In some very real sense, morality is objective, outside the individual—or to be more precise, in some very real sense, morality appears to be objective, outside the individual (Mackie 1977).

The question, then, is where does the objectivity of morality lie? One solution is to derive it from nature itself. It is somehow out there and given up by trees and rivers and mountains and planets. The trouble is—and, as we have seen, Hume once again is important here—that deriving morality from nature seems to involve what philosophers call a category mistake. You are going from the way things are to the way things should be—from *is* to *ought*. That seems to be an unjustifiable leap. "I like untouched rainforests" and "untouched rainforests exist but are threatened" are not the same claims as "you ought to preserve untouched rainforests." And if you turn to evolution for help here, then as T. H. Huxley showed, you seem to be digging yourself into an even deeper hole. In a lecture given in 1893, two years before his death, he pointed out that what we label bad things seem just as much a product of evolution as what we label good things. "The thief and the murderer follow nature just as much as the philanthropist. Cosmic evolution may teach us how the good and the evil tendencies of man may have come about; but, in itself, it is incompetent to furnish any better reason why what we call good is preferable to what we call evil than we had before" (Huxley 2009). Huxley points out also that even though Darwin's mechanism often is translated as the "survival of the fittest"—the light skin of a mouse proves itself fitter than the dark skin of a mouse because the predator cannot see the light skin against the sandy background, whereas the dark-skinned mouse stands out—this is no reason to conclude that biological fitness at once equals moral virtue. In fact, the opposite is often true, and goodness demands that we go against our evolved natures. "In place of ruthless self-assertion it demands self-restraint; in place of thrusting aside, or treading down, all competitors, it requires that the individual shall not merely respect, but shall help his fellows; its influence is directed, not so much to the survival of the fittest, as to the fitting of as many as possible to survive. It repudiates the gladiatorial theory of existence" (82). And that spells the end of naive evolutionary attempts to justify ethics.

If not a natural source for objective morality, what about a nonnatural source? It doesn't necessarily have to be theological. G. E. Moore (1903), another big critic of naturalism in ethics, thought morality consisted of nonnatural properties that somehow we intuit. The trouble lies in where we are to find these properties or things, how they relate to us, and why we should obey them. Is one to take a Platonist position and think them like mathematics, existing in some solitary eternal heaven? How do we become aware of them? If you say we intuit them, how is this done? Is it something that involves part

of the brain, like seeing buildings and people? Brain researchers are now starting to dig into these sorts of questions, and
so far the need to posit nonnatural properties has not seemed
compelling. In moral thinking, we do use our brains, different
parts connecting to emotions and reasons, but there is no sign
yet of connection to outside properties.

Is Evolution the Answer?

Natural solutions don't seem to be the answer. Nonnatural
solutions don't seem to be the answer. Is God the default position? Or can one find another plausible reason for the objectivity of morality? A small but growing band of philosophers and
biologists today think that this is possible (Ruse 1986, 2009).
The secret lies not in the objectivity as such, but in the appearance of objectivity. One cannot justify such objectivity naturally, but one can explain why we think it is there, and once
done, we realize that there is nothing to be justified. Thanks
to modern advances in the understanding of the evolution
(through natural selection) of social behavior, we now know
that altruism—helping each other—is a major factor in animal
interactions. Sometimes altruism comes about because in helping relatives, one is indirectly helping one's own genes to be
passed on (because relatives share copies of the same genes);
sometimes altruism comes about because help to others gets
reciprocated ("you scratch my back, and I'll scratch yours");
sometimes altruism comes about because other organisms
manipulate us into helping. Humans, for all that they have a
violent side, are very good at altruism—we are a highly social
species. And for humans, ethics is part of this mix (Ruse 2012).
A major factor in human sociality is this shared belief that
we ought to help others. But think about it. If we saw at once
that ethics has only the function of keeping us social, then the
temptation to cheat would be overwhelming. You scratch my
back, but while I pretend to scratch yours, I am in fact enrich-
ing myself at your expense. Before long, everything would

collapse in selfish chaos. Suppose, however, that part of the experience of morality was that it is binding, that it is objective. Then the temptation to cheat is reduced or eliminated, and morality keeps functioning. Within the morality system, we can make judgments about right and wrong, just as much as within the soccer system, we can judge a goal scored or a kick offside. It is just that the objectivity of morality, on this reading, is an illusion put in place by our genes to keep us social—as much an illusion as the perfection of the boy or girl with whom we have just fallen in love. It may all seem rather cynical on the part of nature, but whoever said that nature had to be upright and fair! This is the world of nonbelief, and such are the consequences.

9

ALTERNATIVE RELIGIONS

Is There Only One Right Belief?

Let us pull back for a moment and widen our gaze, out from Christianity toward other religions. As atheists rightfully keep pointing out nonstop, at once we come up against a major problem, namely, that faith is apparently altogether too culture dependent. Contrast with science. Historians of science and others have shown us the extent to which scientific claims are embedded in culture, but there is still much in Karl Popper's (1972) characterization of science as "knowledge without a knower," meaning the characteristics of the person who does the science are irrelevant to the truth content. There is no such thing as German science or Jewish science or feminist science—at least not with respect to testing and acceptance. Robert Boyle was an Irishman. His gas law is true and for the same reasons, whether you are Irish or English, Protestant or Catholic. Albert Einstein was a Jew, but his theory of relativity is the same for Jew or Gentile. Lynn Margulis discovered that complex cells (eukaryotic cells) were formed by the fusion of simpler cells (prokaryotic cells). Men can appreciate that truth, and the DNA evidence is the same for them as for women. The trouble is that faith doesn't work that way, or rarely. The children of Protestants tend to have a Protestant take on things, and the children of Catholics have a Catholic perspective on their faith claims. Jews and Muslims grow up very comfortably not believing at all in the divinity of Jesus, and Hindus and Buddhists are ever further away. Are we simply to argue that everyone who does not share our perspective is as wrong as the atheists?

That is Plantinga's (2000) position. He is what is known in the trade as a religious exclusivist. It is my way or the highway. People like him turn to the Bible for justification of their conviction that Christianity is the truth and the only truth. It was apparently Jesus' position: "Jesus said to him, 'I am the way, and the truth, and the life. No one comes to the Father except through me'" (John 14: 6). It was also apparently the position of St. Paul, who was against not only belief in other religions, but practices of Christianity that did not accord with his particular version: "As we have said before, so now I repeat, if anyone proclaims to you a gospel contrary to what you received, let that one be accursed!" (Galatians 1: 9). It is probably fair to say that this today is still very much an Evangelical position. More liberally minded Protestants like Quakers would feel very uncomfortable with such a stand. Also interestingly, although Catholicism used to hold to such exclusivity—*Extra ecclesiam nulla salus* ("Outside the Church, there is no salvation")—while it still thinks you are wrong not to be a Catholic, it no longer thinks that the keys to the kingdom could never be yours. Let us not forget that Jesus praises the Good Samaritan and tells us that God has a place for those of us who care for the sick and visit the imprisoned.

But supposing you want to stand firm on these matters, how do you justify your position over those of others? If you are into natural theology in various ways (broadly conceived as any argument involving reason), one could make a start. I suspect that the average Christian would think that being an average Christian, rather than (let us say) a Jehovah's Witness, was basically a matter of common sense. The claims that blood transfusions are unbiblical are for most people reason enough to reject the system, and that is before you get to all of the stuff about the 144,000 who are going to go to heaven to rule with Jesus. Morally, too—for all of their unbelievable fortitude in face of oppression during the Third Reich—Jehovah's Witnesses' attitudes toward women and homosexuals make subscription to the church rather less than edifying. But is this enough? Sophisticated religions like Judaism tend to have worked out the kinks and don't lead with their chins, as do new religions like Mormonism and the Jehovah's Witnesses. And this is apart from the fact that an influential strain of Protestantism doesn't want to get into natural theology at all. At such a point, and for all that he is into natural theology Plantinga endorses this, you simply have to fall back on the conviction that your faith—your *sensus divinitatis*—is reliable and those who disagree with you are not. Original sin has corrupted their God-given powers.

The best response to Plantinga and his fellows is directing them to Descartes's *Meditations*. Descartes likewise wanted to guarantee truth ("clear and distinct" ideas) by using God as a filter and a support. Unfortunately, this comes in the *Third Meditation*, and in the *First*, as part of his process of systematic doubt (that was supposed to lead us to God as the only secure foundation for knowledge), Descartes lets loose an evil demon who can deceive us on just about anything: "I shall then suppose, not that God who is supremely good and the fountain of truth, but some evil genius not less powerful than deceitful, has employed his whole energies in deceiving me; I shall consider that the heavens, the earth, colours, figures, sound, and all other external things are naught but the illusions and dreams of which this genius has availed himself in order to lay traps for my credulity; I shall consider myself as having no hands, no eyes, no flesh, no blood, nor any senses, yet falsely believing myself to possess all these things" (Descartes 1964, 80). How can Plantinga assure us that he is not being deceived by such a demon? Presumably, he would say that faith gives him the equivalent of a Cartesian clear and distinct idea, something that is self-validating. But that is the whole point of the demon. If it can make us believe that $2 + 2 = 5$, and apparently the demon can do even this, it can surely deceive Alvin Plantinga about the validity of his God experiences.

Or Are There Many Paths to the Truth?

I worried at the beginning of this book about being Eurocentric, in the broad sense of focusing unduly on cultures that are either European or greatly influenced by Europe (notably North America). Epistemological issues apart, there is something deeply morally offensively Eurocentric about suggesting that the Tibetan monk is blinded by sin in a way that is not true of the Florida Baptist. What is the alternative? Some kind of religious inclusiveness. Thanks to his experiences of living and working in the English city of Birmingham, a place that since the Second World War has seen a huge influx of people from foreign lands with foreign faiths, the philosopher of religion John Hick (1980) was passionately committed to such a program. Somehow he thought we have to distill the essential, shared truths that underlie all of the great religions. Prima facie, this is not a very appealing prospect. Can you really argue that beneath the varied claims there is some core of shared belief and understanding? This is not very plausible even within Christianity. Is God a necessary being outside space and time, as claimed by the great (Catholic) philosophers, or is God a person, a position that finds favor with many Protestants? Once you start comparing Christianity with other religions, you are in even deeper trouble. Is Jesus Christ the son of God (Christian position) or not (everyone else's position)? This is not exactly a fringe question. However, perhaps you can make some progress on morality—by and large, religions share commitments to reciprocity—and with respect to the God question, a shared sense of the divine, whatever that might mean. I suspect the basic claims I highlighted in the discussion on science and religion might be pertinent here. This fits in with Hick's suggestion: "God is to be thought of as the divine noumenon, experienced by mankind as a range of divine phenomena which take both theistic and nontheistic forms" (Hick 1980, 110). This language flags us that Hick wanted to go down some kind of Kantian—perhaps better described as neo-Kantian—route. He pointed out that the essence of Kant's philosophy is that we interpret absolute reality—the "thing in itself" or the *Ding an sich* (what Kant called the noumenal world, as opposed to the world of experience, the phenomenal world)—through various categories or constraints of the mind. We think causally, not because we see causes out there—Hume had convinced him that that is not right—but because we cannot think rationally at all if we do not think in terms of causes. In other words, all thought is a matter of the world out there and the world in here—a something external to us viewed through various constraints of interpretation that we add to the stew.

For Kant, these constraints are not optional. All rational people have and must have the same ones. Hick seems to think that, with respect to religion, this part is flexible. (That is why I call him a neo-Kantian.) Christianity and Judaism and so forth are different (phenomenal) ways of approaching and interpreting the same (noumenal) reality. Although Hick was too old-fashioned to get into the trendy philosophy of social constructivism, as when Michel Foucault argued that our take on reality is all a matter of who controls the reins of power, one can see that this is the direction in which he was pointed. "The natural world has a small or non-existent role in the construction of scientific knowledge" (Collins 1981, 3). And that is Becher's Brook—a notoriously difficult fence in the English steeplechase, the Grand National. Apart from philosophical problems with notions like the *Ding an sich*, most people—and you don't have to be particularly conservative to be part of "most people"—find it profoundly implausible to suggest that a sun-centered planetary system, a four-plus-billion-year-old Earth, and a human ancestor that was a fish are claims in which the "natural world has a small or non-existent role" in their validity. I, for one, take the fossil record very seriously, and I don't think the Burgess Shale (that magnificent Canadian collection of fossils so well described by Stephen Jay Gould in his *Wonderful Life*) is a matter of my imagination.

There seems to be something objective, shared by scientists, that is not true for religious believers. To take the first of the claims I highlighted, a Creator God exists, this is affirmed by Christians, Jews, and Muslims, but, as we shall see in a moment, is absolutely and explicitly denied by some in other religions. This is not to say—quite apart from one's huge respect for a man who was grappling with real-life issues of religious tolerance in a city that was desperate for such men of goodwill—that everything Hick argued was for naught. You don't have to be an out-and-out constructivist to recognize a point that has been made repeatedly in this book: metaphor plays a huge role in science. The Scientific Revolution can be reduced to a change in metaphors, from an organism to a machine (Ruse 2010). There are metaphors in all branches of science, and they are in some sense all cultural or social. Darwin, for instance, makes much of the division of labor, and that is right out of Adam Smith and eighteenth-century political economy. One doubts that the genetic code would have had its fascination had it not come in the decade after the brilliant work with Enigma at Bletchley Park. So in some sense science—the very best science—is culture-dependent. But this is far from saying that it is just a matter of culture. There was a code, and it was cracked! The big question is that although religion is no less metaphor-impregnated—the Lamb of God, the Whore of Babylon, the Holy Ghost—whether this brings religion close enough to science to say of it, too, that there is a reality of which it would be unfair to say that it plays but a "small or non-existent role in the construction" of its central claims. Perhaps this is an exercise best left to the reader. But it needs to be tackled, and one suspects that a lot of people will find the process painful. And until this is done, the reader might be forgiven for thinking that the plurality of religions is a significant problem for claims about the veracity of Christianity.

Jewish Atheism?

But what of the religions themselves? Do they throw light on the matter of nonbelief? Do they embrace atheism or give us reasons to think that atheism might be true? Part of the problem here is the difficulty I hinted at when I talked of my beliefs and those of my wife, Lizzie. Both of us in a sense can be described as nonbelievers, but there any similarity ceases. I was raised in an intensely Christian atmosphere, and any issues I have had with Christianity have been molded, perhaps clouded, by this. For me, nonbelief is very real. She was raised in a nonreligious home, and for her the whole question of belief was really a nonstarter. It was not that she thought about these things and rejected them. She never thought about them in the first place. For her, nonbelief is nothing. We find similar issues when we turn to other religions. One starts with a very different position from the Christian, and so one may well end up with a very different position, masked by the same language. Or as is likely in this day and age, one has an end position that owes more to encounters with Christianity than from anything within the religion itself.

Judaism illustrates all of this very well (Berlinerblau 2013). Outside encounters with Christian-dominated societies, it is not easy to see atheism at all within the Jewish religion and its society. Secularism makes sense, meaning moving away from a religion-dominated culture—dropping keeping kosher and that sort of thing—but that is not quite the same thing. Paradoxically and somewhat inconveniently, one thinks one has found genuine atheists, and then it turns out that they are quite committed to an existent God—even though they may not care for him! The already mentioned chap in the Psalms—the fool hath said in his heart there is no God—is the prototype: someone who is kicking against the traces, perhaps not even believing in the God of Israel, but no atheist in our sense. He could as well believe in—would be more likely to believe in—many gods as in none at all. Elisha ben Abuya, born in the first century of the modern era, was a rabbi who was often (especially by writers of the Talmud) picked out for the role of atheist, but although he was undoubtedly heretical, his non-belief in God is far from established. The sort of thing he did was to stress charity to the poor over the virtues of learning, of knowledge of the Torah. One can see why this upset the staid and mighty—why, indeed, God might have felt it necessary to consume his grave with fire—but this doesn't exactly translate as nonbelief in God. As always, the cry of atheist—and revealingly, the Jews did not really have such a term—was more a political and moral move than one of epistemological exactitude.

Coming down to the modern era, much the same applies. The great philosopher Spinoza (1632–1677) was called an atheist by his fellow Jews, but a more God-intoxicated individual would be hard to find, for all that his philosophy of "God or Nature" was close to pantheism. Real atheism perhaps only begins to emerge in the nineteenth century, when many European Jews were becoming ever more secular. Toward the end of the century, movements like Marxism (note, like Freudianism, due to a Jew) started to make significant inroads. Zionism also played a part for many, although it was often mixed with a desire to stress Jewish identity, which, of course, had its roots deep in the religion—the biblical teaching about the patriarchs, particularly. Most interesting was the response to the Holocaust. There were those who thought that God died at Auschwitz. Theologian Richard Rubenstein (b. 1924) wrote of God being "totally unavailable as a source of meaning and value" (Rubenstein 1966, 205). He referred to God as "the Holy Nothingness" and lamented the empty, unfeeling world within which we live. Yet he was not just a rabbi but in a sense a deeply committed believer, working through his anguished response to his creator. And even those who break from God entirely often feel that some kind of kinship with their own is not only inevitable but also morally obligatory. I am sure I am not alone in having very secular Jewish friends who nevertheless fast at Yom Kippur. The death of Anne Frank demands a spiritual response. God may not have been at her side, but we should be.

Muslim Atheism?

Much the same story holds of Islam, although finding the truth can be incredibly difficult because any kind of apostasy brings condemnation and death (Schielke 2013). Look at the troubles of the novelist Salman Rushdie (b. 1947) for supposedly making fun of the Prophet in his novel *Satanic Verses*. From early on in the history of the religion, there were challenges to Islam, particularly the prophecies that play such a large role in the theology. Abu al-Husayn Ahmad ibn Yahya ibn Ishaq al-Rawandi (860–912) was swingeing in his attacks on the big names in the religion—he spoke of the miracles of Abraham, Jesus, and Muhammad as "fraudulent tricks"—and dismissed the Qu'ran as the words of an "unwise being." It doesn't mean that he was an atheist in our sense, nor was another critic, Abu Bakr Muhammad ibn Zakariya al-Razi (865–925), for all that he, too, went after prophecy. He was big on the religious pluralism issue. "How come do you deem it necessary that God would single out some for prophecy and some not, and give them privilege over the people as their guides, and make people dependent on them?" (Schielke 2013, 640). Razi was no atheist, although he was a keen deist, as we would understand the term.

Moving to the nineteenth century, we enter the era when the Islamic world was brought face-to-face with Western civilization—think of the British conquest of India—and as with Judaism, we start to find those who can be called atheists in our sense. Not all. In mid-nineteenth-century Iran, the Bab (Siyyid `Alí Muḥammad Shírází, 1819–1850) led (until he was captured and executed) a movement that stressed new revelations and daring social programs like the emancipation of women. But it was a matter of one conception of God replacing another, as is testified by the Baha'i faith into which his movement evolved. What is significant is that secularism, which hit several Islamic societies, notably Turkey, did not necessarily spell the end of belief. Kemal Atatürk (1881–1938), for instance, was much more interested in harnessing religion to his secular ends than in banning or destroying it. Where one does seem to find real atheism is where Western science and hopes of progress have made inroads. Isma'il Adham (1911–1940)—admittedly with a European Protestant mother as well as a Muslim Egyptian father—declared for atheism outright. "I left religions, and abandoned all (religious) beliefs, and put my faith in science and scientific logic alone" (Shielke 2013, 643). Not that any of this brought him much joy; depressed by reading Schopenhauer and Nietzsche, he committed suicide at the age of twenty-nine.

Today, particularly since the fall of the Soviet Union, which tried so hard to impose atheism on all of its citizens, Muslims as well as Christians, it is unlikely that even the persuasive powers of Richard Dawkins could make great inroads into Islamic societies. Some, like Saudi Arabia, are simply frozen in the past when it comes to religious beliefs. Countries that have trouble with women driving are hardly likely to encourage or countenance sentiments of nonbelief. But those that have felt the winds of change, even of revolution, are not necessarily those where atheism plays or will play a major role. A lot of this is the cultural role that Islam plays in such societies, as with Jews being part of the defining heritage, particularly against others (namely, Western Christians), and also as always very much bound up with morality. Without religion, all will collapse into anarchy and lawlessness. Expectedly, even those who would characterize themselves as atheists—although as always these run the gamut from out-and-out nonbelievers through agnostics to spiritual but against formal religion—make morality the foundation of their position. In explanations of their thinking, "justice and injustice play a key role in all of these accounts, be it in the form of gender equality, war and peace, social justice, the injustice of hell, or the inconsistent and contradictory behavior of religious people" (Schielke 2005, 645).

What about Buddhism?

Are we not being a little coy by refusing to jump straight to the Far East and in particular to the Buddhist religion? After all, everyone knows that Buddhism is an atheistic religion. It has no place for God. Indeed, Sam Harris spent more than ten years in the East studying meditation with Buddhist teachers. You cannot have a better validation than that! But the truth is rather more subtle than this. Buddhism is certainly atheistic inasmuch as it denies the existence of a supreme being, God, who created heaven and earth and so forth. It certainly denies the Christian God who cares for us and whose house has many rooms, that Jesus went on his way to get things ready for us. After that, things start to get a lot more complex (Harvey 1990; Skilton 2013).

Buddhism, like Hinduism, with which it shares various features, was one of the religions developing in the East in the years before Christ. Specifically, it dates from the life and teaching of Gautama Buddha, who was born and lived in Nepal around and after 550 BC. As with Christ, finding out the exact details of his life is not easy, but it seems that the Buddha (this is a generic title, for there were and will be others) was somewhat of a St. Francis figure. He was born to wealth and comfort and married and had a child before he recognized the misery and suffering in the world and renounced his heritage to live a life of simplicity and service to others and to follow the quest for ultimate truth. Having at some point achieved enlightenment, he spent the rest of his life teaching his ever-growing band of disciples and died in peace at about the age of eighty. As is well known, the Buddha was committed to the idea of reincarnation—that we have multiple lives in succession (samsara)—and (as we shall see) that actions and thoughts in this life can have implications for the life that we will live next. Ultimately, the aim is to break out of this ongoing cycle of existences and achieve something called *nibbana* (also called nirvana). One is released from suffering—*dukkha*—and achieves a kind of state of nonbeing. It would seem, therefore, that there is a radical difference from Christianity, a religion that promises some kind of eternal existence, a conscious state of ecstasy in the presence of the Lord. However, without wanting artificially to bring the two systems together, simple nonexistence does not really do justice to *nibbana*. Part of the problem is that encountered in other religions—namely, talking of that which in a certain sense is beyond human comprehension—but there are positive things said of *nibbana*: that it is endless and wholly radiant, the "further shore," the "island amidst the flood," the "cool cave of shelter" (no small thing given the Indian climate), the "highest bliss" (Harvey 1990, 63).

All of this is placed in a rather complex ontology that puts one in mind of modern cosmology. There are apparently an infinite number of universes, with galaxies, themselves clustered into thousandfold groups. There are innumerable planets, and on them we find inhabitants much like our planet and its denizens. Everything is subject to change, decay, and rebirth—often taking vast quantities of time (eons). A cloth stroking a mountain, wearing it away, would finish its work of destruction before an eon is over. No matter, because there were indefinite eons before the one we are in, and there will be indefinite eons after us. In respects, therefore, we have an existence rather like that supposed by the Greeks, where time stretches endlessly backward and forward. As we have this temporal dimension, so we have other dimensions because it transpires that our level of existence is but one of five or six, and part of the process of rebirth is moving up or down these levels according to our behavior in this life. Right at the bottom is the hell realm, *niraya*, with vile beings tortured and subject to horrible nightmares. Above this comes the level of *petas*, ghostly creatures, somewhat akin to the phantom spirits of Western lore. The *wilis* (girls who die of heartbreak from being jilted) of the ballet *Giselle* would be eminently qualified here. Next up is the animal realm, obviously sharing space with humans but in major respects lower forms of life. Humans come next, and then above us are one or two levels for the gods—the *asuras*, the lesser gods, and then the *devas*, which include the *brahmas*, the very highest form of being. Note, however, that everyone, at all levels of existence, is subject to life, death, and rebirth. *Dukkha* is omnipresent, and the aim for all is *nibbana*.

As the Abrahamic religions have their moral directives, so with Buddhism we find combined with the ontology a complex ethical theory. Naturally, this is bound up with achieving *nibbana*, as the Christian moral system is bound up with our eternal salvation. The Four Holy (or Noble) Truths point the way. First, we must understand the unsatisfactory nature of our lives. We must understand our greed and our other desires and the failure to satisfy them. We must understand *dukkha*. Then next, we must understand the reasons for *dukkha* and our incomplete and selfish natures. We must grasp how it is that we can never feel full happiness in our lives. Third comes understanding how *dukkha* can be ended and *nibbana* achieved. "This, monks, is the holy truth of the cessation (nirodha) of dukkha: the utter cessation, without attachment, of that very craving, its renunciation, surrender, release, lack of pleasure in it" (Harvey 1990, 60–61). Finally comes the eightfold path of action: seeing reality as it is, renouncing desires, speaking truthfully, doing no harm, living in a wholesome way, trying to improve, making an effort to see oneself clearly, meditating. This is all part of karma, the actions taken that can affect future lives. Sometimes Buddhism can seem almost fatalistic about what happens, but there are definite strands suggesting that one does have freedom and that one's decisions and actions matter. Lower forms of life apparently have less choice, and higher forms of life less need of choice. They have not achieved *nibbana* but can enjoy the fruits of what led to their exalted status.

Is Buddhism Atheistic?

Asking such a question brings to mind the caution I expressed earlier in this chapter. In a way, it is an odd question to ask of so spirit-infested a system. You just don't think of Buddhism in the kinds of negative terms that one implies when one says "God is dead" or "the universe is a meaningless confusion of atoms moving randomly." The Buddhist world picture is bursting with life. This said, clearly in a sense Buddhism is atheistic. There is no creator God who set everything in motion, and there is no providential God who hovers over his creation and who is prepared to intervene when things go drastically wrong. For the Buddhist, there is no ultimate meaning to life in this sort of way. Life just is, always has been, always will be. That is the nature of things. So one can see why, at least in this respect, Sam Harris was able to fit into the Buddhist system. Yet this is obviously but part of the story, because in other respects Buddhism is not only theistic but also polytheistic. Moreover, this is not just a matter of lip service. Go to Buddhist temples, and you will find space for worship of the various gods. Some rather tricky thinking is needed to justify gifts to the gods, but somehow it is thought that they confer individual merit.

Exploring in more detail, one gets further and at times amusing insights. It turns out that at least in early Buddhism, there was one major god, the Great Brahma. Some even thought he might have been the creator of Earth, and indeed the Great Brahma himself encouraged such thinking, because when he was first born, he was alone, the only one of his kind. Naturally, he wished for companions, and in the regular course of nature, other beings at his level did appear, simply because they had been born up the scale, as it were. This led the Great Brahma to think that he was responsible for their creation: "I am Brahma, the Great Brahma. . . the All-seeing, the Controller, the Lord, the Maker, the Creator. . . these other beings are my creation." The Buddha, however, scotched this kind of thinking, pointing out that the Great Brahma was mistaken. He was just a being like everyone else. An interesting implication of this exchange is that although the Great Brahma is a higher level of being than the Buddha, a human, it was the Buddha who was wiser and closer to *nibbana*. The Great Brahma is nevertheless warm and friendly, concerned about people's needs. Obviously, because he was not creator, the problem of evil does not arise. He was no more responsible for *dukkha* than anyone else.

For all that Plato thought that existence is eternal, he managed to find room for a creation story (the Demiurge designed things according to the Good). This is a story of design out of existing material rather than out of nothing. So also in Buddhism, we find creation stories about individual worlds out of existing materials. In a way, they parallel the Genesis story of the fall, because apparently higher forms of being hover over newly created worlds—as keeps occurring because of the constant recycling—and then these forms somehow get entangled with the physical aspects of these new worlds and themselves become human, with the various faults we have. Note that as with Christianity, there is an odor that very human things like sexuality are not altogether good things, but rather part of our fallen nature, demanding renunciation. This is but part of a general trend toward asceticism in Eastern religions, where giving up earthly pleasures like good food (including meat), personal property, and even attention to bodily hygiene are often seen as ways to achieve desirable spiritual ends. Interestingly, although the Buddha for a while practiced such asceticism, he came to see that it was not ultimately fruitful and pulled back from the extremes. One suspects that Jesus of Nazareth, who enjoyed good food and drink, would have understood fully.

My aim here is to contrast Christianity against other religions and not really dig into their truth statuses in their own right. Obviously, some of the problems raised against Christianity—for instance, about the persistence of personal identity—are found with regard to Buddhism. Other problems are not so pressing. The problem of evil has been mentioned. No doubt Buddhism has problems that Christianity does not have. The main point is that although we can surely speak of Buddhism as atheistic in respects, we should tread very warily in making such a claim and recognize that it is hedged in various important ways.

What Is the Moral of the Story?

There is little point in trawling endlessly through various religions searching for atheism. Buddhism is certainly not unique in basically accepting the universe as it is and going from there. Jainism, another Indian religion that developed in the centuries before the Christian era, noteworthy for its reverence for all living things, shares the belief that the universe just is, eternal and not created. It is deeply ethical and deeply spiritual, so much so that (as for Buddhism) it seems odd to think of it as atheistic, although (for all that like Buddhism there are superior god-like beings) by Western criteria in some important sense it obviously qualifies. What is fascinating is the way that the moral prescriptions about the sanctity of life are bound up with refusal to accept a Christian-like god. Suffering is part of the living condition and thus our obligations to alleviate or minimize it for all beings. In the words of the *Acaranga Sutra*, one of the oldest scriptures (around the third century BC): "as sorrow and pain are not desirable for you, so it is to all which breath, exist, live or have any essence of life. To you and all, it is undesirable, and painful." There would never be such a condition of suffering were there an all-loving, all-powerful god. The idea of such a god is not just wrong, but sinister even (Vallely 2013).

Hinduism is a fusion, or perhaps more accurately a range, of different belief systems, some of which certainly contain gods and creation stories and much more, including all sorts of moral prescriptions. In the more philosophical of the religious writings, the *Upanishads*, Brahman is the ultimate creative spirit, a sort of ground of our being, as noted by American transcendentalists like Waldo Emerson not entirely unlike the Plato-inspired philosophical God of Christianity, although one needs to be awfully careful about simple identifications (Quack 2013). It is true nevertheless that like Buddhism there is in Hinduism a strong traditional streak that (by Western standards) would undoubtedly be thought atheistic. In one of the earliest *Vedas* (some include the *Upanishads* in the *Vedas* but most of the *Vedic* writings predate the *Upanishads* and are more spiritually focused), composed centuries before the creation stories of Genesis, there are passages that certainly can be read in an atheistic spirit.

Then was not non-existent nor existent: there was no realm of air, no sky beyond it. . . .Who really knows and who here can say it, when it was born and whence flows this creation? The Gods are later than this world's production. Who knows then whence it first came into being? (*Rigveda* 10: 130)

Later thinkers came up with a farrago of reasons why there could be no god, many sounding familiar to Western ears, as for example the difficulties of understanding the notion of a god who has emotions and the worthlessness of a god who does not have emotions, problems of evil, whether a god is needed for moral conduct, and so forth. As always, this kind of thinking was almost always bound up strongly with ethical concerns, anticipating the New Atheists in feeling that a life without gods is morally superior to a life with gods (Frazier 2013).

There has been much debate about whether Confucianism is a religion (Yao 2000)—the early Jesuits saw it more as a moral system that could coexist harmoniously with Christianity, whereas the Dominicans and Franciscans thought that ancestor worship was central and pagan. Either way, it is not a system with a creator God who sustains and who is significant in human life. All of which rather confirms the sentiment that if there is any message to be drawn from Buddhism and other systems, it is that although atheism can be found in various forms in other cultures, the *problem* of atheism does seem to be very much a Western phenomenon, essentially a Western Christian phenomenon. Atheism is certainly not a problem for Buddhism, however much you may consider Buddhism to be an atheistic religion. The same goes for other Eastern religions. That atheism is primarily a Christian issue also seems to be borne out by the fact noted earlier that if one is considering atheism across the world today, usually the starting point is a particular culture's first encounter with the West and with Western ideas. Often, there was no word for atheism as such, and even today survey takers have to use ingenuity to find questions that make sense in non-Western cultures. In Japan, for instance, atheism was simply not an issue until the middle of the nineteenth century and the beginning of the Meiji Era (1868–1912). It was then that Japan started to open up to the West, and European and American teachers started to go there and, conversely, young Japanese started to go abroad for higher education (Whylly 2013). Very quickly, scientific and other ideas started to capture the imagination of the young, especially the intellectuals, and thoughts of progress and other Enlightenment values began to make their way through the ranks. As in America, Herbert Spencer (1820–1903) was a major influence. (He was also in China and in British India. One of the Indian characters in Rudyard Kipling's great novel *Kim* is an ardent Spencerian.) And in the wake of such new ideas came Western squabbles about religion and, in particular, thoughts of atheism.

Interestingly, although perhaps expectedly, such thoughts were often directed against the Christian religion exclusively, and critical thinking was used less to make theological points and more to make political points about the undesirability of imposing various Western religions and ideologies on the native culture. It was not so much that people were anti-God—they often didn't believe in God in that sense anyway—but that they were against the Christian God. This, for instance, was the position of Inoue Tetsujiro (1855–1944), the first Japanese professor of philosophy at Tokyo University. His *Collision between Religion and Education* (1893 (see Godart [2011])) was explicitly motivated by nationalistic concerns—he didn't think Christians showed the right deference to the emperor—and almost paradoxically brought his training in Germany in that country's idealism to bear in an attack on the very idea of the Christian God. He was not the only one, but although obviously all of this is interesting not only in its own right but for understanding what happened to Japan (and other countries) in the twentieth century, it is not really of direct concern to us here, so now we can conclude our brief survey and move on.

10

NATURALISTIC EXPLANATIONS

Explanations?

In the light of the issues detailed in the critical chapters, if you are a nonbeliever, you are going to ask how on earth we got ourselves into this kind of mess. Religion obviously has had and in major respects still does have a huge hold on the human imagination. How can this be? Some naturalistic case for belief must be offered, a case where the truth value of the beliefs can be overridden; otherwise, the case is incomplete. If you are lucky, perhaps, you might even have a naturalistic explanation that suggests the religious beliefs are erroneous. In and after the First World War, many people went to spiritualists to communicate with the recent dead. And they did! "It's aright mum. I'm happy now. I'm just waiting for you and dad to pass over." I suspect that an explanation of these messages in terms of psychological stress combined with fraud gives both a causal answer to the responses and instills considerable skepticism about their authenticity. For the atheist or the skeptic, this is the philosopher's stone—an explanation that simultaneously explains and debunks.

The reflective believer is hardly going to be indifferent to these issues. Granted that ultimately it is God's gift of faith (and perhaps reason) that leads one to belief, how has God made it possible that we believe in the face of the difficulties? What is

it that makes belief compelling? This is not to say that nonbeliever and believer will necessarily approach this question in
exactly the same ways. One presumes that the religious person
may be somewhat more circumscribed in his or her range of
possible naturalistic causes. For the nonbeliever, almost anything is allowable. The only criterion is—Does it work? The
believer presumably would be uncomfortable with an account
of religion's origin that necessitated huge amounts of human
suffering—although in the light of the Old Testament, one
wonders just how big something has to be before it qualifies
as huge. Obviously also, the believer would be uncomfortable
with an explanation that carried within it a debunking of the
main claims of religion. Supposing we accept that spiritualism
can be shown false in all respects, a believer would be wary
of a similar explanation of more conventional religion. Part
of the problem here is about how similar "similar" has to be
before you reject the claims. We know that egregious fraud
was involved in the origins of one of those religious movements that sprang up in America in the nineteenth century.
Ellen G. White (1827–1915), more influential than any other in
the founding of the Seventh-day Adventists, claimed to have
had visions that told her of such things as the literal six-day
creation of the universe and the need to keep Saturdays, the
Sabbath, sacred and not to be used for work. More than a hundred years later, historian Ronald Numbers (b. 1942), raised
a good Adventist, discovered that White had taken most of
her recorded visions, line for line, from the writings of others
earlier in the century. It shook his faith, but most of his coreligionists simply argued that, whatever the source, the content
was true.

There is an important question here about whether ultimately all naturalistic explanations are going to point to the
falsity of religion, or, if not all, then at least all that today
have any plausibility. I suspect that if we spend our time trying to set up conditions for acceptable natural explanations

of religion, we shall probably never emerge from the morass. After all, if we are worrying about who got the ideas first, we saw that general opinion among New Testament scholars is that Matthew and Luke almost certainly drew on an unknown source labeled Q—after the German word for "spring," *Quelle*—and if we are talking about sinners involved in the founding of religions, let us start with Peter, who denied his Lord, and Saul (as Paul was then known), who held the coats of those stoning Stephen. So we simply move on from this threateningly indeterminable discussion of conditions for explanation to actual explanations. We can judge as we go along if they disprove religion. Unfortunately, however, thus far we haven't really prepared ourselves to speak to the more empirical level about the origins and hold of religion. We have been concerned with the more philosophical and theological side to things. We haven't really seen religion in the flesh, and this puts us at a disadvantage when it comes to judging explanations. Let's try to remedy this. As Aristotle said, one swallow does not make a summer, but putting religion in action before our eyes may aid understanding. From many possibilities, because we do know so much about it but at the same time it is sufficiently distant from us that we can be relatively disinterested, I will take the English Catholics in the years just before the Reformation, something that came to England in the 1530s (MacCulloch 2004; Duffy 1992).

What Was It Like Five Hundred Years Ago?

The Wars of the Roses came to an end with Richard III (1452–1485) killed in the Battle of Bosworth Field and with England and Wales then united under the first of the Tudors, Henry VII (1457–1509). What was life like back then? One thing we can say with certainty is that it was hugely more difficult and dangerous than anything we encounter today—at least, anything that comfortable, middle-class Westerners encounter today (Dyer 1994). Of course, some were doing much better in society and acquiring more of its goods than were others, not just the nobles and the landowners, but merchants and tradespeople in the cities and towns. Travel around parts of Suffolk today, Lavenham and Long Melford, and gaze at the huge parish churches, completed in the fifty years before the break. The incredibly wealthy wool families had used their profits in part to the glory of their communities. But other people, by far the majority, lived lives literally and metaphorically close to the land, farming or providing services like blacksmithing. Housing was primitive to say the least, work was back-breaking—at forty, one was an old person—and always disease and death stalked. Most people did not survive childhood, and those who did were haunted by a host of dangers and ailments. The Black Death, the bubonic plague, had hit Europe in the middle of the fourteenth century, wiping out up to half of the population. The rate in England was a little lower but still frighteningly large. And it kept repeating, right up to the Great Plague of London in 1665. Truly did the philosopher Thomas Hobbes, even in the seventeenth century, speak of "the life of man, solitary, poor, nasty, brutish, and short."

But this is a qualified description. This is humankind in a state of nature, without culture and society and all else that makes for civilized living. With these, and above all with religion, things are very different, and this was so for medieval England. Our ancestors—my ancestors at least, for I was born in Britain—led hard lives, but lives rich in meaning and value, with joy and laughter as well as sadness and tears, and it was religion that made it all possible. This was true of all levels of society, for although most were illiterate—with the coming of printing, this was changing even before literacy shot up with the translation of the Bible into the vernacular—thanks to sermons and images and just general gossip and talk, everyone could share in the community beliefs and experiences. Epitomizing this popular and shared dimension to religion were the mystery plays, short sketches based on biblical happenings, often presented in succession on movable carts by different guilds (tradesmen like the coopers), traditionally on the feast day of Corpus Christi (late May to early June). As a schoolboy, I had a (very minor) role in a revival of the York Mystery Plays (an unknown Judi Dench was the Virgin Mary), and still I remember vividly the beautiful and stirring language, the fall of Satan, the immensity of the crucifixion, the power and dread of the final judgment—and the humanity and humor of the saints and sinners, patriarchs and their wives, kings and commoners, disciples and traitors. The devil-as-serpent tempting Adam and Eve was seductive, scary, and very, very funny in his asides to the audience as he broke down their resistance.

Life was ordered by the church calendar: Advent, Christmas, Easter, Pentecost, and a host of other festivals, usually connected with the Virgin or the many, many saints. Frequently there were thinly veiled appropriations from pre-Christian festivals; one celebrated the end of the year and the beginning of the new, the coming of spring, the high points of summer, and most particularly, especially in rural areas, the end of the harvest and thanks for bounties given. Rogation days, taken almost directly from Roman pagan practices, involved processions around a parish, "beating the bounds," as people marked out their lands as separate from those of neighbors. The Virgin and the major saints, Peter and Paul particularly, were shared by all. Others were more connected with and venerated by localized groups of people. In England, the martyred Thomas à Becket (1118–1170) had a special place in people's hearts. Pilgrimages, as Chaucer described the one to Canterbury, had an important role, at least for those who could leave the land and afford the trip. Some saints were more generic, worth praying to for a medley of ills. Others were more specific. Saint Apollonia was burned alive after she had her teeth smashed in by a club. A little tweaking, and like Dorian Gray, she became once again young and beautiful, and a little more tweaking and her teeth were pulled out one by one. She was, therefore, very obviously the saint to whom one prayed when one had toothache.

Festivals were linked with practices and obligations. At certain times, Lent for instance, one was expected to abstain from flesh and perhaps even all animal products. Twenty-first-century philosophy graduate students did not invent the vegan diet, although one hopes back then it was not quite as awkward for hosts as it is now. Afterwards came times of dining and feasting. Often these were occasions when the fortunate and wealthy in society could show Christian charity by distributing alms to those less fortunate. Sunday, of course, was the time for the mass, and the sacredness of the ceremony was a focal point of the week, especially as the priest lifted the host to be adored and recognized as the body of the savior. Prayers were prescribed for the onlookers.

> Ihesu Lord, welcome thow be,
> In forme of bred as I the se;
> Ihesu! for thy holy name,
> Shelde me to day fro synne & schame. (Duffy 1992, 117)

For the laity, communion was usually a once-a-year phenomenon, at Easter. It had to be preceded by confession, and this led to a searching of the soul and—very important socially for binding the community—a recognition of one's sins. This was a time when one made peace with neighbors and tried to mend one's ways and made special efforts to reach out to those in need.

Birth, marriage, and, above all else, death, are the big events in a person's life. It was important to be welcomed into the church, and given the dangers of childbirth, special provisions were made so that laypeople could do the honors if need be. Marriage was the solemn commitment that it is today, although impossible to escape if things went wrong or one had made an unwise choice. This was remedied to a certain extent by the fact that survivors probably went through more than one relationship before the end. Widows having had three or four husbands were not unknown. Most important, there was death. This was, if anything, the most social event of one's whole existence, with much concern not to die alone and friendless and most particularly to have made amends with one's creator before leaving this earthly abode. People were terrified lest they leave without the last rites, and saints such as Catherine (c. 282–305), who were supposed to have the power to prevent such an awful happening, found that their good offices were much in demand. Interestingly, the English-language prayers (as opposed to those in Latin) tended to focus on the prevention of so dreadful an end.

Purgatory—the idea that, between death and entry into heaven, one needs to go through a period of suffering and purification—is an ancient idea. But it really came into its own in the medieval period. The detailed descriptions of what awaits one veer toward (actually pass right into) the sadistic. It is hard to see how being burned by red-hot coals makes one a better person. Fortunately, however, one was not entirely helpless in this matter. Prayers and other good deeds done in one's name, especially after death, could significantly reduce the days spent in agony. Thus legacy after legacy was directed toward such ends. One sees here with full clarity the social nature of religion. Death is a group phenomenon, now and even more in the future. The living have concern for and obligations toward the dead. In turn, the dead have made provisions for the living. Charitable bequests to the poor, donations to the church, payment for prayers—all of these make the departed as much a part of the community as the living.

Why Religion?

Once you start to lay out things in the raw, with the ceremonies and the eating and drinking and birthing and marrying and dying, you can see why so much has been written about the supposed naturalistic underpinnings of religion. A rich culture like this just cries out for interpretation and understanding. Indeed, from around 1850, religion was often both cause and effect of the growth of the social sciences. The great French sociologist Émile Durkheim (1857–1917), writing a hundred years ago, was more penetrating on the natural causes of religion than any thinker before or since. He saw the extent to which religion gives meaning to life, makes the hardships of existence not just possible but in important respects explicable. With religion—and this surely screams out from my brief description of late medieval Christianity—we have a culture binding people and helping people and giving hope to all. "A religion is a unified system of beliefs and practices relative to sacred things, i.e., things set apart and forbidden—beliefs and practices which unite in one single moral community called a Church, all those who adhere to them" (Émile Durkheim 1912, Book 1, Ch. 1). Durkheim wrote of the collective consciousness that binds society together in a functioning whole. This fits medieval Christianity exactly. Think of how we have just seen rich and poor connect through shared roles, expectations, and obligations in pre-Reformation Britain. Religion for these people was totally and utterly a unifying force and experience. Birth was a time of group celebration as the baby was shown around and through the church welcomed into the community. Marriage again, very much a group celebration (as it is still today), was ordered and blessed by religion. Death, as we saw so clearly and emphatically in the last section, was above all embedded in culture and tradition. Because of the church, its rituals, its demands, its customs, this most terrifying of human events could be accepted and handled. The fears were shared and ameliorated.

Durkheim was not alone in writing about religion. Marx told us that religion is the "opiate of the people," Frazer examined shared myths across cultures in an effort to understand our religion, and Freud declared that God is a father figure, an illusion invented to help us curtail our animal passions. Much that has been written is highly controversial and today finds little favor. Perhaps the most famous, or notorious, of all the naturalistic claims about religion was that of the sociologist Max Weber (1864–1920), who argued that the rise of Protestantism and the rise of modern capitalism are inextricably linked—that the changes in society after the period we have just been looking at were all part of a single pattern, as people tried to show their devotion to God by accumulating capital rather than simply spreading the bounty through society. Even today, a hundred years after he advanced this thesis, scholars argue about its truth. Yet even when one questions some of the more striking claims about the natural causes of religion—Freud, for instance, suggesting that Moses was an Egyptian who brought monotheism to the Jews, for which he was killed, and his role and beliefs long suppressed—one encounters many penetrating insights. Our story of late medieval England starts to fall into place. For example, Weber stressed the significance of immediate personal deities or people with special access to the deities. One of the most striking things about the medieval picture we have been sketching is the extent to which the common people ignored or found irrelevant the rather ethereal, distant God articulated by the great philosophers like Anselm and Aquinas and substituted the Virgin and the familiar friendly saints, personal beings with whom they could have direct social intercourse. Psychologically and sociologically, there is something wrong with the philosopher's God, for all the fancy arguments otherwise. (We shall meet this feeling again in our own time.)

Nothing stands still. Recent work by American sociologists has questioned the kinds of explanations offered by Durkheim and his successors. It is one thing to explain a society where one and only one religion prevails, as in England and Wales before Henry VIII. It is another to explain societies with multiple religions, as is the case in the United States. Perhaps not surprisingly, economic models seeing rival sects as competing for customers in the marketplace have found much favor (Stark and Bainbridge 1996). Following such developments, however, would sidetrack us. Keeping our focus, let us turn to suggestions made by today's atheists (including the New Atheists) who have argued that religion can be explained—generally explained away—naturalistically. For reasons that are perhaps as much historical as conceptual, we shall see that evolutionary biology plays a large role in such discussions.

Does Religion Start with Mistaken Perceptions?

The classic naturalistic account of religion's origins—one that appears again and again in one guise or another—is that of David Hume in his *Natural History of Religion*: "We find human faces in the moon, armies in the clouds; and by a natural propensity, if not corrected by experience and reflection, ascribe malice or good-will to everything, that hurts or pleases us" (Hume 1963, 78). In other words, religion begins in mistaken identification of the inanimate with the living. From there, presumably, it is all uphill (or downhill, as the fancy may take you) to a full-blown religious system. This kind of thinking was picked up a hundred years later by Charles Darwin in the *Descent of Man*. By this stage of his life (the *Descent* appeared in 1871 when Darwin was sixty-two), Darwin had slid into a fairly easy agnosticism, and it is surely significant that, although he devoted considerable time to the origins and nature of morality, he dealt with religion almost briskly. He wasn't scared to talk about it; it was just that as a late Victorian he was getting a bit bored in talking about it. Borrowing heavily from Hume (Darwin first read *Natural History* in the late 1830s), he thought it was all a matter of chance and confusion, thinking that the "tendency in savages to imagine that natural objects and agencies are animated by spiritual or living essences" was illustrated by the mistaken actions of his dog (a beast, Darwin tells us, who is "a full-grown and very sensible animal"). Snoozing on the lawn, the dog was upset by a parasol moving in the wind. Going on the attack "every time that the parasol slightly moved, the dog growled fiercely and barked. He must, I think, have reasoned to himself in a rapid and unconscious manner,

that movement without any apparent cause indicated the presence of some strange living agent, and that no stranger had a
right to be on his territory" (Darwin 1871, 1: 67).

More recently, anthropologist Scott Atran has proposed
a similar kind of byproduct explanation of religion, thinking that it is all bound up with our mechanisms for detect-
ing danger and showing fear. "Natural selection designs the
agency-detection system to deal rapidly and economically
with stimulus situations involving people and animals as
wired to respond to fragmentary information under conditions of uncertainty, inciting perception of figures in the
clouds, voices in the wind, lurking movements in the leaves,
and emotions among interacting dots on a computer screen."
He thinks that this kind of adaptation can all too easily go
astray. "This hair-triggering of the agency-detection mechanism readily lends itself to supernatural interpretation of
uncertain or anxiety-provoking events" (Atran 2004, 78).

Why Does Religion Persist?

Agree that religion may have started life with no direct biological function. This in itself does not make religion false. As it
happens, although by the time Hume and Darwin were writing on the subject neither had any religious beliefs that were
particularly pressing, both stressed that their arguments did
not and could not disprove religion as such. Today we have
Christian anthropologist-psychologist Justin Barrett, who
combines a deep faith commitment with a scientific position
much like that sketched in the last section. He argues that religion comes very much in a Humean fashion from the over-
activity of what he calls "agency detection devices" (ADDs).
"Our ADD suffers from some hyperactivity, making it prone
to find agents around us, including supernatural ones, given
fairly modest evidence of their presence. This tendency encour-
ages the generation and spread of god concepts and other religious concepts" (Barrett 2004, 31). Faces in the moon, armies

in the clouds. Eventually, all of this gets blown up into a fully functioning religion. And it could all be simply God's way of getting religion naturalistically. "Suppose science produces a convincing account for why I think my wife loves me—should I then stop believing that she does?"

One thing we can say with some confidence is that if religion did start as a byproduct, this does not mean that it stayed that way. Indeed, if it had no function or even a slight negative function, it would be unlikely to persist for long. Very well known in evolutionary biology is the move to a positive function for which a feature was not originally designed—what have been called *exaptations* (Gould and Vrba 1982). Vertebrates did not first grow four legs because that is the most stable land configuration. They began life in the sea, and two limbs fore and two limbs aft was the best way of moving up and down in the water. Only later did the fourness of the limbs become adaptive on land. Likewise, whatever the function or not of religion as it began, it could be picked up quickly by natural selection and turned to other uses. And if Durkheim and the other social scientists who think his way are even half right, the use is obviously some kind of group cohesion, where people benefit from being part of a society and not individuals alone. To quote Franklin on the signing of the Declaration of Independence: "We must all hang together, or assuredly we shall all hang separately." Does this kind of thinking lend itself to an evolutionary interpretation? Many would think not. Surely the struggle for existence means that Hobbes was right; everyone is turned against everyone else. But from Darwin on, as was noted earlier, it has been realized that this is a simplistic understanding of the workings of natural selection. Often cooperation, what biologists call *altruism*, is a highly effective adaptive strategy, simply because the benefits of working together outweigh the costs (Ruse 2006).

Harvard-based Edward O. Wilson (b. 1929), evolutionary biologist and nonbeliever, has been prominent among those who emphasize that altruism is widespread through the animal world, that it is distinctively characteristic of humans, and that religious belief and practice is at the heart of all of this. He thinks (in major respects echoing Durkheim) religion is adaptive because of its power to confer group membership. "In the midst of the chaotic and potentially disorienting experiences each person undergoes daily, religion classifies him, provides him with unquestioned membership in a group claiming great powers, and by this means gives him a driving purpose in life compatible with his self interest" (Wilson 1978, 188). Wilson does admit that there may be something to cultural causes, but (and here he goes beyond Durkheim) essentially he thinks that it all comes back to biology. "Because religious practices are remote from the genes during the development of individual human beings, they may vary widely during cultural development. It is even possible for groups, such as the Shakers, to adopt conventions that reduce genetic fitness for as long as one or a few generations. But over many generations, the underlying genes will pay for their permissiveness by declining in the population as a whole" (178). Culture can play variations on the themes, but ultimately these themes are biological.

Without judging too severely the particular causal input of biology over culture, we can grant Wilson his empirical case. Had the medieval British had modern science and technology, perhaps they would not have needed their religion. But they didn't have it, and one does suspect strongly that if they simply lived existences bereft of meaning, just going about their duties day in and day out, they would have functioned a lot less efficiently than they did in real life. And this is quite apart from the meaning to their lives. (A matter we shall take up in more detail in the final chapter.) What is fascinating and suggestive is how much of the religion revolved around precisely the sorts of things that evolutionary biologists think important. Marriage is an important part of the Christian life, the commitment to the other and the expectation of family. (There were lots of saints who were specifically into the fertility business.) Notice that there was no theological nonsense about multiple marriages down here leading unacceptably to multiple spouses in the hereafter. A man with children whose wife has just died in childbirth needed a new mate, not the consolations of the promised hereafter, and the same goes for a woman whose husband has fallen from a tree and broken his neck. The Christmas story cherishes the arrival of a new member into the group: "Make we joy now in this feast. In quo Christus natus est: E-ya!" And don't forget the loving parents. For all that God pushed him aside when it came to impregnating Mary, Joseph has a major part in the story, caring for his wife and child, stressing the importance of the father in the family. Is it too outlandish to suggest that in an age when, because of short life spans, social relationships and obligations often took over from biological relationships and obligations, Joseph was an exemplary role model?

As noted before, confession was usually once a year (then one could take communion), a time to examine one's conscience and to forge or remake relations with family, friends, and neighbors. People who get on with each other, prepared to give a hand when needed, function far better than those alone and distrusting, hating and hated. For the more literate, there were guidebooks on how to take stock of one's life and behavior, with hints for improvement. Rogation days and beating the boundaries mean that parishioners know what is theirs and what is the property of others. The biological meanings of various temporal rituals and beliefs—notably the resurrection of the savior, identified with that epitome of spring, the lamb, and then the subsequent harvest festivals— are almost too obvious to be worth mentioning. Remembering the Sabbath and keeping it holy means that one has a break from the tedium and labor of daily life, a time to refresh and renew, enjoy family life, relate to friends and neighbors. The same is true of the various religion-mandated holidays. Food choices and taboos have long fascinated students of human culture, biological or not. At a general level, they are easy to understand. You need to learn early and quickly what is suitable and what is not, what can be used readily at almost any time and what needs cherishing and careful harvesting.

Note the way that our medieval folk focused on proper eating; for instance, Lent taught them self-control and moderation—quite apart from coming at a time of year when supplies are low and conservation a priority—and on feast days, food could be shared, and the rich and successful could show charity to those in need. It is so much easier to have a structured society when people accept their roles, and while have-nots are always going to bear resentment toward those who have, matters are much improved if there is a sense that even the most successful are mindful of everyone.

A happy picture. Still, one is yet haunted by Gould's criticism of all such biological approaches to culture (Gould and Lewontin 1979). Are we not simply making up plausible accounts to fit the facts? Gould reminded us of the *Just So Stories* of Rudyard Kipling—fantastic tales (the elephant got its long nose because the crocodile seized it and pulled) that truly have no connection to reality. I don't think that as a general criticism this is well taken. It is hard to imagine that incest taboos are not in some way a function of the horrendous effects of close inbreeding. One can perhaps plausibly think that tales of St. Apollonia in predentistry times had a function, even if it was only the placebo effect. But Gould's critique still has bite. What about purgatory, an idea that had so large a grip on the medieval imagination? With the coming of the Reformation, purgatory was swept away as without biblical warrant. A hundred and fifty years later, the descendants of our good Catholic population happily flourished, believing that it was straight from this life to the next. Did purgatory therefore have no adaptive significance, and if not for something so major, what price the rest of the religious culture? There is surely something to our naturalistic explanations of religion. The unanswered question is how great is this something?

Does Evolution Show Religion False?

Truly pertinent to our discussion is what this all means with respect to the truth content of religion. Having given an adaptive explanation of religion in evolutionary terms, does this now mean we can dismiss religion as false? Is religion, as was suggested might be the case for morality, no more than the collective illusion of the genes to keep us reproducing efficiently? Wilson has pursued this line of thinking, arguing that now traditional religion can be seen as dispensable. He thinks that humans are by nature religious and that we must have a religion. But with evolution having shown traditional religion false, we must turn now to new alternatives. "But make no mistake about the power of scientific materialism. It presents the human mind with an alternative mythology that until now has always, point for point in zones of conflict, defeated traditional religion." We must now have a kind of secular religion, based on evolution. "Its narrative form is the epic: the evolution of the universe from the big bang of fifteen billion years ago through the origin of the elements and celestial bodies to the beginnings of life on earth" (Wilson 1978, 192). He concludes: "Theology is not likely to survive as an independent intellectual discipline."

One can only respond that although traditional religion may be false, although we may be on the way to replacing it with an evolutionary alternative, and although theology may not survive, Wilson has certainly not shown any of these things to be true. Even though interestingly Durkheim would in principle have agreed with Wilson, historically, we should be wary of tales of science just pushing religion aside. Durkheim's ancillary thesis about religion (indebted to August Comte's threefold analysis of progress—from the religious to the metaphysical, from the metaphysical to the positive) was that as society develops, it becomes more secular, and religion falls out. Perhaps this is true, and we do certainly find this kind of casting off of religion a significant feature of the modern world, but, as it happens, the example of pre-Reformation Christianity shows that things have to be more complex than simply a trip from dark to light. The reason the medieval system sketched earlier came to an end had little or nothing to do with the Scientific Revolution. In part, its demise was certainly a function of the Protestant Reformation, for instance, in the decline and fall of beliefs about purgatory, which people like Luther condemned as without biblical warrant and also disliked because of the power (and cost in the form of indulgences) that the belief gave the church over common people. The main reason for its fall, however, was political. Henry VIII (1491–1547) wanted a male heir, his Catholic wife Catherine of Aragon (1485–1536) gave him only a daughter, she who was to earn the epithet Bloody Mary, and so he wanted a divorce. When the pope, in the thrall of the Spanish monarchy (Catherine's family) refused, Henry simply took his country and went home. Less metaphorically, he let loose Thomas Cromwell (1485–1540), and the old religion was swept away in favor of the new, autonomous English religion.

So it wasn't just a matter of science pulverizing all before it. History shows that internal issues of theology and external issues of politics can count for much. Philosophically, one might also doubt Wilson's claim about the inevitable triumph of evolutionary materialism. Go back for a moment to morality, an absolutely fundamental part of medieval Christianity. You ought to cherish your children. You ought to be faithful to your spouse. You ought to care about those less fortunate than you. You ought to say prayers for the dead. An earlier chapter argued that from a naturalistic perspective, the objectivity of morality may be an illusion, and there is ontologically nothing but the genes doing their thing. But even if we assume that this argument is well taken and that it scotches the argument for God's existence from the fact of morality, none of this prevents the believer (who presumably believes on other grounds) from interpreting it all from a Christian perspective (Ruse 2010). It is one thing to say that morality does not necessarily have to have God's backing; it is another thing to say that morality could not have God's backing. One simply argues that this is how God gets us to be moral, through the genes rather than (as may be the case with mathematics) through reading some script on the Platonic wall. In fact, traditional Catholic teaching about morality—natural law theory, going back to Aquinas, who in turn went back to Aristotle—is that morality doesn't exist out there independently, but is a matter of doing what is natural, where what is natural is dictated by the way things are. A mother suckling her hungry baby is a good thing because that is the way the human body is designed. Quarreling with your neighbors is a bad thing because it disturbs the functioning of society, and everyone (including the malcontent) suffers. If you want a theological reading of morality—and you may or may not—then this natural law position perfectly complements the Darwin explanation. (No big surprise really, given that Aristotle was a biologist before he turned philosopher.) Likewise in the case of religion. That it exists because it is adaptively useful suggests in some sense that it is natural, and while religion may not be true, there is nothing to stop the religious from arguing on other grounds that it is.

But What if Religion Is a Bad Thing?

Something like purgatory suggests that, even if one sees religion as generally biologically adaptive, matters could backfire and religion work against biological interest. In the extreme case, we saw how Wilson takes note of the Shakers, whose prohibition on sexual activity has led to their extinction. One might tack all the way and argue that, far from having a positive cultural or biological value, religion is dangerous and exists because in some sense it manages to pervert the proper order of things. Perhaps our medieval peasants were taking too many holidays from their labors. They took forty to fifty feast days, a matter of some tension with employers, and something the Reformers clamped down on—they were particularly keen to keep things moving through the prime agricultural months of summer—causing significant if understandable resentment (Duffy 1992, 40). Student of culture Pascal Boyer thinks this is the norm, rather than the exception;

religion in some way subverts features and habits that in their own rights are perfectly adaptive and functioning. "The building of religious concepts requires mental systems and capacities that are there anyway, religious concepts or not. Religious morality uses moral intuitions, religious notions of supernatural agents recruit our intuitions about agency in general, and so on. This is why I said that religious concepts are parasitic upon other mental capacities" (Boyer 2002, 311).

Writing in much the same vein, we have the New Atheists. Dawkins, as a biologist, is particularly sensitive to this issue. His explanation goes as follows: "When a child is young, for good Darwinian reasons, it would be valuable if the child believed everything it's told. A child needs to learn a language, it needs to learn the social customs of its people, it needs to learn all sorts of rules—like don't put your finger in the fire, and don't pick up snakes, and don't eat red berries. There are lots of things that for good survival reasons a child needs to learn" (Dawkins 1997). So natural selection steps right up to the plate. "Be fantastically gullible; believe everything you're told by your elders and betters." Which, of course, is fine much of the time but open to invasion by parasites with their own interests in mind. It is the same sort of thing that happens with computers. Viruses invade with their own agendas, not necessarily in the interests of the hosts. Unfortunately, religion is right up there with the worst of the invaders. Humans are wide open to such silly ideas as: " 'You must believe in the great juju in the sky,' or 'You must kneel down and face east and pray five times a day.' These codes are then passed down through generations. And there's no obvious reason why it should stop." Even worse is the fact that those viruses that are really good at their job are precisely those with the most awful and dangerous messages. "So, if the virus says, 'If you don't believe in this you will go to hell when you die,' that's a pretty potent threat, especially to a child."

Dawkins is offering a somewhat scaled-down version of what is perhaps today's most sophisticated theory of gene-culture coevolution. Peter Richerson (b.1943) and Robert Boyd (1948) argue that biology informs and directs culture with two innate rules: follow the norms and practices of your society ("When in Rome, do what the Romans do") and, if in doubt, do what the leaders and the influential do: "Determining *who* is a success is much easier than to determine *how* to be a success. By imitating the successful, you have a chance of acquiring the behaviors that cause success, even if you do not know anything about which characteristics of the successful are responsible for their success" (Richerson and Boyd 2005, 124). All of this certainly seems to fit nicely with our picture of pre-Reformation England. Your mum and dad went to confession once a year; you should go to confession once a year. The squire or the wealthy wool merchant gives freely at feast time; you should treat your cowman or milkmaid with the same kind of thoughtfulness. Notice, however, that none of this implies that religion is necessarily false or dangerous. Of course, it could be. Do the bread and wine really turn into the body and blood of Christ? Let us grant at least that the truth status of this belief is up for grabs. And yet you believe in it because everyone else does. And sometimes beliefs could be really unsound. One doubts that forking over large sums to the church to avoid time in purgatory really served anyone but the beneficiaries. But all of this is surely to do with the truth content of the claims and not with natural reasons for holding the claims. The same sorts of reasons could be applied to beliefs our medieval people would have had that we surely think true, for instance, that parents have obligations to their children, and you ought to try to work things out with your neighbors. Dawkins has biased the discussion by slipping in the weasel word *gullible*. Yet, although we are all gullible sometimes, learning from others is not necessarily being gullible. As was the case for Edward O. Wilson's explanatory suggestions, whether religion is true or false, even a more developed theory of gene-culture coevolution does not give a definitive answer.

What about Memetics?

Philosopher Daniel Dennett also pursues a negative line of thinking. He invokes the notion of a meme, an invention of Richard Dawkins (1976) intended to represent a heritable unit of culture analogous to the gene, a heritable unit of biology. Based on an understanding of religion that is (at the most charitable) sketchy, Dennett's conclusion is that religion is a meme of a rather unpleasant kind. With Boyer and Dawkins, he thinks it is a parasite, a virus on humans, just as much as the liver fluke is a parasite on sheep. "You watch an ant in a meadow, laboriously climbing up a blade of grass, higher and higher until it falls, then climbs again, and again, like Sisyphus rolling his rock, always striving to reach the top." Why does this happen? The ant gets nothing out of all of this activity. "Its brain has been commandeered by a tiny parasite, a lancet fluke (*Dicrocelium dendriticum*), that needs to get itself into the stomach of a sheep or cattle in order to complete its reproductive cycle. This little brain worm is driving the ant into position to benefit *its* progeny, not the ant's" (Dennett 2006, 3–4). Religion likewise serves its own ends without regard for the well-being of the host in which it resides. It leads Muslims, Christians, and Jews to devote "their lives to spreading the Word, making huge sacrifices, suffering bravely, risking their lives for an idea" (Dennett 2006, 4). Huge sacrifices perhaps, but as earlier with the implication that the sacrifices are for naught. For all that it is false—perhaps because it is false—religion can and does do immense harm, and the naturalistic explanations show why.

Unfortunately, even sympathizers wonder if meme talk is anything but common sense wrapped up in fancy language (Ruse 2009). Memetics seems not to have led to new and surprising predictions, the sine qua non of good new theories. Moreover, Dennett is playing the same trick as Dawkins, sliding in negative implications under the cover of supposed objective discussion. Talking of parasites and viruses is using what we in the philosophical trade call "persuasive definitions." We have analogy and not the literal truth. In any case, who said that all viruses are bad? Viruses (bacteriophages) that attack harmful bacteria have their virtues. This is not to say that religions are like bacteriophages, but it is not to rule this out either. To be fair to Dennett (and to Dawkins), approaches like theirs are suggestive about how religions can get into flights of fancy and at times prove positively dangerous, to practitioners and to others. But because an idea is transmitted as a meme, it does not follow that all religion is false. It may be false. Let us grant that this is true of purgatory. It may be true. Love your children. Or it may almost certainly be false but have good consequences. Pray to St. Apollonia because you have tooth-ache. The placebo effect (of which, of course, you are unaware) may make you feel better.

What Should We Conclude?

Given the ease with which religion can be made to fit the vari-ous naturalistic explanatory theories, one is reminded of a warning from Karl Popper (1963). A theory that can explain everything explains nothing. In like manner, one hears still the voice of Gould from beyond the grave. With reason, most people will be a little wary of these naturalistic expla-nations, the negative ones as much as the positive ones. Like the religions they purport to explain, there are so many that one suspects that many, if not most, must be off the mark in some respect. One cries out for quantitative predictions and attempts to test them. Perhaps the right conclusion is the fol-lowing. There is surely enough now to the naturalistic expla-nations to religion to think that there must be some adequate explanations, whether we are close to finding them or still far away. The nonbeliever need have no fears here. There is no rea-son to think that one must invoke a supernatural explanation. However, there is breathing room for the believer. Perhaps religion is a byproduct, perhaps not. Perhaps religion is func-tional, perhaps not. Or more likely it is a bit of everything. But that is the nature of the world in which we live. The bottom line is that there is nothing in naturalistic explanations of religion per se that suggests all religion is false or that it must necessarily be false, and there is nothing inherent in the more plausible explanations that we now have to change this conclusion. In short, naturalistic explanations give comfort to the nonbeliever, but whether they refute the believer is another question.

11

IS RELIGION EVIL?

Why Aren't We Finished?

We have gone through the history. We have dug through the facts and figures. We have looked at the arguments for and against. We have peered into the naturalistic reasons for belief. Why aren't we finished? The simple and true answer was given in our opening pages. Atheism, for or against, has never been just a matter of the facts. There have always been the moral issues, personal issues, the social issues. In the last chapter, we touched briefly on the possibility that religion is something bad. Remember, Richard Dawkins doesn't just think that religion is false. He thinks that bringing a kid up Catholic is a form of child abuse. Sam Harris thinks that Islam is responsible for 9/11. And everyone endorses Steven Weinberg. Say it yet again: "Good people will do good things, and bad people will do bad things. But for good people to do bad things—that takes religion." Don't be scared of the bullies. Martin Luther scotched purgatory. Would that he had done the same for the rest of the false, frightening nonsense. No God is going to descend on you. "There probably is no god, so stop worrying and get on with your life."

Well, let's start off with the question of whether religion is morally pernicious. In the next and final chapter, I will reverse the tables and ask whether a life without religion can be fulfilling, morally and in any other way.

Is Religion Evil?

You can certainly make a pretty good case for this. As a child in England, for a couple of years I went to Queen Mary's Grammar School in a town in the British Midlands (Walsall). We were very proud of our school, for uniquely it was founded in 1554, during the short reign (1553–1558) of the queen of that name. This has filled me with a lifelong sneaking regard for Queen Mary. There is very good reason for me to keep my regard sneaking, for she worked hard to merit her sobriquet of Bloody Mary. Remember, Mary was the oldest child of King Henry VIII, his daughter by Catherine of Aragon. After Anne Boleyn (1501–1536), who gave birth to Elizabeth (1533–1603), finally with his third wife, Jane Seymour (1508–1537), Henry produced a male heir, the fiercely Protestant Edward VI (1537–1553). When Edward died while still a teenager, the Protestant faction at court put Lady Jane Grey (1537–1554) on the throne, but the people would have none of this, and within nine days the Catholic Mary was queen. Jane's days were numbered, although whether her execution was because of her usurping the throne or because she was Protestant remains a nice point. No such nicety was needed for Thomas Cranmer (1489–1556), archbishop of Canterbury; Nicholas Ridley (1500–1555), bishop of London; and Hugh Latimer (1487–1555), bishop of Worcester. They went to the stake because of their Protestantism. As did another three hundred of Mary's subjects. It makes for gruesome reading as one brave person after another—many of them very ordinary people: clerks, cobblers, hatters—died for their faith. What is striking is how many of those who went to their deaths were women.

And in the end, it was all so pointless (MacCulloch 2004). Mary died, probably of stomach cancer, in 1558, and her Protestant half-sister Elizabeth was queen of England. She in her turn set about showing that Protestants were pretty good at putting down Catholics. There was a brisk trade in disemboweling, hanging, and quartering her subjects, especially those who made the mistake of going abroad to be ordained into the Catholic priesthood and then returned home to practice. English men and women being put to death in the most horrible ways, because they differed on such things as whether Jesus was actually present in a piece of bread, and if he was what that meant and if he wasn't what that meant.

If anything, so much of the gruesome killing backfired—or perhaps rather went on doing harm long after it was all over. Cranmer was pressured into renouncing his faith, but then at the last moment declared for Protestantism, famously thrusting his right arm into the flames as punishment for having been the vehicle of his signed recantation. Latimer turned to Ridley as the flames licked their feet: "Be of good comfort, and play the man, Master Ridley; we shall this day light such a candle, by God's grace, in England, as I trust shall never be put out." I learned these words in primary school in England in the late 1940s, and it was undoubtedly a factor in the underlying sense of anti-Catholicism that still marked that society. Four hundred years of prejudice by people who claimed to worship the same God as those they belittled. Not that the Catholics would have been much better. In the past two centuries, there has been a lot of beatification and subsequent canonization by popes of their martyrs, as English Catholics have started to assert their places in society. If you know just how high the English regard for Good Queen Bess is, if you know the joy with which every November 5 the English light bonfires and burn the effigy of Guy Fawkes, a Catholic who tried to blow up the English House of Parliament, then you know how provocative an action this is.

I am writing of just a few that stick in the memory because we know so much and they proved so important historically. If you are talking about the Reformation and its aftermath as a whole, then the English Civil War in the seventeenth century took at least 100,000 lives, perhaps twice that number. The Peasants' Revolt in Germany (1524–1525) took at least 100,000 lives and perhaps three times as many. And the Thirty Years' War (1618–1648) on the Continent killed from 3 or 4 million to at least 10 million. No one would say that these conflicts were purely religious. In England, a lot of the tension was over who would rule the country, king or parliament. But anyone who thinks that Calvinism had no causal role in the actions of Oliver Cromwell and the Roundheads or that other forms of Protestantism did not factor into the actions of Charles I and the Cavaliers had better return to the history books.

Was the Modern Era Worse?

You might say that awful as these conflicts were, they pale in comparison to conflicts like the First and Second World Wars, conflicts that were not ostensibly religious at all. There is some truth in this. The death total in the First World War was about 10 million military deaths (Hart 2013). The first day of the Battle of the Somme (July 1, 1916) saw twenty thousand Britons lying dead on the fields of France and another forty thousand wounded. Brought low by enemy gas, my grandfather coughed his lungs out for twenty-five years, dying a few days before I was born (in June 1940). Two months later, sitting on a box outside our shattered home in a suburb of Birmingham, my mother held me in her arms, as my father dashed home to see if we had survived the German bombing attack. In the Second World War, there were about 20 million military deaths and more than that number of civilian deaths (Beevor 2012). Terrible numbers, although I am not quite sure why this is taken to let religion off the hook. In any case, it is not as if religion comes out pure and uncontaminated from these events. We all know about the padres on both sides in the Great War earnestly praying to God to bring down death and destruction on the enemies. "Gott strafe England." (A slogan incidentally from a German Jew, something that even then did not entirely endear him to his fellow religionists.) The Second World War is no better, perhaps in respects far worse, although more complex. Two thousand years of anti-Semitism by the Catholic Church and four hundred years by Protestants had to have an effect and be a causal factor in the persecution and killing of the Jews. The Goldhagen thesis so beloved of Sam Harris has to have some truth. However, Germany of all places was the country that in the nineteenth century had made greatest strides with Jewish emancipation (Evans 2003). On the verge of the First World War, there were thirty-five mixed marriages for every hundred purely Jewish marriages, so obviously the separation and hatred was not universal. Far more at fault causally was the intense anti-Jewish indoctrination in the years of the Third Reich of young people—at school, in the media, and above all in the Hitler Youth (*Hitler-Jugend*) and the girls' equivalent, the Band of German Maidens (*Bund Deutscher Mädel*). As one of the major historians of the era (Richard Evans) has said, by the early 1940s, when it came to "lesser" races, young Germans were no longer "ordinary men," to use the term used by one recent historian trying to understand the awful events of the Second World War (Browning 1998). To this day, my aged German stepmother, the child of people who loathed Hitler and all he stood for, wrestles with this dreadful legacy. The monsters of manipulation left their marks on the young and vulnerable.

In the Second World War, some of the churches, the branch of the Protestant Evangelische Kirche known as the German Christians, went along with and indeed encouraged the Nazis. Others, the branch of the Evangelische Kirche known as the Confessing Church, were as much as possible a major voice of opposition. Karl Barth, although Swiss, was the primary author of the Barmen Declaration, the church's statement of dissent from the Nazi state. The Catholic Church's response, although there was no formal split, was likewise mixed. A major factor was that Eugenio Pacelli (1876–1958), first papal nuncio to Germany, then cardinal secretary of state, and finally (1939) Pope Pius XII, was always first and foremost a diplomat. Given the rise of the Nazis, he was intent on keeping as much of the church structure and organization (and power) in place in Germany as he could. To be candid, this met with but mixed success, but the downside was a failure to come out bluntly in moral condemnation of the regime. The church protested bravely at the Nazi program of selective elimination of the physically and mentally handicapped, but other than for converts did little or nothing to help the Jews. Overall, not a sterling record.

Are things any better today? The New Atheists protest that they are not. Christians may not be killing each other in the name of their Lord in the numbers of yesterday—although remember Northern Ireland—but as a function of their religion, they are still responsible for huge amounts of harm, either because of the beliefs or because of the social structure. Above all, there is the Catholic Church and the problem of sexual abuse of the young. It is hard to know where to start. In America, the first trickle was when a priest in Louisiana in 1985 pled guilty to eleven counts of sexual molestation. By the 1990s, the trickle had become a torrent. The dam had broken. One authoritative survey found that in the second half of the twentieth century, about 4,500 priests—4% of the active priesthood—were the subject of 11,000 allegations (John Jay Report 2004). Eighty percent of the victims were male, about 25% of the victims were ten or younger, and another 50% were under fifteen. Surely significant, pointing to the life of a supposed celibate as a causal factor, is that fewer than 10% of the offending priests had histories of being sexually abused. These were not men who entered the priesthood emotionally crippled, whatever the effects on them later. Certainly, a lot of the cases were basically fondling (often to climax), but let there be no mistake: many of the sexual acts involved oral and anal penetration. Men of God sodomizing ten-year-olds.

Other countries have equally sordid tales to tell. What compounds the great wickedness of people in power and

authority, claiming to speak for a savior who died in agony
on the cross, is the unbelievable behavior of the church hier-
archies. Again and again, the tale is of actions covered up, of
police uninformed or pressured, of priests moved to new loca-
tions where their behavior started all over again, of denials in
the face of evidence, and above all of a determination not to
give way financially or in any other way until extreme legal
pressure forced otherwise. The response of Bernard Cardinal
Law of Boston beggars belief. One abusive priest after another
was moved around, always one step ahead of the authorities.
And when he was finally caught out and forced to resign, Pope
John Paul II gave him a post in Rome. As a cardinal, he par-
ticipated in the election of Benedict in 2005. More recently, he
is reported as one of those pushing most strongly for punitive
action against activist American nuns.

Is There Nothing to Be Said for Religion?

And yet, of course, there is the other side to the story. The tales
of love and compassion, of giving and of sacrifice, of suffering even unto death, all done genuinely by Christians in the
name of their Lord. Since we started the downside in England,
let us return there for the upside. The earliest antislavery pro-
tests started in the New World in the late seventeenth century.
Soon they spread to England, and like many of the American
protesters, the earliest antislavery campaigners were members
of the Religious Society of Friends, Quakers. The first formal
movement was the Society for Effecting the Abolition of the
Slave Trade, founded in London in 1787. Nine of the twelve
founding members were Quakers, the others Anglicans. As
is well known, certainly to every schoolchild in Britain, par-
liamentary leadership was taken over by William Wilberforce
(1759–1833), a man who had undergone an extreme conversion to evangelical Christianity and whose whole life was
dedicated to what he thought was the directive of his faith.
A member of the British parliament, he began introducing

bills for the abolition of the slave trade, explicitly basing his actions on his Christian commitment. "Never, never will we desist till we have wiped away this scandal from the Christian name, released ourselves from the load of guilt, under which we at present labour, and extinguished every trace of this bloody traffic, of which our posterity, looking back to the history of these enlightened times, will scarce believe that it has been suffered to exist so long a disgrace and dishonour to this country" (Speech before the House of Commons, April 18, 1791, in Clarkson 2010, 448). It took forty years for slavery to be abolished through the British Empire, and final success was only achieved days after the death of Wilberforce. But without the efforts of these deeply committed Christians, the abolition of slavery in the empire would not have occurred as soon (Hochschild 2006).

Wilberforce and his fellow campaigners—who included the Wedgwood family of pottery fame (to which the mother and wife of Charles Darwin belonged)—could be dreadful prigs at times, as well as often showing a remarkable lack of interest in the well-being of their own native working population (Desmond and Moore 2009). Yet they were not alone in their Christian-driven urges to reform. Elizabeth Fry (1780–1845), another Quaker, labored incessantly for the betterment of the lives and well-being of women in prison. She also founded shelters for the homeless and started a training school for nurses (some of whom were to go to the Crimea with Florence Nightingale). Faced with criticism for her efforts as a woman—a role that stemmed naturally from the equality of the sexes in Quakerism—she found a formidable ally late in life in her new monarch, Victoria. The Seventh Earl of Shaftesbury (who so hated German theology) was a notable evangelical and social reformer, one who started by working for the reformation of how the mentally disabled were treated and then went on to play a major role in the improvement of the conditions of workers, especially children, in factories and related occupations. The Mines and Colliers Act of 1842 finally banned women and children from going down the mines, and boys under ten years old were also barred. It took another thirty years before Shaftesbury was able to ensure the elimination of boy chimney sweeps (like Tom in Charles Kingsley's *Water Babies*), a particularly vile occupation, dangerous in itself—a popular way of getting the wretches to move on was to light a fire under them—and with horrible effects later in life, notably scrotal cancer.

Do we find parallels, stories of light and goodness in the other areas I showed the dark and evil side to religion? Of course we do. The story of Pastor Martin Niemöller (1892–1984) is well known (Evans 2005). A First World War hero, he was a sailor in the U-boats, and he followed his father in becoming a Lutheran pastor. From a conservative background, initially he welcomed the rise of the Nazis, but soon he fell afoul of them over the Aryan policies, becoming one of the founders of the Confessing Church. For his outspoken opposition, he spent much of the Third Reich in concentration camps, Sachsenhausen and Dachau. He is best known for his famous statement that he and his fellows had stood aside and let the forces of evil have their way—they came for the communists, the trade unionists, the Jews, the Jehovah's Witnesses, the incurables—and then? "Then they came for me, and there was no one left to speak for me." Pastor Dietrich Bonhöffer (1906–1945) is an even greater Christian hero. Another founding member of the Confessing Church, he returned from abroad to work alongside his fellow Christians. Imprisoned by the Nazis, he died strangled by piano wire for his involvement in plots against Hitler. Always driven forward by his faith, Bonhöffer explicitly saw the imitation of Christ here on earth as our first, foremost, and indeed only obligation. Deeply influenced by the Pietism movement in German thought and tradition, he argued that only by engaging as Christians within the world can we show our true allegiance to our savior. Among those greatly influenced by Bonhöffer was Martin Luther King, Jr. And finally, if you want a third person—or group—there is the story almost too painful to recount of Sophie Scholl (1921–1943) and the White Rose group (Newborn and Dumbach 2007). A small band of Christians—Sophie was Lutheran but much moved by Catholic writing and preaching—they distributed antiwar pamphlets at the University of Munich in 1942 and 1943. Inevitably, they were discovered, condemned to death, and executed. As she walked to the guillotine, her last words were: "How can we expect righteousness to prevail when there is hardly anyone willing to give himself up individually to a righteous cause. Such a fine, sunny day, and I have to go, but what does my death matter, if through us, thousands of people are awakened and stirred to action?" (Hanser 1979).

And so to the Catholic Church. Does one talk of Vincent de Paul (1581–1660), who founded charities, who built hospitals, who ransomed galley slaves from the Arabs? Does one mention the great teaching orders, most notably the Jesuits, who founded no less than twenty-eight universities and colleges in America, including Fordham, Georgetown, and Gonzaga? Do not forget Dorothy Day (1897–1980), devout Catholic convert, who served the poor and homeless during the Depression. Or does one speak of Maximillian Kolbe (1894–1941), the Franciscan friar who calmly took the place of a condemned prisoner and died in Auschwitz? Take the Christian Brothers. An Irish congregation, they have spread across the world, founding schools in all of the many countries in which they find themselves. In Canada, rightly, for the abuses that they perpetrated at an orphanage in Newfoundland, they have a dreadful reputation. (All too typically, the archdiocese had been aware of what was happening and simply covered things up until they exploded into the public domain.) Put this against the story of a man I am proud to call my friend, Michael Matthews (b. 1946), who virtually single-handedly has reformed science education by bringing to bear the insights of the history and philosophy of science. He was raised by a single mother in Sydney, Australia, and when he was on the verge of adolescence, the headmaster of the local Christian Brothers school announced that (without cost) Michael would be enrolled as a pupil the next Monday. And he was, and his life was launched—through the dedication of men for whom the life of a Christian was reason enough. No doubt telling this story will embarrass Michael, but I do so to deflect interest in my own parallel story involving the kindness of members of the Religious Society of Friends. My education was paid for by Kit Kat bars, produced by the Quaker philanthropists, the Rowntree family.

Does the Good Outweigh the Bad?

Christians will not be surprised by any of this, the bad and the good. "I do not understand my own actions. For I do not do what I want, but I do the very thing I hate" (Romans 7: 15). We are made in the image of God, but we are deeply tainted by sin. But how are we to evaluate things? Does the good outweigh the bad, or is it the other way? Richard Dawkins will say that the bad far outweighs the good. Many Christians (not all) will say the good outweighs the bad. They will point out also that we are not just dealing with morality, but with culture generally, and this includes the arts. Could one imagine a world without the cathedral at Chartres, without a Raphael Madonna (or for that matter without a Grunewald Crucifixion), without the Bach Passions? Dawkins responds that there is no need of religion for any of this: "the *B Minor Mass*, the *Matthew Passion*, these happen to be on a religious theme, but they might as well not be. They're beautiful music on a great poetic theme, but we could still go on enjoying them without believing in any of that supernatural rubbish" (this was a series of talks and debates organized by the Science Network in association with the Crick-Jacobs Center at the Salk Institute, La Jolla, California, November 5–7, 2006). I confess that I am not entirely certain about this, although admittedly a purely secular and worthwhile culture is possible. My favorite opera is Mozart's *Cosi*

Fan Tutte, which is about as non-Christian and Enlightenment cynical as it is possible to imagine. I find *Parsifal* very tedious, and the quasi-Christian mysticism is a major part of what makes it so.

The simple fact is that one is asking an impossible and unanswerable question. What kind of calculus is one to use to weigh Bloody Mary killing three hundred Protestants against the sacrifice of Sophie Scholl in Munich in 1943? Somehow, a simple body count seems highly inappropriate. How does one measure those going to their death absolutely secure in their belief in the hereafter and of God's love and praise against someone who dies worried and scared and not completely sure, or at least was that way until the last moment—someone like Blanche in Poulenc's *Dialogues of the Carmelites*? For that matter, how do you measure the death of Sophie on the guillotine against the death of Jesus on the cross? Alvin Plantinga is convinced that the latter is overwhelmingly the greatest act of moral goodness ever. I am not so sure. New Atheists will argue that such calculations are irrelevant. As the example of one child suffering is argument enough against the existence of the Christian God, so the sexual abuse of one child is argument enough against the value of religion. The evils of religion are just too awful, and religion must be abandoned. This is the morally right thing to do. Others, not necessarily all Christians, will argue that evil things are going to happen whatever the state of society—think of what happened in the atheistic societies of Russia and China—and that perhaps on balance religion ameliorates this. The aim is not to eliminate religion but to improve it.

What about Islam?

Are we not missing the elephant in the room? The focus in this book is the Christian faith. Agree if you must that on the evil question it is a draw, or at least that there are arguments for and arguments against. But Christianity is not the only religious faith, and no contemporary discussion of whether religion is a bad thing would be complete without at least a brief look at the religion of Islam. Since the attack on the World Trade Center's towers, 9/11, a major theme running through the writings of those opposed to religion is that Islam presents a special and particular danger. So insistent is this theme that critics have suggested that a form of Islamophobia is at work, because surely no religion could be this bad, and, even if it is, the skimpy research (to be generous) of the atheists precludes them from having an opinion.

I will not get into that charge here. The New Atheists are pretty ecumenical in their dislikes. The question is whether there is something particularly pernicious about Islam. One thing we can say is that simple blanket condemnations of Islam are just plain stupid. No one can deny that, taken overall in the 1,500 years since the life of Muhammad (c. 570–632), Islam has seen and supported and been part of great civilizations—with law and order, justice, music, arts, literature, philosophy, and, above all, science. As a philosopher and historian of science, I know how much we all owe to the Muslims. In straight philosophy, too, Islamic culture flourished when Europe truly was in the Dark Ages. And if you doubt art and architecture, go to Spain and visit the Alhambra. Better than Chartres? I don't know, but certainly it is not a silly question. Yet there is ongoing violence. That fateful morning, it was Muslim fanatics who flew the planes into the towers (and who hijacked two other planes). To be balanced, violence seems often directed toward coreligionists as much as toward anyone else, but that compounds the problem. There is something instinctively violent about Islam. There are other aspects of Islamic culture that also seem less than desirable: the status of women, for instance. But—recognizing that this might be another reason for your hostility to religion on moral grounds—let us leave this one. What about the violence issue?

It seems fair to say a number of things (Kelsay 2007). First, perhaps purely because of history, there does seem to be something distinctive about Islam with respect to fighting and territory. It is a religion founded by fighting men, and its early history was very much one of aggression and expansion. In a way, this is in the lifeblood of Islam. (What follows are commands by Muhammad to fighting forces.) "Fight in the name of God and in the path of God. Fight the mukaffirun [ingrates, unbelievers]" (Kelsay 2007, 100–101). This is not a Sermon on the Mount kind of religion. (Many would say, with reason, neither is Christianity.) However, this brings up the second point, that Muslims are not and never have been barbarians. Their fighting forces were never SS units doing their thing in Eastern Europe. The notion of Just War has always been as central to Islam as it is to Christianity. "Do not cheat or commit treachery, and do not mutilate anyone or kill children." This is from the mouth of the Prophet, although notice that these things are all very circumscribed. Muhammad goes on to give directions about how you should accept surrender and how to treat people you have conquered. "Whenever you meet the mushrikun [idolaters], invite them to accept Islam. If they do, accept it and let them alone. You should then invite them to move from their territory to the territory of the émigrés. If they do so, accept it and leave them alone." But if they don't go along with what you want, then things change, and you, as a good Muslim, have a duty to treat them sternly even unto death.

Third, related to all of this, especially with respect to territory, there is a sense that once a part of the world becomes Muslim, it should stay that way for all eternity. After all, there is but one God, and he rules over everything. Our pushing outward with his rule is but doing his will. This, of course, was just fine when Islam was in expansionist mode, but in the last third of its history, it has seen more and more encroachment on its territory. One thinks of the Iberian Peninsula, conquered by the Muslims by 750 and then increasingly lost until the rule came to an end around 1500. One thinks of the British occupation of India, the Raj, with many Muslims under its control, although this was reversed somewhat with the creation of Pakistan. And most recently, one thinks of the creation of the state of Israel in 1948, on land previously owned and occupied by Muslims.

So, fourth, expectedly, there is a divide between ideology and realpolitik. Basically, although one does hear some fanatics making the territorial claim, there is not a major desire in the world of Islam to retake Madrid in the name of the Prophet. But what about Israel, especially given that since the war of 1967, it seems to be in an expansionist mode with respect to land occupied by Muslims? I am not now talking about the rights and wrongs of Israel but about how its very existence sets up tensions for Islam. There don't seem to be quite the same tensions in Christian lands. It is true that France and Germany have pushed back and forth on the disputed provinces of Alsace-Lorraine, but no one seems terribly concerned to retake East Prussia for the present German Republic. And this is so, for all that the displacement of the Germans in the east seems to have been at least as brutal as any displacements when Israel was founded.

Fifth and finally, there is no one Islamic authority to make decisions in the name of everyone. One can hardly blame Islam too much here. Western Christianity since the Reformation has been divided, and this leads to differences about major moral issues. But it does mean that people like Osama bin Laden (1957–2011) feel empowered to step up and take action when and where they think others are failing or compromised (for instance, by their alliances with the West) or simply taking the wrong course of action. Do note that this does not mean that such people are ipso facto justified by Islam. By its very nature, Islam has always been a religion in which authority is respected and obeyed. That, too, is rooted in early history. The law is not there to be taken into your own hands, and there is the already mentioned concern about a just war. It is hard to see 9/11 falling within these limits. It is here more a question of why these things happen as they do. With fragmented authority, and Muslim state set against Muslim state—think Iraq and Iran—it is little wonder that fanatics step in to take their own courses of action.

So to conclude, the issue here is not about how to deal with the threat of Islamic terror in today's world. The question is whether there is something evil about Islam, over and above the norm for religion (whatever that norm might be). The answer is that there do seem to be factors that make for violence unique to Islam and that these would be triggered in today's world. But things are complex, by no means inevitable (given Islam), and there are controlling factors, which may or may not be observed. An atheist will pick up on this and argue that this is yet one more argument against religion, and perhaps an atheist should. Yet note that we have focused only on religion and whether religion is that only or most important factor, and not whether we should take into account things like poverty and jealousy of other nations that seem to be pushing Muslims around. This is surely a question that needs discussion. However, it is not our discussion at this place and at this time.

So, What's the Answer?

What is the connection between religion and evil? That there is a connection is well taken, hardly a surprise, given the extent to which religion invades our lives in so many respects, personal and public. That the connection is complex is equally no surprise. After that, the matter is still open for debate. Some, like Peter van Inwagen (2011), mentioned earlier, will see overall that religion has been a force for good. Others, like the New Atheist Christopher Hitchens (2007), the subtitle of whose book was *How Religion Poisons Everything*, will see overall that religion has been a force for ill. Increasingly, students of human history and nature—represented most recently and most forcefully by the Harvard evolutionary psychologist Steven Pinker (2011)—are starting to conclude that (even taking into account the dreadful events of the twentieth century) there has been a significant decline in violence in human history. Pinker is inclined to find the causes in the rise of modernity—the rule of a democratic law-bound state, the development and application of liberal philosophies about the status and rights of individual humans, and the like. Against Hitchens, he argues that religion has on occasions obviously been a force for good, but certainly not uniformly. "The theory that religion is a force for peace . . . does not fit the facts of history" (677). Perhaps in the end there is no one answer but a host of answers, depending on the circumstances. Better perhaps is the question whether one sees certain trends that tend to lead to good or ill. When the authority of the priesthood goes unquestioned, perhaps there is more scope for ill. When, as Pinker suggests, the role of women is raised, perhaps more kindly factors prevail. Certainly, one might expect a more balanced approach to sexuality and gender roles. That is the best that can be said, but that can still be a great deal.

12

THE MEANINGFUL LIFE

The End of Religion?

If the arguments of Sextus Empiricus were so penetrating, if the dialogues of David Hume were so devastating, if the rhetoric of Richard Dawkins was so powerful, why on earth does anyone go on believing? Why is Christianity not on the garbage dump of human ideas like phlogiston theory or the Hippocratic theory of humors? Since the Scientific Revolution, certainly since the Enlightenment, religion has been under attack, from philosophy, from science, and indeed from the ranks of religion itself. Are we seeing the decline and fall of religion? Has the atheist only to sit tight and watch the results with satisfaction? If not in our lifetimes, then in a century or two, will it appear as alien and quaint as crinolines or blood-letting or (in civilized countries) capital punishment? In one sense, you might think that the evidence is pointing that way and that the attacks have had their effect. Certainly in countries of the West, the number of nonbelievers of various kinds has increased and goes on increasing. There has to be some moral drawn from the bestseller status of the New Atheist books. The buyers cannot all be church reading groups determined to root out flaws. Atheism is on a roll.

And yet obviously in a broader sense, this is silly talk. The churches of America are still filled, and if not in Europe, then across Asia and also in Africa one finds huge numbers of believers, fervent in their faith and faithful in their practice. It really does not look as though religion is going to go away very soon. Let us not deny the force of the arguments of the past few chapters—with good reason one nineteenth-century critic (David Brewster) said of David Hume that he was "God's greatest gift to the infidel"—but ask why they do not have the effect that one might expect. No one spoke more eloquently on the problem of evil than the Russian novelist Fyodor Dostoevsky (1821–1881) in his *The Brothers Karamazov*, yet he remained a Christian. If we were to hand out free copies of *Dialogues Concerning Natural Religion* to everyone in America, why wouldn't we expect instant conversion to the creed of Dawkins? The answer surely is that many people think—for many people, it is true—that religion gives meaning to their lives. Without religion, all is cold and flat and without purpose. Without religion, life is as a landscape by the nineteenth-century German artist Caspar David Friedrich, harsh and uninviting. But don't take my word for it. We saw this meaning in the case of pre-Reformation Britain. Unfortunately, although the upside to going back five hundred years is that we could be reasonably objective, the downside is that critics might argue that it is no longer relevant today, in the age of science and technology. Let's look at a contemporary group where religion is a very major factor. For more-or-less obvious reasons—they are among the noisiest and most fervent—I choose a subset of American Evangelicals today. I am not pretending that this is in some sense significantly significant, but it will help to answer some of the questions we might have.

Why Do Evangelicals Believe?

The early days of many now-staid religious movements were often very different, marked by behaviors and beliefs almost expressly designed to upset the comfortable and respectable. Today, it would be hard to imagine a more sober and middle-class group of people than the Quakers, with meetings (at least as it seemed to me as a child) dominated by the pontificating of what are known semi-affectionately as "weighty Friends." In the middle of the seventeenth century, they were at the least rabble-rousers and at worst serious threats to law and order and proper government: "a man, a Quaker, came naked through the [Westminster] Hall, only very civilly tied about the privates to avoid scandal, and with a chafing-dish of fire and brimstone burning upon his head. . . crying, 'Repent! Repent!'" (Samuel Pepys, *Diary*, July 29, 1667). The thought of my headmaster, stark naked but for a rag around his genitals, makes me long to return to the seventeenth century. He was good on the repent business, though.

The Vineyard Christian Fellowship fits the pattern (Luhrmann 2012). Dating back to the 1960s, the hippy movement, and other manifestations of that time, it started as pastors reached out to young people caught up by the fashions—booze, drugs, sex, Eastern philosophies—that faded and showed themselves false friends, leaving their devotees lonely, crushed, miserable. These truly Christian men offered an alternative: Jesus. Not the Jesus of the traditional churches—the somewhat ethereal and distant son of God, sitting at the right hand of the father, ready to judge and condemn. Certainly not the Jesus who is a being eternal, impersonal, known only by analogy. Rather (as Max Weber led us to expect) a Jesus who is here now, a Jesus who is God and yet to whom one can talk, who listens and who does not judge but befriends and helps. A Jesus who is supernatural but at the same time deeply human. A Jesus, as psychological anthropologist T. M. Luhrmann suggests, who is the Jesus of the Gospel of Mark, who does not fully understand his own powers, who gets angry and frightened, and who in respects goes to his death unsuspecting.

From the start and as it has grown, with many branches in America and elsewhere, the movement has been firmly and unambiguously evangelical. It is deeply Bible-based: "The Bible is God's Word to us. It was written by human authors, under the supernatural guidance of the Holy Spirit. It is the supreme source of truth for Christian beliefs and living. Because it is inspired by God, it is the truth without any mixture of error." (This and the following quotations are taken from the church's website.) It is unambiguously Augustinian when it comes to original sin. "Under the temptation of Satan, our original parents fell from grace, bringing sin, sickness and God's judgment of death to the earth." And the church's theology makes no bones about the role of Jesus in all of this: "In His sinless, perfect life Jesus met the demands of the law and in His atoning death on the cross He took God's judgment for sin which we deserve as law-breakers." Expectedly, given its origins and its great contemporary appeal—there are no hang-ups about evolution—this very old-fashioned theology is promoted in modern dress, in ways that tie right back in with religion long ago and far away. Above all, it is a group experience, with services characterized by singing and praising, with heartfelt preaching, and with much extemporaneous prayer. In short, with the kind of enthusiasm that makes High Church Anglicans shudder and, since they have traveled a long way since the founding, leads today's members of the Religious Society of Friends to give thanks to God (if such there be) that they are not as other men. Theologically, what is distinctive to the point of being innovative about the Vineyard church is the relationship with God. "The kingdom of God is not a geo-political territory, nor is it the people of God. Rather, the kingdom of God is a dynamic realm. When one enters the kingdom she/he experiences the dynamic reality which exists within the triune God—Father, Son and Holy Spirit." This is a deity to whom one speaks and who speaks right back. "The experience of the kingdom of God (and thus, the experience of God's presence) is central to our faith and Christian life."

This doesn't mean that, without training or preparation, you can sit right down and chat with God. One of today's great theological wonders is the evangelical embrace of C. S. Lewis, a conservative Anglican and author of children's books, an acquired taste that, rather like chitlins and greens, some of us are rather glad not to have acquired. He is the authority here. Lewis tells us that coming to faith is not easy and often you will encounter ideas or practices that make little sense until you have in some sense internalized them. You cannot believe in them until you believe them. You have to learn to pray. Here again, incidentally, although ultimately it is you and the deity, the learning and practicing is very much a group experience, and you are guided in the practice and taught how to do it effectively. Seemingly paradoxically but perhaps not really, the spiritual exercises of the founder of the Jesuits, St. Ignatius Loyola (1491–1556), are a big favorite. The trick is to practice what is known as *kataphatic* prayer, where one uses one's imagination to get close to God, imagining him as a person who can be seen and spoken to and who responds back. (None of your Platonic otherness here.) The Spanish soldier-turned-priest asked his followers to put themselves beside Jesus and become part of the very experience, the situation. Take, for instance, the events leading up to the crucifixion. After the supper, Christ goes to pray, and the story starts to unfold: "He sweats sweat as drops of blood, and after He prayed three times to the Father and wakened His three Disciples, and after the enemies at His voice fell down, Judas giving Him the kiss of peace, and St. Peter cutting off the ear of Malchus, and Christ putting it in its place; being taken as a malefactor, they lead Him down the valley, and then up the side, to the house of Annas" (Spiritual Exercises of St. Ignatius Loyola). You must imagine yourself there, imagine yourself suffering along with Christ. Think about the physical agony and mental despair. Think about the place itself. "It will be here to consider the road from Mount Sion to the Valley of Josaphat, and likewise the Garden, whether wide, whether large, whether of one kind, whether of another." Then "ask for grief with Christ in grief, anguish with Christ in anguish, tears and interior pain at such great pain which Christ suffered for me." Do not "try to bring joyful thoughts, although good and holy, as, for instance, are those on the Resurrection and on heavenly glory, but rather to draw [yourself] to grief and to pain and anguish, bringing to mind frequently the labors, fatigues and pains of Christ our Lord, which He suffered from the moment when He was born up to the Mystery of the Passion in which [you] find [yourself] at present."

Whether you approve of any of this or not, you can start to get a sense of how it works, whether for the Jesuit novitiate or the Protestant evangelical. The theological context in which the two would embed their experiences would not be the same. For the Jesuit, doing all of this leads one deeper into the nature and purpose of Jesus and his suffering. Little wonder that the Jesuits were the shock troops of the Counter-Reformation, often themselves suffering horrendously for their faith. For the evangelical, it is not exactly "all about me," but it is something to open the way to contact with the Almighty. "Honestly, I think I'm closer to Jesus than I've ever been. I've been a Christian since—since I was sixteen, which is wild. The Ignatian stuff, for me, had to do with really drilling down into what I really believe. Jesus's ministry, resurrection, and death. I don't know if I fully believed until I did the exercises" (Luhrmann 2012, 183, quoting a woman who was following the exercises). You are part of God's scene, and in a converse way, he is part of yours. For some indeed, God is so far part of their world, they actually hear his voice—someone external speaking. This is not the experience of everyone, and it is not necessarily something repeated, but it does happen and can change lives. "Speak, for your servant is listening" (1 Samuel 3: 10).

Are They Crazy?

However empathetic, the nonbeliever will look back to (let us say) the religion of the Middle Ages if not with condescension, at least with a sense of superiority grounded on five centuries of science and philosophy. One understands why people thought and behaved as they did, but as modern medicine has moved on from the folk beliefs of that day, so modern thinking about God must move on. Our ancestors were decent enough people, but they were naifs. Fair enough, perhaps, but what are we to say of today's believers? To be candid, you do not have to be a Richard Dawkins, inclined to put all religious belief down to emotional instability, to have an immediate reaction in terms of mental health. There is a word for people who hear voices—*schizophrenic*. The webpage of the National Institute of Mental Health plunges right in: "Schizophrenia is a chronic, severe, and disabling brain disorder that has affected people throughout history." Continuing: "People with the disorder may hear voices other people don't hear." And what do folk hear? "The voices may talk to the person about his or her behavior, order the person to do things, or warn the person of danger." Even if a newcomer enters the doors of the Vineyard Christian Fellowship in good mental health, by the time the group has finished messing around with his or her mind, it is little wonder that madness has set in. There is minimal difference from a healthy person who enters an opium den and decides to stay for a year or two or ten.

The C. S. Lewis response will be brought out here. Until one does it, one cannot really understand what it is all about. Moreover, it is hardly a fault if people have to go through fairly rigorous training and only then get what is hidden to most people. Is this any different from a radiologist who has to learn to read an X-ray? Perhaps more pertinently, is this any different from what Plato argues in the *Republic*, that only certain people have the ability to gaze on the Forms and then only after a long training involving much mathematics and like mind-enhancing activities? At a less rhetorical and more empirical level, Luhrmann finds that those who hear voices or feel in immediate contact with God do not show greater tendencies toward mental illnesses. She does find, however, that they are not entirely typical of average members of society, showing an increased tendency toward absorption.

People with this character trait, perhaps expectedly, tend to appreciate the moment and to have imagination and appreciation. Such people "take pleasure in music and literature and the arts." The higher you score, "the more likely you are to be a reader, and the more likely you are to immerse yourself in rich, imaginative worlds; the more likely you are to be the kind of person who can lose him- or herself in movies or literature, the kind of person for whom the story can feel more real than the everyday" (Luhrmann 2012, 199). She stresses that such people tend, if anything, to use their natures positively, being socially skilled, warm, giving, artistic, likable, interesting. (Rats! I thought this was my story.) She does note, however, that things can backfire, and high scorers can more easily "remember" sexual abuse, real and imaginary, as well as abduction by aliens! In the Vineyard context given, with the prominent place played in its theology by the fallen angel Satan, it is little wonder that some members have troubles with demons and getting them out of their thoughts. This kind of thinking can lead to real breakdowns.

Is Good Comfort Enough?

Drowning out the avuncular tones of C. S. Lewis, one hears the stern moralizing of W. K. Clifford. Granted, people of earlier generations found comfort in their religion. Who is to blame them, particularly given their premodern age and beliefs? Granted, people today can work themselves up to believe the stuff of the Vineyard Christian Fellowship and it, too, gives comfort and meaning to their lives. But how can one believe it all in this day and age? How can one bring oneself to believe in it all? And most particularly, how dare those such as Lewis tell people to set about deliberately to bring on a state of false belief? If ever one questioned the immorality of this sort of thing, look again at what is going on: people letting emotion cloud their judgment and people of authority encouraging it.

Yes, you say, but what is the alternative? What about the troubles with atheism? Probably the biggest worry about atheism—leaving aside now truth or falsity issues—is that it seems such a cold and unfriendly sort of business. You may eke out a life, but given atheism, you can hardly have a very joyous life, and any sense of a life with some kind of meaning seems impossible entirely. If there is no God to make sense of things—if death is death and there is no hereafter and eternity—is anything worth anything? "Eat, drink and be merry, for tomorrow we die." Who cares about standards! That is to play the Christian's game. Just enjoy yourself, or at least indulge your senses to and beyond the full. That is meaning enough to life. When you are dead, you are dead. The ethics of belief really don't come into the equation because either you were right that there is a hereafter or you were wrong and it no longer matters.

As a matter of historical fact, the impression one gets is that there tends not to be a great deal of eating, drinking, and merriment by nonbelievers. They sound like a cross between Jonathan Edwards and Immanuel Kant when it comes to these kinds of things. One thinks of John Stuart Mill. One thinks of Charles Darwin filling up page after page of his *Descent of Man* with musings about morality. One thinks, above all, of the great nineteenth-century novelist George Eliot.

> I remember how, at Cambridge, I walked with her once in the Fellows' Garden of Trinity, on an evening of rainy May; and she, stirred somewhat beyond her wont, and taking as her text the three words which have been used so often as the inspiring trumpet-calls of men—the words *God, Immortality, Duty*—pronounced, with terrible earnestness, how inconceivable was the *first,* how unbelievable the *second,* and yet how peremptory and absolute the *third.* Never perhaps have sterner accents affirmed the sovereignty of impersonal and unrecompensing Law. I listened, and night fell; her grave, majestic countenance

turned toward me like a sibyl's in the gloom; it was as though she withdrew from my grasp, one by one, the two scrolls of promise, and left me the third scroll only, awful with inevitable fates. And when we stood at length and parted amid that columnar circuit of the forest trees, beneath the last twilight of starless skies, I seemed to be gazing, like Titus at Jerusalem, on vacant seats and empty halls—on a sanctuary with no Presence to hallow it, and heaven left lonely of a God. (Myers 1881, 62)

This sounds like the Wee Frees (a particularly dour breakaway group of the Presbyterian Church) on a wet Sunday in January. Contrast it with a harvest festival in Suffolk around 1500.

Reading the New Atheists is not much better. Their writings are certainly not things designed to leave you with a warm and cuddly feeling. It is all so dire and bleak. Dawkins is stark: "In a universe of blind physical forces and genetic replication, some people are going to get hurt, other people are going to get lucky, and you won't find any rhyme or reason in it, nor any justice. The universe we observe has precisely the properties we should expect if there is, at bottom, no design, no purpose, no evil and no good, nothing but blind, pitiless indifference" (Dawkins 1995). Not much joy or meaning here. You might as well start drowning your sorrows in alcohol before you slip off to Belgium to have yourself put down. Contrast this with the richness of the religious culture of the modern-day Evangelical. You may look down on such people, laugh at them perhaps, but they have something that you do not have. The Mormons may believe things you think totally false; they may have secret rituals that to the outsider seem embarrassingly bizarre, their dietary restrictions that go beyond beer and wine to tea and coffee may seem totally ludicrous, and their taste in underwear makes the long johns of the Sears Catalog seem positively risqué, but the closeness and the richness of their family lives is legendary. It is all very well to talk about duty in the abstract, but would that others could provide such an alternative in this world of alcoholism and drug use, of broken families and absent fathers, of crime and vandalism.

Is Humanism the Answer?

In the face of this existential bleakness, one might wonder if pure atheistic naturalism is possible (Blessing 2013; Farias 2013). Can one live this way? Surely, we are bound to start making a new religion or religion-substitute to compensate for what we have lost. New Atheists and fellow travelers indignantly deny that this has or must happen. And they are surely right in some respects. There is no explicit Church of Atheism and, although he sometimes behaves that way, Richard Dawkins is not its primate. It is true that (as we saw in chapter 2) people have tried to make secular religions—the followers of Comte, for example, and the creators of ethical societies, particularly in America. Moreover, some existing religions have been taken over by nonbelief, incorporating into already existing social structures. One thinks, for instance, of the Unitarian Universalists. They denied the Trinity, but they used to be fervent believers in a deity. No more. Now we just get ethical principles: "The inherent worth and dignity of every person"; "Justice, equity and compassion in human relations"; "Respect for the interdependent web of all existence of which we are a part"; and that sort of thing (information taken from the Unitarian-Universalist website). But this religiosity is certainly not to every nonbeliever's taste. Having given up Christianity, rather than tying ribbons on trees, they would rather spend their Sunday mornings reading the papers and going out to brunch.

This is not to say that atheists have no creed to substitute for that of Christians. Thomas Henry Huxley, Darwin's great supporter, joked about the earnestness of secular true believers, yet no one worked harder that he to provide a kind of nonreligious framework for living to challenge and supplant

Christianity (Ruse 2005). He and his fellows—including Florence Nightingale (1820–1910)—worked incessantly in the second half of the nineteenth century to bring Britain (and then America) up to the social and moral standards required of an industrial society. Huxley was much involved in education—he sat on the first London School Board and was dean at the new science university founded on the profits of the Great Exhibition of 1851. Others like Sir Michael Foster (1836–1907), a Huxley student, were involved in training doctors, and yet others in such areas as sanitation and local government. Whether articulated or not, they were putting into practice a philosophy that has come to be known as humanism. As we saw, this term, first used in the nineteenth century, talked of Renaissance scholars and thinkers like Erasmus. It was appropriated in the 1930s for more secular ends, but the philosophy itself had certainly been formulated by the mid-nineteenth century, and the term would have found favor with Huxley. To quote a fairly representative, recent endorsement, it is "the ethical outlook that says each individual is responsible for choosing his or her values and goals and working towards the latter in the light of the former, and is equally responsible for living considerately towards others, with a special view of establishing good relationships at the heart of life, because all good lives are premised on such" (Grayling 2013, 139).

Expectedly, science has always been close to the heart of humanists. The second half of the nineteenth century saw the founding of the great museums of natural history—the British Museum (Natural History) in London, the American Museum of Natural History in New York, and (a little later) the Royal Ontario Museum (ROM) in Toronto. The extent to which a conscious effort was being made to push religion out of society is shown overwhelmingly by the neo-Gothic architecture of the new structures. In Toronto, you hardly know whether you are entering a museum or Durham Cathedral. Instead of going to church on Sunday morning and gaping at the raised host, the modern family was expected to go to the museum on Sunday afternoon and gape at the stupendous new fossil dinosaurs being brought back from the digs in the American and Canadian West. But it was science backed by morality. The museum displays almost always had a message about proper living or human relationships. Good hygiene is a perennial theme, as is the horror of warfare. Hardly surprisingly for Huxley (who was known in the popular press as Pope Huxley), it was evolutionary theory that lay at the back of his ethical thinking—at least until in his old age he rather repudiated everything (Desmond 1994, 1997). This theory was taken almost in a metaphysical vein; its supposed upward nature leading to humankind was the key premise. The Christian had providence, the belief that save through the blood of the lamb we are doomed. The modern thinker had progress, the belief that through our own efforts we can better ourselves and society. From culture to biology and then in a happy circular fashion back to culture (Ruse 2005).

Far more than Darwin, in England, North and South America, and elsewhere in the world, Herbert Spencer was the philosopher of the day. "Now we propose in the first place to show, that this law of organic progress is the law of all progress. Whether it be in the development of the Earth, in the development of Life upon its surface, in the development of Society, of Government, of Manufactures, of Commerce, of Language, Literature, Science, Art, this same evolution of the simple into the complex, through successive differentiations, holds throughout" (Spencer 1857, 245). This view of evolutionary progress, in biology and in culture, carried through to the twentieth century. Thomas Henry Huxley's oldest grandson, Julian Huxley (1887–1975), was a well-known biologist in his own right. He was also a very prominent atheist who endorsed the upward direction of history and found within it his own humanistic worldview. He even went so far as to write a book called *Religion without Revelation* (1927). As tends to be the case with religion and apparently with religion substitutes, his particular ethical directives were tailored to his times. He was much in favor of large, government-sponsored technological projects and even wrote a book praising the Tennessee Valley Authority (Huxley 1943). Most recently, it has been Edward O. Wilson at work. He argues for his pet projects—biodiversity and saving the Brazilian rainforests (Wilson 2002)—and he does so in the name of evolutionary progress. He thinks humans are at the pinnacle (his word) of evolution, hence we have a moral obligation to preserve the species, and promoting biodiversity is a very good start.

Is Pure Atheistic Naturalism Possible?

One hates to put a damper on this happy picture, but one fears that the nonbelievers are having flights of fancy to equal any of those of the believers. Evolutionary progress—that history shows an upward climb from the blob to the human—is a notion much disputed. Gould, despite thinking (somewhat inconsistently) that humanlike creatures would almost inevitably evolve, called it "a noxious, culturally embedded, untestable, nonoperational, intractable idea that must be replaced if we wish to understand the patterns of history" (Gould 1988, 319). Humans are certainly among the end points of evolution, but who is to say that evolution was a climb up to us? For all that I am the proud owner of a trilobite tattoo, I would rather spend the afternoon with a human than with a bunch of smelly marine invertebrates, unless, like the Walrus and the Carpenter, I was eating them. But that is my choice, not something dictated by evolution. Remember how Jack Sepkoski (a student of both Wilson and Gould, incidentally) thought that cows might in some circumstances be top dogs, to mix metaphors. The trouble is that we are slipping into the very problem Hume spotted (and that Huxley, to his credit, came to realize)—namely, trying to get value out of the natural state of things—and that is not possible. We are imposing our values that progress exists and that it is a good thing. This we may not do. In any case, after the horrors of the twentieth century, dare anyone say (Pinker's optimism notwithstanding) that history shows progress or that, if in respects it does, that this is always a good thing? It wasn't just that the country of Kant, of Goethe, of Beethoven sank to the evil that it did, but the philistine vulgarity of the Third Reich, despite—often because of— its embrace of modernity, whether the massive quasi-Roman architecture so beloved of Hitler, the grotesque misreading of the *Ring* as a harbinger of what was to come, or how Goebbels made such brilliant use of film and radio.

I have been at pains to say that I do not claim that all humanists are on the way to making or joining a secular religion. Some are, so much so that it is one of the major reasons that Paul Kurtz, who proudly proclaimed himself a humanist, broke with some of the very organizations he had been party to founding. I am also not saying that all humanists necessarily believe in some kind of progress—although I suspect many more do than they realize. The question for me is whether you can have any world picture that is shorn of all outside value and whether such a picture would be too oppressively bleak. Even at this stripped-down stage, people like Alvin Plantinga (1991, 1997) think that all naturalism, and hence modern science, forces you into some kind of religious-like commitment. Either that or you just give up on naturalism and go straight to theism. This is certainly false. However, Plantinga's bad arguments should not stop us from asking if naturalism/science requires some kind of leap beyond the directly visible. Of course it does! For a start, naturalism supposes that the future is going to be like the past. Boyle's law held yesterday; it will hold tomorrow. This is not an evidence-based claim, nor is it justified deductively. The same is true of a huge amount more that goes into science, for instance, that a theory that explains a lot of things is probably better than a theory that explains only one thing and that a theory that predicts surprising things (then found true) is probably better than a theory that explains only the already known. You can keep going. The reason prey flee the predator is that (contra Descartes) they feel pain on being caught and don't want that, and the reason people commit certain standard logical fallacies is that they thought about them and their reasoning misled them. I don't know how you could do the social sciences if you thought everyone was just a zombie—no pain, no sentience—but how you prove absolutely and definitively that they are not escapes me.

Does this mean that science is just faith-based like religion? Not at all. The point about the assumptions of science is that they work. They justify themselves pragmatically. The future does turn out to be like the past. Theories that correctly predict the unexpected do turn out to be powerful tools of understanding. Assuming that animals feel pain makes sense of evolutionary and ecological claims. Assuming that people are trying to reason, successfully or otherwise, makes sense of psychology. The trouble with religious faith claims is that they don't work that way. You cannot rely on them in the same way. You may have faith enough to walk on water but you would be a damn fool to try. I don't mean that faith cannot give you a meaning for life, because it obviously can. But science doesn't invest in beliefs without some empirical reward, some backup. Karl Popper (1959) used to say that the demarcation between science and nonscience is that only the former is genuinely falsifiable. He got a lot of flak for that, mainly from our fellow philosophers. But he did have a point. The medical scientist predicts that a certain syndrome will have a certain effect. If it doesn't, he is wrong. The wise preacher knows that he had better not get into that game at all. You have cancer and you recover? God loves you and spared you. You have cancer and you will not recover? God loves you and is calling you to him. Either way, God wins and you feel comforted, but the cost is that it is just not science.

Let us grant that you can have a worldview that is not religious in any sense. Does subscribing to such a view mean leaving behind much that makes life worthwhile and renouncing the world rather like a Cistercian monk entering a monastery of a virulently spartan kind? John Stuart Mill's answer would be that even if this is so, if you really believe there is no God, you have no choice but to go this way. "It is better to be a human being dissatisfied than a pig satisfied; better to be Socrates dissatisfied than a fool satisfied. And if the fool, or the pig, are of a different opinion, it is because they only know their own side of the question" (Mill 1863). Does one have to choose? I argued in the last chapter that one can have music and literature and art. I don't see why the atheist should not enjoy a Bach passion for what it is or a noble cathedral as a testament to the human spirit. I certainly don't let thoughts of the Greek and Roman gods get in my way when I visit Italy and Greece. And if you are really uncomfortable, there is much secular work to enjoy. Baron Haussmann's Paris is not exactly spiritual, but I can walk the streets endlessly in amazement and sheer joy. I don't mean that there won't be times when you are overcome by the existential worthlessness of it all—although I suspect that many Christians have those sorts of times, too—but that I don't see why you cannot live a life of happiness and fulfillment. To refer for one final time (!) to my wife, Lizzie, she is not religious in any meaningful way, within or without a conventional church. Yet I cannot imagine anyone with a richer life, with family, with friends, with enjoyment of life and what it has to offer—even though it means sometimes being dragged off to the Metropolitan Opera by her husband for four hours of screeching in Italian.

"The LORD gave, and the LORD has taken away. Blessed be the name of the LORD" (Job 1: 21). David Hume does the same in reverse. He leads us into the land of skepticism, whether about the nature of experience, the foundations of morality, or the meaning of it all. But in the end, he points out, our psychology steps in to save us.

> Most fortunately it happens, that since reason is incapable of dispelling these clouds, nature herself suffices to that purpose, and cures me of this philosophical

melancholy and delirium, either by relaxing this bent of mind, or by some avocation, and lively impression of my senses, which obliterate all these chimeras. I dine, I play a game of backgammon, I converse, and am merry with my friends; and when after three or four hours' amusement, I would return to these speculations, they appear so cold, and strained, and ridiculous, that I cannot find in my heart to enter into them any farther. (Hume [1739–1740] 2000, 175)

In respects, this is the most important passage in this whole book. Don't kid yourself. If you become a nonbeliever, then you have left the security of your childhood. There is no ultimate meaning. And secular attempts to find a substitute, like relying on progress, simply aren't going to do it. It's gone forever. But don't panic or despair. There may be no objective morality and no ultimate meaning, but nature (meaning in today's terms our psychology as molded through evolution by natural selection) has made us such that we can be kind and giving, enjoy life, and find it worthwhile. And as within the system we can separate Sophie Scholl and Adolf Hitler, so within the system we can separate Socrates and the fool. Blessed be the name of David Hume.

Is Religion Good for You?

Hume is all well and good. Today, can we back up the unsubstantiated claims of an eighteenth-century Scotsman? What do the social scientists have to tell us? Can you find meaning without God? Close to religion or far from religion, is the nonbeliever going to be a person apart? A kind of spiritual leper in society, unhappy and rightly despised or pitied by others who see her or him as a threat to the whole? There are studies all over the place about the religious, the spiritual (assuming that this can be separated from the religious), the secular, the atheistic, and how they compare (Hwang 2013). We saw earlier evidence that on balance believers are happier than nonbelievers. The difference is not great, and nonbelievers seem to score higher on some things they probably cherish. For instance, they have a greater willingness to try out new ideas, seek new challenges, and try new activities. Predictably, many happy hours have been spent inquiring into the sex lives of atheists as opposed to the religious. Perhaps as one might expect, religion is associated with guilt and repression, and the more heavy-handed the religion, the greater the guilt and repression (Ray and Brown 2011). However, biology is pretty powerful. One of the more delicious findings is that Utah, the home of the Mormons, is the state with the highest on-average consumption of online pornography (Edelman 2009). Making public answers to questions that some might think ought not even be entertained in private, one learns that atheists are into earlier and more sex, more partners, voyeurism (at least as compared to the religious), and (among heterosexuals) greater variation and inventiveness (Farias 2013). Apparently anal sex is an atheistic favorite. One presumes that all of those jokes about the missionary position might have a kernel of truth. In fairness to the nineteenth century and to George Eliot, in case you are worried that they had nothing but gloom and doom— and duty!—one should note that the great novelist spent most of her adult life living with a man to whom she was not married and, when he died, married a man twenty years younger than she.

From a health viewpoint, there is indeed a general finding that being religious is better for one's health, although claims like these are fraught with difficulties and exceptions (Miller and Thoresen 2003; Powell, Shahabi, and Thoresen 2003; Seeman, Dubin, and Seeman 2003). This is particularly so if one thinks less of beliefs with actual religious content and more in terms of having a generally spiritual approach to life, feeling that in some sense it is all meaningful. There is fairly solid evidence that the religious do eat more sensibly, take more exercise, and smoke and drink less, although (and

I am not joking) apparently those churches that go in for fre-
quent potluck suppers put a nasty upward blip in the obesity
figures. What table 12.1 suggests is that being part of a supportive group of coreligionists, friends, does give one a zest for living that pays off. This seems fairly reasonable. What the table
also suggests is that believing Jesus died on the cross for your
sins does not protect you against cancer. Many would think

Table 12.1 From Powell, L., L. Shahabi, and C. Thoresen. 2003. "Religion and
Spirituality: Linkages to Physical Health." *American Psychologist* 58: 36–52.
Hypotheses Tested and Summary of Strength of Evidence for Them

	Strength of Evidence	
Hypotheses	**Mediated Model**[a]	**Independent Model**[b]
1. Church/service attendance protects against death.	Persuasive	Persuasive
2. Religion or spirituality protects against cardiovascular disease.	Some	Some
3. Religion or spirituality protects against cancer mortality.	Inadequate	Inadequate
4. Deeply religious people are protected against death.	Consistent failures	Consistent failures
5. Religion or spirituality protects against disability.	Inadequate	Consistent failures
6. Religion or spirituality slows the progression of cancer.	Consistent failures	Consistent failures
7. People who use religion to cope with difficulties live longer.	Inadequate	Inadequate

(Continued)

Table 12.1 (*Continued*)

Hypotheses	Strength of Evidence	
	Mediated Model[a]	Independent Model[b]
8. Religion or spirituality improves recovery from acute illness.	Consistent failures	Consistent failures
9. Religion or spirituality impedes recovery from acute illness.	Some	Some
10. Being prayed for improves physical recovery from acute illness.	Some	Some

[a] Studies include adjustment for the demographic confounders of age, gender, ethnicity, education, poor health, and disability.

[b] Studies include adjustment both for the demographic confounders of age, gender, ethnicity, and education, poor health, and disability and for established risk factors including aspects of a healthy lifestyle (e.g., smoking, alcohol, physical activity, diet), social support/integration, and depression.

that this also seems fairly reasonable. Perhaps expectedly, as opposed to those who stay put, more mental health stress is found among those who switch religions or switch in and out of religion. Conversely, the least depression is found among those at the ends of the scale—people who are firm believers and people who are firm nonbelievers or (if agnostic) know exactly where they are and why. Being secure in your belief or nonbelief really counts. As you might expect, whether you are comfortable with your belief or nonbelief is in part a function of the society within which you live. It is easier to be an atheist in a society like Britain that is relaxed about that sort of thing than in some Middle Eastern countries that take belief very seriously indeed—and nonbelief even more seriously. As it is for gays, in the United States it is easier to be an atheist if one lives in New England or on the West Coast than if one lives in the Deep South. Do not ask for credit—or to host a Christmas party—as a refusal might offend!

Is Religion Good for Society?

Switching the emphasis from the individual to the society is very revealing. There is a general presumption by believers that belief in God is good for society. That Platonic Form of sentimentality, the movie *It's a Wonderful Life* starring Jimmy Stewart as a man on the verge of suicide until his guardian angel shows how much difference he has made to people's lives, is taken as a paradigm. Belief in God leads to Bedford Falls, the town within which the hero lives, which is warm, friendly, caring. No belief in God leads to Pottersville, named after the greedy, grasping villain of the story, a place of hatred, poverty, despair. Note that it is not just the social benefits of religion that are thought important—schools, hospitals, and the like—but the very belief in a deity, or rather the Christian deity (although obviously this is a major theme in Judaism and Islam, too).

Is it true? Not quite! Judging on people's self-reported beliefs, practices, and so forth, you can draw up lists of the most and least theistic countries. The top twenty most theistic on one well-regarded study are (not ranked order) Nigeria, Uganda, Philippines, Pakistan, Morocco, Egypt, Zimbabwe, Bangladesh, El Salvador, Colombia, Senegal, Malawi, Indonesia, Brazil, Peru, Jordan, Algeria, Malta, Mexico, and Sierra Leone. Least theistic (again, not ranked order) are Sweden, Denmark, Czech Republic, Norway, Finland, China, South Korea, Estonia, France, Vietnam, Russia, Bulgaria, Japan, Netherlands, Slovenia, Germany, Hungary, Great Britain, New Zealand, and Belgium (Zuckerman 2013, 500). As always with this kind of exercise, one can wonder about precise rankings, and they are not uniform in the groups. Some countries, for instance, are much less theistic than others. But the information is pretty solid overall.

Turning now to indications of well-being, one finds that study after study reports that the nontheistic countries come out way ahead of the theistic countries. It is far better to be a mother—proper care at birthing, maternity benefits, and so forth—in the nontheistic countries. Every one of them scores higher than the theistic countries. The same story is true of peacefulness, judged by engagement in war, levels of crime, availability of weapons, and the like. Homicide tells a similar story. The figures speak for themselves: El Salvador (homicide rate of 71 per 100,000 inhabitants), Colombia (33 per 100,000 inhabitants), Brazil (26 per 100,000), and Mexico (18 per 100,000) versus Sweden, Japan, Norway, and the Netherlands (all with homicide rates that are less than 1 per 100,000). General well-being, including health, wealth, life expectancy, and education, gives the same result. The nontheistic countries are up at or toward the top. The theistic countries are at or toward the bottom.

There are anomalies, but generally they are exceptions that prove the rule. North Korea is nontheistic and by anyone's standards a pretty dreadful place to live, however judged. But note that this is a dictatorship and not a democracy. Once you take that into account, then the story changes. Generally, dictatorship is bad for your health and much else. I still remember visiting Franco's Spain in 1961, driving through the countryside from Barcelona to Gibraltar. I (and my fellow student traveling companions), coming from the British welfare state, simply could not believe the appalling conditions under which people, especially in the rural areas, were having to live. We had never before seen village after village of children literally in rags and barefooted. Yet as is well known, Spain under the fascists was deeply religious, and the Catholic Church had a major role.

What about the United States? The ten states with the highest levels of theism are Louisiana, Arkansas, Alabama, Mississippi, Georgia, South Carolina, North Carolina, Kentucky, Tennessee, and Oklahoma and Utah (tied). The ten states with the lowest levels are Maine, Vermont, Connecticut, New Hampshire, Rhode Island, Massachusetts, New York, Alaska, Oregon, and California. Of course, this being America, we are not looking for widespread atheism in the lowest ten: 59% of people in Maine believe in God "with absolute certainty." It is a matter of ratios: 91% of people in Mississippi believe in God "with absolute certainty." It is also a matter of lifestyle and standard of living. Study after study, index after index, shows that internally the United States mirrors the world externally. For education, wealth, health, and life expectancy, it is better to live among the infidels than among the true believers.

What is the causal connection? Does theism depress life, or does an elevated life lead to nonbelief? Social scientists are all over the map on this. There is some evidence to support a common-cause explanation—education leads to both societal success and diminished belief. The strongest trends, however, are toward societal benefits leading to nonbelief rather than conversely. It could well be that religion functions as a substitute or panacea when the going is rough (Pasquale and Kosmin 2013). What may qualify this simple conclusion is that some of the most developed nontheistic societies today come historically from very religious backgrounds. One thinks of Scandinavia. Perhaps religion was very important in getting things going, even if it drops off at a later point. Whether it was the religion that got things going or other factors like education and science is another matter. Perhaps religion retards things in this respect. Could we here have an explanation of a fact that may seem anomalous? In the United States, religion is good for one's health and yet the less religious states have the better health care statistics. It seems plausible to suggest that religious people are more likely to turn inward to their group for help than outward to the state. This explains why overall health care is better in nonreligious states. But within any state, religious or not, the religious are more likely to get group support and hence do better than their fellows.

And the Answer Is?

So, does any of this speak to whether the atheist can have a meaningful life or if the religious are bound to have a life that is meaningful in itself and comparatively more meaningful than that of the atheist? My suspicion is that your answer depends on where you started. Clearly, religious people can and do have lives that they find rich and meaningful. As clearly, nonreligious people can find meaning in their lives. For religious people, that is answer enough, although usually they would like nonreligious people to share in it, too. History shows and philosophy and psychology confirm that it is not always easy being nonreligious, and there are surely those who find their lives empty and bereft of meaning. At this point perhaps the best one can say is that, psychology aside, there is the moral demand, something that pays little heed to personal happiness. Nothing can be of worth based on a falsity, and if the only meaning is thin and threadbare, then that is an end to it. But many do find peace, contentment, and real value in life, and the nonbelief contributes to this. My father was not unique. Hume was right, you can find fulfillment without external supports, and while (as for Darwin and my father) self-worth and contentment comes in part from denying a god one does not much care for—sick of being judged in this life, one does not want more of it in the next—at least part of the fulfillment comes from recognizing the illusion of external supports. It is the reward for putting away childish things and seeing through the glass clearly.

ENVOI

Early in the writing of this book, I realized that I could not conceal my own thinking on the subject. My values and beliefs were bound to color what I wrote. Pretending that I do not have them or that they do not affect my writing would be false because, whether by intention or not, I am sure I would be introducing such values and beliefs covertly. Better therefore to make them public but to try for balance despite, or perhaps because of, them. Whether there is such balance I leave for you to judge. Part of being a philosopher is being fair to the opinions of others and accepting their good points if well taken. I have tried hard to do that and not to claim more than I should. The theological and philosophical issues seem to me to destroy the central claims of Christianity and indeed of related religions. Whether this entirely negates any kind of religious claim or still leaves open space for some genuine form of skepticism or agnosticism I cannot say. I am with Haldane on this. If there is an ultimate truth, it is going to be a lot stranger than I can imagine. I do think that the science and religion relationship is more complex than many atheists think, the same is true of the significance of naturalistic explanations, and very much the same holds for the value status of religion. Like my father, as I move through the eighth decade of my life, I find that a gentle nonbelief gives me great personal comfort and sense of self-worth. Readers must judge for themselves where they stand and what all of this means in the long run. Above all, if the case for atheism is well taken, then this must be for good arguments, not bad ones.

As I said at the beginning of this book, my biggest worry was about being boring. Whether I have avoided that pitfall, I also leave for you to judge. I told you that the first reader of any book I write is myself and never more than this book. I can say simply that I have learned a lot, and I hope the same will hold for you. I stress one more time the overall theme of this book: atheism is an intensely moral issue. It is not just a matter of facts, for and against. It is a matter of you as a person, what you believe and what you should believe. It is a matter of how you live your life, how you act toward others, and the roles of you and others in society. Regardless of whether there is a God, it is you who will be judged. "Ask not for whom the bell tolls, it tolls for thee."

And now, at least as far as I am concerned, you have in your hands *Atheism: What Everyone Needs to Know*!

REFERENCES

Anonymous. 1944. The plot against Hitler. *Bulletin of International News* 21: 626–632.

Anselm, St. 1903. *Anselm: Proslogium, Monologium, An Appendix on Behalf of the Fool by Gaunilon; and Cur Deus Homo.* Translator S. N. Deane. Chicago: Open Court.

———. 2008. *The Major Works.* Translators B. Davies and G. R. Evans. Oxford: Oxford University Press.

Aquinas, St. T. 1952. *Summa Theologica, I.* Translators Fathers of the English Dominican Province. London: Burns, Oates and Washbourne.

Aristotle. 1984. De Anima. In *The Complete Works of Aristotle.* Editor J. Barnes. Princeton, N.J.: Princeton University Press.

Atkins, P. W. 1995. The limitless power of science. *Nature's Imagination: The Frontiers of Scientific Vision.* Editor J. Cornwell, 122–132. Oxford: Oxford University Press.

Atran, S. 2004. *In Gods We Trust: The Evolutionary Landscape of Religion.* New York: Oxford University Press.

Augustine, St. 1961. *Saint Augustine Confessions.* Translator R. S. Pine-Coffin. Harmondsworth, Middlesex: Penguin.

———. 1982. *The Literal Meaning of Genesis.* Translator J. H. Taylor. New York: Newman.

Barrett, J. 2004. *Why Would Anyone Believe in God?* Lanham, Md.: AltaMira Press.

Barrow, J. D., and F. J. Tipler. 1986. *The Anthropic Cosmological Principle.* Oxford: Clarendon Press.

Barth, K. 1957. *The Word of God and the Word of Man.* Translator D. Horton. New York: Harper.

Bavinck, H. 1951. *The Doctrine of God.* Translator W. Hendricksen. Grand Rapids, Mich.: Eerdmans.

Beevor, A. 2003. *The Fall of Berlin 1945.* New York: Penguin.

———. 2012. *The Second World War.* Boston: Little, Brown.

Behe, M. 1996. *Darwin's Black Box: The Biochemical Challenge to Evolution.* New York: Free Press.

Berlinerblau, J. 2013. Jewish atheism. *The Oxford Handbook of Atheism.* Editors S. Bullivant and M. Ruse, 320–336. Oxford: Oxford University Press.

Berton, P. 1965. *The Comfortable Pew: A Critical Look at Christianity and the Religious Establishment in the New Age.* Toronto: McClelland and Stewart.

Blessing, K. A. 2013. Atheism and the meaningfulness of life. *The Oxford Handbook of Atheism.* Editors S. Bullivant and M. Ruse, 104–118. Oxford: Oxford University Press.

Boyer, P. 2002. *Religion Explained: The Evolutionary Origins of Religious Thought.* New York: Basic Books.

Boyle, R. [1686] 1996. *A Free Enquiry into the Vulgarly Received Notion of Nature.* Editors E. B. Davis and M. Hunter. Cambridge: Cambridge University Press.

———. [1688] 1966. A disquisition about the final causes of natural things. *The Works of Robert Boyle.* Editor T. Birch, 5: 392–444. Hildesheim: Georg Olms.

Bremmer, I. N. 2007. Atheism in antiquity. *Cambridge Companion to Atheism.* Editor M. Martin, 11–26. Cambridge: Cambridge University Press.

Brown, C. G. 2013. The twentieth century. *The Oxford Handbook of Atheism*. Editors S. Bullivant and M. Ruse, 229–244. Oxford: Oxford University Press.

Brown, D. 2003. *The Da Vinci Code*. New York: Doubleday.

Brown, P. 1967. *Augustine of Hippo: A Biography*. London: Faber and Faber.

Browning, C. 1998. *Ordinary Men: Reserve Police Battalion 101 and the Final Solution in Poland*. New York: Harper.

Buckley, M. J. 1987. *At the Origins of Modern Atheism*. New Haven, Conn.: Yale University Press.

Bud, R. 2013. Life, DNA and the model. *British Journal for the History of Science* 46: 311–334.

Budd, S. 1977. *Varieties of Unbelief: Atheists and Agnostics in English Society, 1850–1960*. London: Heinemann.

Bullivant, S. 2010. The new atheism and sociology: Why here? Why now? What next? *Religion and the New Atheism: A Critical Appraisal*. Editor A. Amarasingam, 109–124. Boston: Brill.

Bullivant, S., and M. Ruse, Editors. 2013. *The Oxford Handbook of Atheism*. Oxford: Oxford University Press.

Bultmann, R. 1958. *Jesus Christ and Mythology*. New York: Charles Scribner's Sons.

Calvin, J. [1536] 1960. *Institutes of the Christian Religion*. Editor H. T. Kerr. Philadelphia: Westminster Press.

Churchland, P. M. 1995. *The Engine of Reason, The Seat of the Soul*. Cambridge, Mass.: MIT Press.

Churchland, P. S. 1986. *Neurophilosophy: Towards a Unified Science of the Mind and Brain*. Cambridge, Mass.: MIT Press.

Clark, A. 2000. *Mindware: An Introduction to the Philosophy of Cognitive Science*. New York: Oxford University Press.

Clarkson, T. [1808] 2010. *The History of the Rise, Progress and Accomplishment of the Abolition of the African Slave-Trade, by the British Parliament*. Lenox, Mass.: HardPress.

Clifford, W. K. 1879. *Lectures and Essays*. Editors L. Stephen and F. Pollack. London: Macmillan.

Collins, H. M. 1981. Stages in the empirical program of relativism— Introduction. *Social Studies of Science* 11: 3.

Collins, R. 1999. A scientific argument for the existence of God. *Reason for the Hope Within*. Editor M. J. Murray, 47–75. Grand Rapids, Mich.: Eerdmans.

Conway-Morris, S. 2003. *Life's Solution: Inevitable Humans in a Lonely Universe*. Cambridge: Cambridge University Press.

Cooper, J. M., Editor. 1997. *Plato: Complete Works*. Indianapolis, Ind.: Hackett.

Cragun, R. T., J. H. Hammer, and J. M. Smith. 2013. North America. *The Oxford Handbook of Atheism*. Editors S. Bullivant and M. Ruse, 601– 621. Oxford: Oxford University Press.

Craig, W. L. 2013. Slaughter of the Canaanites. www.reasonablefaith. org/slaughter-of-the-canaanites.

Darwin, C. 1859. *On the Origin of Species by Means of Natural Selection, or the Preservation of Favoured Races in the Struggle for Life*. London: John Murray.

———. 1871. *The Descent of Man, and Selection in Relation to Sex*. London: John Murray.

———. 1985. *The Correspondence of Charles Darwin*. Cambridge: Cambridge University Press.

Darwin, E. 1794–1796. *Zoonomia; or, The Laws of Organic Life*. London: J. Johnson.

Davies, B. 2004. *An Introduction to the Philosophy of Religion* (Third Edition). Oxford: Oxford University Press.

———. 2010. Simplicity. *The Cambridge Companion to Christian Philosophical Theology*. Editors C. Taliaferro and C. Meister, 31–46. Cambridge: Cambridge University Press.

———. 2016. Not understanding God in the *Summa Theologiae*. *The Cambridge Critical Guide to Aquinas's 'Summa Theologiae.'* Editor Jeffrey Hause. Cambridge: Cambridge University Press.

Davies, B., and E. Stump, Editors. 2012. *The Oxford Handbook of Aquinas*. Oxford: Oxford University Press.

Davis, S. T. 2010. Resurrection. *The Cambridge Companion to Christian Philosophical Theology*. Editors C. Tallaferro and C. Meister, 108–123. Cambridge: Cambridge University Press.

Dawkins, R. 1976. *The Selfish Gene*. Oxford: Oxford University Press.

———. 1986. *The Blind Watchmaker*. New York: Norton.

———. 1995. *A River Out of Eden*. New York: Basic Books.

———. 1997. Religion is a virus. *Mother Jones*. November.

———. 2003. *A Devil's Chaplain: Reflections on Hope, Lies, Science and Love*. Boston: Houghton Mifflin.

———. 2006. *The God Delusion*. New York: Houghton Mifflin Harcourt.

Dawkins, R., and J. R. Krebs. 1979. Arms races between and within species. *Proceedings of the Royal Society of London, Series B* 205: 489–511.

Dembski, W. A. 1998. *The Design Inference: Eliminating Chance Through Small Probabilities*. Cambridge: Cambridge University Press.

Dembski, W. A., and M. Ruse, Editors. 2004. *Debating Design: Darwin to DNA*. Cambridge: Cambridge University Press.

Dennett, D. C. 1984. *Elbow Room: The Varieties of Free Will Worth Wanting*. Cambridge, Mass.: MIT Press.

———.1992. *Consciousness Explained*. New York: Pantheon.

———. 2006. *Breaking the Spell: Religion as a Natural Phenomenon*. New York: Viking.

Descartes, R. [1637] 1964. Discourse on method. *Philosophical Essays*, 1–57. Translator L. J. Lafleur. Indianapolis, Ind.: Bobbs-Merrill.

———. [1641] 1964. Meditations. *Philosophical Essays*, 59–143. Translator, L. J. Lafleur. Indianapolis, Ind.: Bobbs-Merrill.

———. 1985. *The Philosophical Writings*, Volume I. Translators J. Cottingham, R. Stoothoff, and D. Murdoch. Cambridge: Cambridge University Press.

Desmond, A. 1994. *Huxley, the Devil's Disciple*. London: Michael Joseph.

———. 1997. *Huxley, Evolution's High Priest*. London: Michael Joseph.

Desmond, A., and J. Moore. 2009. *Darwin's Sacred Cause: How a Hatred of Slavery Shaped Darwin's Views on Human Evolution*. New York: Houghton Mifflin Harcourt.

D'Holbach, P. H. T. [1770] 2007. *The System of Nature; or the Laws of the Moral and Physical World*. Teddington, U.K.: Echo Library.

Diels, H., and W. Kranz. 1952. *Die Fragmente der Vorsokratiker*. Berlin: Weidmann.

Dijksterhuis, E. J. 1961. *The Mechanization of the World Picture*. Oxford: Oxford University Press.

Duffy, E. 1992. *The Stripping of the Altars: Traditional Religion in England 1400–1580*. New Haven, Conn.: Yale University Press.

Durkheim, E. 1912. *Elementary Forms of Religious Life*. Oxford: Oxford University Press.

Dyer, C. 1994. *Everyday Life in Medieval England*. London: Hambledon and London.

Edelman, B. 2009. Markets: Red light states: Who buys online adult entertainment? *The Journal of Economic Perspectives* 23: 209–220.

Edwards, J. [1741] 2005. *Sinners in the Hands of an Angry God and Other Puritan Sermons*. New York: Dover.

Edwards, M. 2013. The first millennium. *Oxford Handbook of Atheism*. Editors S. Bullivant and M. Ruse, 152–163. Oxford: Oxford University Press.

Edwards, R. M. 1978. The pagan dogma of the absolute unchangeableness of God. *Religious Studies* 14: 305–313.

Ehrman, B. D. 2001. *Jesus: Apocalyptic Prophet of the New Millennium*. Oxford: Oxford University Press.

———. 2012. *Did Jesus Exist? The Historical Argument for Jesus of Nazareth*. New York: Harper.

Evans, R. J. 2003. *The Coming of the Third Reich*. New York: Penguin.

———. 2005. *The Third Reich in Power*. New York: Penguin.

Farias, M. 2013. The psychology of atheism. *The Oxford Handbook of Atheism*. Editors S. Bullivant and M. Ruse, 468–482. Oxford: Oxford University Press.

Feenstra, R. J. 2010. Trinity. *Christian Philosophical Theology*. Editors C. Taliaferro and C. Meister, 3–14. Cambridge: Cambridge University Press.

Findlay, J. N. 1948. Can God's existence be disproved? *Mind* 57: 176–183.

Fischer, J. M., R. Kane, D. Pereboom, and M. Vargas. 2007. *Four Views on Free Will.* Malden, Mass.: Blackwell.

Frazer, J. G. 1890. *The Golden Bough: A Study in Comparative Religion.* London: Macmillan.

Frazier, J. 2013. Hinduism. *The Oxford Handbook of Atheism.* Editors S. Bullivant and M. Ruse, 367–379. Oxford: Oxford University Press.

Godart, C. 2011. Inoue Tetsujirō (1855–1944). *Japanese Philosophy: A Sourcebook.* Editors J. W. Heisig, T. P. Kasulis, and J. C. Maraldon, 611–618. Honolulu, Hawaii: University of Hawaii Press.

Goldhagen, D. 1996. *Hitler's Willing Executioners: Ordinary Germans and the Holocaust.* New York: Knopf.

Gosse, P. H. 1857. *Omphalos; An Attempt to Untie the Geological Knot.* London: John Van Voorst.

Gould, S. J. 1985. *The Flamingo's Smile: Reflections in Natural History.* New York: Norton.

———. 1988. On replacing the idea of progress with an operational notion of directionality. *Evolutionary Progress.* Editor M. H. Nitecki, 319–338. Chicago: University of Chicago Press.

———. 1989. *Wonderful Life: The Burgess Shale and the Nature of History.* New York: W. W. Norton.

———. 1999. *Rocks of Ages: Science and Religion in the Fullness of Life.* New York: Ballantine.

Gould, S. J., and R. C. Lewontin. 1979. The spandrels of San Marco and the Panglossian paradigm: A critique of the adaptationist programme. *Proceedings of the Royal Society of London, Series B: Biological Sciences* 205: 581–598.

Gould, S. J., and E. S. Vrba. 1982. Exaptation—A missing term in the science of form. *Paleobiology* 8: 4–15.

Graham, G. 2010. Atonement. *The Cambridge Companion to Christian Philosophical Theology.* Editors C. Taliaferro and C. Meister, 124–135. Cambridge: Cambridge University Press.

Gray, A. 1876. *Darwiniana*. New York: D. Appleton.

Grayling, A. C. 2013. *The God Argument: The Case against Religion and for Humanism*. London: Bloomsbury.

Gunton, C. E., Editor. 1997. *The Cambridge Companion to Christian Doctrine*. Cambridge: Cambridge University Press.

Haldane, J. B. S. 1927. *Possible Worlds and Other Essays*. London: Chatto and Windus.

Hall, A. R. 1954. *The Scientific Revolution 1500–1800: The Formation of the Modern Scientific Attitude*. London: Longman.

Hanser, R. *A Noble Treason: The Revolt of the Munich Students against Hitler*. New York: Putnam.

Harris, S. 2004. *The End of Faith: Religion, Terror, and the Future of Reason*. New York: Free Press.

Hart, P. 2013. *The Great War: A Combat History of the First World War*. Oxford: Oxford University Press.

Harvey, P. 1990. *An Introduction to Buddhism: Teachings, History and Practices*. Cambridge: Cambridge University Press.

Hasker, W. 2010. Eternity and providence. *The Cambridge Companion to Christian Philosophical Theology*. Editors C. Taliaferro and C. Meister, 81–91. Cambridge: Cambridge University Press.

Haught, J. F. 2008. *God and the New Atheism: A Critical Response to Dawkins, Harris, and Hitchens*. Louisville, Ky.: Westminster John Knox Press.

Heidegger, M. 1959. *An Introduction to Metaphysics*. Translator R. Manheim. New Haven, Conn.: Yale University Press.

Hesse, M. 1966. *Models and Analogies in Science*. Notre Dame, Ind.: University of Notre Dame Press.

Hick, J. 1961. Necessary being. *Scottish Journal of Theology* 14: 353–369.

———. 1978. *Evil and the God of Love*. New York: Harper and Row.

———. 1980. *God Has Many Names*. Philadelphia: Westminster Press.

Hitchens, C. 2007. *God Is Not Great: How Religion Poisons Everything*. New York: Hachette.

Hitler, A. 1941. *My New Order*. Editor R. de R. de Sales. Introduction by R. G. Swing. New York: Reynal and Hitchcock.

Hochschild, A. 2006. *Bury the Chains: The British Struggle to Abolish Slavery*. London: Pan.

Hume, D. [1739–1740] 2000. *A Treatise of Human Nature*. Editors D. F. Norton and M. J. Norton. Oxford: Oxford University Press.

———. [1757] 1963. A natural history of religion. *Hume on Religion.*, *31–98*. Editor R. Wollheim, London: Fontana.

———. [1777] 2007. *An Enquiry Concerning Human Understanding*. Editor P. Millican. Oxford: Oxford University Press.

———. [1779] 1947. *Dialogues Concerning Natural Religion*. Editor N. K. Smith. Indianapolis, Ind.: Bobbs-Merrill.

Huxley, J. S. 1927. *Religion without Revelation*. London: Ernest Benn.

———. 1943. *TVA: Adventure in Planning*. London: Scientific Book Club.

Huxley, T. H. 1894. *Science and Christian Tradition*. London: Macmillan.

———. [1893] 2009. *Evolution and Ethics with a New Introduction*. Editor M. Ruse. Princeton, N.J.: Princeton University Press.

Hwang, K. 2013. Atheism, health, and well-being. *The Oxford Handbook of Atheism*. Editors S. Bullivant and M. Ruse, 525–536. Oxford: Oxford University Press.

Hyman, G. 2010. *A Short History of Atheism*. London: Tauris.

Ingersoll, R. G. 1874. *The Gods and Other Lectures*. Peoria, Ill.: Privately printed.

James, A., and A. Wells. 2002. Death beliefs, superstitious beliefs and health anxiety. *British Journal of Clinical Psychology* 41: 43–53.

John Jay College of Criminal Justice. 2004. *The Nature and Scope of the Sexual Abuse of Minors by Catholic Priests and Deacons in the United States, 1950–2002*. Washington D.C.: United States Conference of Catholic Bishops.

John Paul II. 1998. *Fides et Ratio: Encyclical Letter of John Paul II to the Catholic Bishops of the World*. Vatican City: L'Osservatore Romano.

Kant, I. [1781] 1999. *Critique of Pure Reason*. Translators P. Guyer and A. W. Wood. Cambridge: Cambridge University Press.

———. [1785] 1959. *Foundations of the Metaphysics of Morals*. Translator L. W. Beck. Indianapolis, Ind.: Bobbs-Merrill.

————. [1788] 1898. *Critique of Practical Reason*. Translator T. K. Abbott. London: Longmans, Green.

————. [1790] 1951. *Critique of Judgement*. Translator J. H. Bernard. New York: Haffner.

Kelsay, J. 2007. *Arguing the Just War in Islam*. Cambridge, Mass.: Harvard University Press.

Kershaw, I. 1999. *Hitler 1889–1936: Hubris*. New York: Norton.

Keysar, A., and J. Navarro-Rivera. 2013. A world of atheism: Global demographics. *The Oxford Handbook of Atheism*. Editors S. Bullivant and M. Ruse, 553–586. Oxford: Oxford University Press.

Kinnaman, D. 2011. *You Lost Me. Why Young Christians Are Leaving Church. . . and Rethinking Faith*. Grand Rapids, Mich.: Baker Books.

Kors, A. C. 2013. The age of Enlightenment. *The Oxford Handbook of Atheism*. Editors S. Bullivant and M. Ruse, 195–211. Oxford: Oxford University Press.

Kuhn, T. 1962. *The Structure of Scientific Revolutions*. Chicago: University of Chicago Press.

————. 1977. Objectivity, value judgment, and theory choice. In T. Kuhn, *The Essential Tension: Selected Studies in Scientific Tradition and Change*, 320–339. Chicago: University of Chicago Press.

Lakoff, G., and M. Johnson. 1980. *Metaphors We Live By*. Chicago: University of Chicago Press.

Lamy, G. 1679. *Discours anatomiques*. Brussels: Henry Fricx.

Larson, E. J. 1997. *Summer for the Gods: The Scopes Trial and America's Continuing Debate over Science and Religion*. New York: Basic Books.

Larson, E. J., and L. Witham. 1997. Scientists are still keeping the faith. *Nature* 386: 436–437.

————. 1998. Leading scientists still reject God. *Nature* 394: 313.

Lee, L. 2013. Western Europe. *The Oxford Handbook of Atheism*. Editors S. Bullivant and M. Ruse, 587–600. Oxford: Oxford University Press.

Leftow, B. 2010. Necessity. *The Cambridge Companion to Christian Philosophical Theology*. Editors C. Taliaferro and C. Meister, 15–30. Cambridge: Cambridge University Press.

Leibniz, G. F. W. [1714] 1965. *Monadology and Other Philosophical Essays.* Translators P. Schrecker and A. Schrecker. New York: Bobbs-Merrill.

Locke, J. [1689] 1959. *An Essay Concerning Human Understanding.* Editor A. C. Fraser. New York: Dover.

Lodge, D. 1980. *How Far Can You Go?* London: Secker and Warburg.

Luhrmann, T. M. 2012. *When God Talks Back: Understanding the American Evangelical Relationship with God.* New York: Vintage.

MacCulloch, D. 2004. *The Reformation: A History.* New York: Viking.

Mackie, J. 1977. *Ethics.* Harmondsworth, U.K.: Penguin.

Maimonides, M. 1936. *The Guide for the Perplexed.* Translator S. Friedlander. London: Routledge.

Marx, K. 1844. A contribution to the critique of Hegel's Philosophy of Right, Introduction. *Deutsch-Französische Jahrbücher,* 7 & 10 February.

McGinn, C. 2000. *The Mysterious Flame: Conscious Minds in a Material World.* New York: Basic Books.

McGrath, A. E., Editor. 1995. *The Christian Theology Reader.* Oxford: Blackwell.

———. 1997. *Christian Theology: An Introduction* (Second Edition). Oxford: Blackwell.

McGrath, A. E., and J. C. McGrath. 2007. *The Dawkins Delusion: Atheist Fundamentalism and the Denial of the Divine.* Downers Grove, Ill.: InterVarsity Press.

McMullin, E., 1985. Introduction: Evolution and creation. *Evolution and Creation.* Editor E. McMullin, 1–58. Notre Dame, Ind.: University of Notre Dame Press.

———, Editor. 2005. *The Church and Galileo.* Notre Dame, Ind.: University of Notre Dame Press.

McShea, D., and R. Brandon. 2010. *Biology's First Law: The Tendency for Diversity and Complexity to Increase in Evolutionary Systems.* Chicago: University of Chicago Press.

Meister, C. 2010. The problem of evil. *The Cambridge Companion to Christian Philosophical Theology.* Editors C. Taliaferro and C. Meister, 152–169. Cambridge: Cambridge University Press.

Mill, J. S. 1863. *Utilitarianism*. London: Parker, Son, and Bourn.

———. [1874] 1985. The utility of religion. *The Collected Works of John Stuart Mill, X. Essays on Ethics, Religion, and Society*. Editor J. M. Robson, 403–428. Toronto: University of Toronto Press.

Miller, K. 1999. *Finding Darwin's God*. New York: Harper and Row.

Miller, W., and C. Thoresen. 2003. Spirituality, religion and health. *American Psychologist* 58: 24–35.

Moore, G. E. 1903. *Principia Ethica*. Cambridge: Cambridge University Press.

Moser, P. K. 2010. Sin and salvation. *The Cambridge Companion to Christian Philosophical Theology*. Editors C. Taliaferro and C. Meister, 136–151. Cambridge: Cambridge University Press.

Mossner, E. C. 1954. *The Life of David Hume*. Oxford: Oxford University Press.

Myers, F. W. H. 1881. George Eliot. *The Century Magazine*: November, 57–64.

Nash, D. 2013. The (long) nineteenth century. *The Oxford Handbook of Atheism*. Editors S. Bullivant and M. Ruse, 212–228. Oxford: Oxford University Press.

Newborn, J., and A. Dumbach. 2007. *Sophie Scholl and the White Rose*. Oxford: Oneworld.

Newman, J. H. 1870. *A Grammar of Assent*. New York: Catholic Publishing Society.

———. 1973. *The Letters and Diaries of John Henry Newman, XXV*. Editors C. S. Dessain and T. Gornall. Oxford: Clarendon Press.

Nietzsche, F. [1882] 1974. *Vorspiel einer Philosophie der Zukunft (The Gay Science)*. Translator W. Kaufmann. New York: Random House.

Noll, M. 2002. *America's God: From Jonathan Edwards to Abraham Lincoln*. New York: Oxford University Press.

Numbers, R. L. 2006. *The Creationists: From Scientific Creationism to Intelligent Design*. Cambridge, Mass.: Harvard University Press.

Paine, T. [1794] 1907. *The Age of Reason*. New York: G. P. Putnam's Sons.

Paley, W. [1802] 1819. *Natural Theology (Collected Works: IV)*. London: Rivington.

Pasquale, F. L., and B. A. Kosmin. 2013. Atheism and the secularization thesis. *The Oxford Handbook of Atheism.* Editors S. Bullivant and M. Ruse, 451–467. Oxford: Oxford University Press.

Pennock, R., and M. Ruse, Editors. 2008. *But Is It Science? The Philosophical Question in the Creation/Evolution Controversy* (Second Edition). Buffalo, N.Y.: Prometheus.

Pew Research Religion and Public Life Project. 2013. Canada's changing religious landscape. www.pewforum.org/2013/06/27/canadas-changing-religious-landscape/.

Pinker, S. 2011. *The Better Angels of Our Nature: Why Violence Has Declined.* New York: Viking Penguin.

Plantinga, A. 1980. *Does God Have a Nature?* Milwaukee, Wis.: Marquette University Press.

———. 1981. Is belief in God properly basic? *Nous* 15: 41–51.

———. 1991. An evolutionary argument against naturalism. *Logos* 12: 27–49.

———. 1997. Methodological naturalism. *Perspectives on Science and Christian Faith* 49, no. 3: 143–154.

———. 2000. Pluralism: A defense of religious exclusivism. *The Philosophical Challenge of Religious Diversity.* Editors K. Meeker, and P. Quinn, 172–192. New York: Oxford University Press.

———. 2004. Supralapsarianism, or "O Felix Culpa." *Christian Faith and the Problem of Evil.* Editor P. Van Inwagen, 1–25. Grand Rapids, Mich.: Eerdmans.

———. 2011. Comments on "Satanic Verses: Moral Chaos in Holy Writ." *Divine Evil? The Moral Character of the God of Abraham.* Editors M. Bergmann, M. J. Murray, and M. C. Rea, 109–114. Oxford: Oxford University Press.

Plotinus. [250] 1992. *The Enneads.* Translator S. MacKenna. Burdett, N.Y.: Larson.

Popper, K. R. 1959. *The Logic of Scientific Discovery*. London: Hutchinson.

———. 1963. *Conjectures and Refutations*. London: Routledge and Kegan Paul.

———. 1972. *Objective Knowledge*. Oxford: Oxford University Press.

Porterfield, A. 2012. *Conceived in Doubt: Religion and Politics in the New American Nation (American Beginnings, 1500–1900)*. Chicago: University of Chicago Press.

Powell, L., L. Shahabi, and C. Thoresen. 2003. Religion and spirituality: Linkages to physical health. *American Psychologist* 58: 36–52.

Poythress, V. S. 2006. *Redeeming Science: A God-Centered Approach*. Wheaton, Ill.: Crossway.

Quack, J. 2013. India. *The Oxford Handbook of Atheism*. Editors S. Bullivant and M. Ruse, 651–664. Oxford: Oxford University Press.

Ray, D., and A. Brown. 2011. Sex and secularism. www.scribd.com/Doc/ 57318688/Sex-and-Secularism-What-Happens-When-You-Leave-Religion.

Re Manning, R., Editor. 2013. *The Oxford Handbook of Natural Theology*. Oxford: Oxford University Press.

Richerson, P., and R. Boyd. 2005. *Not by Genes Alone: How Culture Transformed Human Evolution*. Chicago: University of Chicago Press.

Robichaud, D. J. J. 2013. Renaissance and Reformation. *The Oxford Handbook of Atheism*. Editors S. Bullivant and M. Ruse, 179–194. Oxford: Oxford University Press.

Robinson, J. A. T. 1963. *Honest to God*. London: SCM.

Rogers, K. A. 2010. Incarnation. *The Cambridge Companion to Christian Philosophical Theology*. Editors C. Taliaferro and C. Meister, 95–107. Cambridge: Cambridge University Press.

Rogerson, J. W. 2000. Higher criticism. *The Oxford Companion to Christian Thought*. Editors A. Hastings, A. Mason, and H. Pyper, 297–298. Oxford: Oxford University Press.

Rubenstein, R. L. 1966. *After Auschwitz: Radical Theology and Contemporary Judaism*. Indianapolis, Ind.: Bobbs-Merrill.

Ruse, M. 1979. *The Darwinian Revolution: Science Red in Tooth and Claw.* Chicago: University of Chicago Press.

———. 1986. *Taking Darwin Seriously: A Naturalistic Approach to Philosophy.* Oxford: Blackwell.

———. 1996. *Monad to Man: The Concept of Progress in Evolutionary Biology.* Cambridge, Mass.: Harvard University Press.

———. 2001. *Can a Darwinian Be a Christian? The Relationship between Science and Religion.* Cambridge: Cambridge University Press.

———. 2003. *Darwin and Design: Does Evolution Have a Purpose?* Cambridge, Mass.: Harvard University Press.

———. 2005. *The Evolution-Creation Struggle.* Cambridge, Mass.: Harvard University Press.

———. 2006. *Darwinism and Its Discontents.* Cambridge: Cambridge University Press.

———, Editor. 2009. *Philosophy after Darwin: Classic and Contemporary Readings.* Princeton, N.J.: Princeton University Press.

———. 2010. *Science and Spirituality: Making Room for Faith in the Age of Science.* Cambridge: Cambridge University Press.

———. 2012. *The Philosophy of Human Evolution.* Cambridge: Cambridge University Press.

———. 2013. *The Gaia Hypothesis: Science on a Pagan Planet.* Chicago: University of Chicago Press.

Russell, B. 1927. *Why I Am Not a Christian.* London: Watts.

Russell, R. J. 2008. *Cosmology: From Alpha to Omega, the Creative Mutual Interaction of Theology and Science.* Minneapolis: Fortress Press.

Schielke, S. 2013. The Islamic world. *The Oxford Handbook of Atheism.* Editors S. Bullivant and M. Ruse, 638–650. Oxford: Oxford University Press.

Schneider, J. 2010. Recent genetic science and Christian theology on human origins: An "aesthetic supralapsarianism." *Perspectives on Science and Christian Faith* 62: 196–212.

Sedley, D. 2008. *Creationism and Its Critics in Antiquity*. Berkeley: University of California Press.

———. 2013. From the Pre-Socratics to the Hellenistic Age. *The Oxford Handbook of Atheism*. Editors S. Bullivant and M. Ruse, 139–151. Oxford: Oxford University Press.

Seeman, T., L. F. Dubin, and M. Seeman. 2003. Religiosity/spirituality and health; A critical review of the evidence for biological pathways. *American Psychologist* 58: 53–63.

Sextus Empiricus. 1953. *Against the Physicists*. Translator R. G. Bury. Cambridge, Mass.: Harvard University Press.

Shapiro, A. R. 2013. *Trying Biology: The Scopes Trial, Textbooks, and the Antievolution Movement in American Schools*. Chicago: University of Chicago Press.

Skilton, A. 2013. Buddhism. *The Oxford Handbook of Atheism*. Editors S. Bullivant and M. Ruse, 337–350. Oxford: Oxford University Press.

Spencer, H. 1857. Progress: Its law and cause. *Westminster Review* LXVII: 244–267.

Stark, R., and W. Bainbridge. 1996. *A Theory of Religion*. Newark, N.J.: Rutgers University Press.

Stirrat, M., and R. E. Cornwell. 2013. Eminent scientists reject the supernatural: a survey of the Fellows of the Royal Society. *Evolution: Education and Outreach* 6: 33; doi:10.1186/1936-6434-6-33.

Sullivan, T. D., and S. Menssen. 2010. Revelation and miracles. *The Cambridge Companion to Christian Philosophical Theology*. Editors C. Taliaferro and C. Meister, 201–215. Cambridge: Cambridge University Press.

Swinburne, R. G. 1970. *The Concept of Miracle*. London: Macmillan.

———. 1977. *The Coherence of Theism*. Oxford: Clarendon Press.

Taliaferro, C., and C. Meister, Editors. 2010. *The Cambridge Companion to Christian Philosophical Theology*. Cambridge: Cambridge University Press.

Taylor, C. 2007. *A Secular Age*. Cambridge, Mass.: Harvard University Press.

Vallely, A. 2013. Jainism. *The Oxford Handbook of Atheism.* Editors S. Bullivant and M. Ruse, 351–366. Oxford: Oxford University Press.

Van Doren, C. 1938. *Benjamin Franklin.* New York City: Viking.

Van Inwagen, P. 2011. Comments on "The God of Abraham, Isaac, and Jacob." *Divine Evil? The Moral Character of the God of Abraham.* Editors M. Bergmann, M. J. Murray, and M. C. Rea, 79–84. Oxford: Oxford University Press.

Vanhoozer, K. 1997. Human being, individual and social. *The Cambridge Companion to Christian Doctrine.* Editor C. E. Gunton, 158–188. Cambridge: Cambridge University Press.

Wainwright, W. J. 2010. Omnipotence, omniscience, and omnipresence. *The Cambridge Companion to Christian Philosophical Theology.* Editors C. Taliaferro and C. Meister, 46–65. Cambridge: Cambridge University Press.

Walls, J. L. 2010. Heaven and hell. *The Cambridge Companion to Christian Philosophical Theology.* Editors C. Taliaferro and C. Meister, 238–251. Cambridge: Cambridge University Press.

Weinandy, T. G. 2000. *Does God Suffer?* Notre Dame, Ind.: University of Notre Dame Press.

Weinberg, S. 1999. A designer universe. *New York Review of Books* 46, no. 16: 46–48.

Weltecke, D. 2013. The medieval period. *The Oxford Handbook of Atheism.* Editors S. Bullivant and M. Ruse, 164–178. Oxford: Oxford University Press.

Whitcomb, J. C., and H. M. Morris. 1961. *The Genesis Flood: The Biblical Record and Its Scientific Implications.* Philadelphia: Presbyterian and Reformed.

Whitehead, A. N. 1929. *Process and Reality: An Essay in Cosmology.* New York: Macmillan.

Whylly, S. 2013. Japan. *The Oxford Handbook of Atheism.* Editors S. Bullivant and M. Ruse, 665–679. Oxford: Oxford University Press.

Williams, B. 1973. The Makropulos case: Reflections on the tedium of immortality. *Problems of the Self.* Cambridge: Cambridge University Press.

Wilson, E. O. 1978. *On Human Nature.* Cambridge, Mass: Harvard University Press.

———. 2002. *The Future of Life.* New York: Vintage.

Yao, X. 2000. *An Introduction to Confucianism.* Cambridge: Cambridge University Press.

Zuckerman, P. 2013. Atheism and societal health. *The Oxford Handbook of Atheism.* Editors S. Bullivant and M. Ruse, 497–510. Oxford: Oxford University Press.

INDEX

eternal nature of (Plato), 183
existentialism, 42
Extra ecclesiam nulla salus (Outside
the Church, there is no
salvation), 170

faith, 147–168
Aquinas and, 85
belief and, 188
defining, 83–84
Ingersoll and, 37
perspectives on, 169–170
reason and, 12
versus action, 20
Fawkes, Guy (1570–1606), 213
festivals (church), 193
Feuerbach, Ludwig (1804–1872),
38
Fides et Ratio ("Faith and Reason,"
Pope John Paul II), 84
fig tree (parable), 71–72
final cause (Aristotle), 9, 91, 116
Finland, 249
Fisher, Geoffrey (1857–1972), 43
Flynt, Larry (b. 1942), 46
Focus on the Family, 136–137
Form of the Good (Plato), 9, 73,
152. *See also* God
Forms/Ideas (Plato's unseen
archetypes), 9, 73–75
Foster, Michael (1836–1907), 239
Foucault, Michel (1926–1984), 173
Four Holy (or Noble) Truths
(Buddhism), 181
France, 54, 62, 249
Franklin, Benjamin (1706–1790), 23
Frazer, James G. (1854–1941),
135, 195
Free Inquiry (journal), 47
free will, 79–80, 128–131
evil and, 156–158
libertarianism and, 129
freedom (and constraint), 130
French Revolution, 33

Freud, Sigmund (1856–1939), 41,
120, 195
Friedrich, Caspar David
(1774–1840), 229
*Fruits of Philosophy, The, or the
Private Companion of
Young Married People*, 37
Fry, Elizabeth (1780–1845), 218
fundamentalism, 28, 107

Galilei, Galileo (1564–1642), 17, 19
Gautama Buddha (circa 550 BC),
179–180
Gay Science (Nietzsche), 39
gender, atheism and, 61
Genesis Flood (Whitcomb), 48, 109
geology, 30
geometry, Plato and, 73
Georgia, 250
Germany, 54, 62, 249
Gilbert, William (1544–1603), 17
Gladstone, William Ewart
(1809–1898), 42, 100
gnosis (Greek word for
knowledge), 33
God, 45, 122–123. *See also*
Demiurge (Plato); *deus*
(Latin word for God);
Form of the Good
(Plato); Supreme Being
attributes of
eternal, 74, 129, 152
ethically unchanging, 133
immanent and providential,
14, 74
ineffable, 76
intervening in creation, 13
knowing, 75–77
loving, 74
miracles, 14
omnipotent, 74, 128–131
omniscient, 74, 128–131
providential, 182
unchanging, 127